GOODBYE JUNIE MOON

A VIETNAM WAR MEMOIR
BY JUNE COLLINS

Publicious

Published in 2012
By June Collins
BLOG: www.memoirofjuniemoon.wordpress.com
Author contact: juniemooncollins@hotmail.com

Published with the assistance
of Publicious Pty Ltd

Layout and cover design
by Publicious Pty Ltd
www.publicious.com.au

**Catalogue-In-Publication details
available on request**

ISBN: 978-0-646-58272-6

Also available as an ebook
ebook ISBN: 978-0-646-58003-6

PREVIOUS BOOKS

The Khaki Mafia (co-authored with Robin Moore)

DEDICATION

To my mother, who by example taught me everything about courage, strength, loyalty, integrity and unconditional love. She omitted sex. Nobody did it in those days. We got our babies from under cabbages,

When I decided to write this book I thought certain revelations would embarrass her, so one day I said "Listen to this chapter about you Mum. If it upsets you, I won't include it." After I read the chapter to her, there was a long silence. Finally, she replied, "It's the truth, June. Go ahead and leave it in."

I never loved her more than at that moment.

TRIBUTE

There were many commercial entertainers in Vietnam from the USA, Australia, Korea, the Philippines and Thailand. Most were young and either adventurous or naïve or both. Some were still teenagers who were exuberantly received by the troops of whom too many were teenagers themselves. I believe all entertainers experienced danger if they stayed for any length of time. A few were wounded and I know of four who were killed. They all displayed courage when they made that initial choice to face the unknown and travel to a war zone. Some left after a few weeks but most stayed. I pay tribute to each one of them.

Most important, I pay tribute to Vietnam Vets everywhere.

ACKNOWLEDGEMENTS

Robin Moore (The French Connection, The Green Beret) and I wrote a fictionalized version of the events of the U.S. Army's Clubs and Messes scandal in Vietnam and my involvement. The Khaki Mafia was an in-depth look at the corruption. As fiction, (Robin liked to call it faction) not all events were entirely true and some characters were composites, however the overall story was fact. The Khaki Mafia kept the story in the public eye long after the headlines had faded.

I have always wanted to write the exact version of my three and a half year involvement in the war and focus on the emotional element. What leads anyone to jeopardize their life and become a whistle blower? There are seldom any rewards and often serious consequences. I respect all whistle-blowers.

I wish to thank R.A.D.F (Regional Arts Development Fund) of Beaudesert Shire, Queensland who gave me a writing grant which encouraged me to get started when self-doubt caused delays.

My dear daughter Anna was of great help whenever I had computer problems. David Moss of The Gold Coast was also kind enough to read and correct my earliest draft. Clancy Covington of Mount Tamborine offered advice and much needed encouragement. At one point Clancy, a Queensland University Lecturer said "I'm not sure about THAT part. It makes you sound like a loose woman."

"It stays" I said, "I was a bit of a loose woman and I take neither pride nor shame in that. I sought life and freedom within the bounds of my own principles, rejecting the need to fit society's mould. I wouldn't change a thing."

Finally, I thank David Scott, a playwright and fellow member of the Tamborine Mountain Writers Group, Harry Youngberry and Richard Meyer, both authors from South East Queensland. Their insight and suggestions were of great help.

AUTHORS NOTE

This book contains some profanity and a graphic sexual opener. Life in a war zone is not filled with cups of tea and polite conversation. This is a warning, not an apology. If the sometimes raw dialogue will offend your sensibilities, then best you skip this one.

PROLOGUE

Vietnam, July 1969

My legs are wrapped around his taut behind, my eyes closed as I move in harmony with his thrusts. The Vietnam air is humid as always and his sweat drips onto my breasts. It is late at night and the silence of the empty NCO club is occasionally broken by his grunts as he pushes into me.

Playing my part, I emit a soft, pretence moan. I have to stop myself from turning my head away when he places his open mouth over mine. But this is necessary I think. To reach my objective I have to gain his trust.

He keeps pumping into me and I am grateful he is not one of the corpulent ones. I could not bear their soft flab draped over my small body but his body is lean and hard. Despite myself, I am surprised when I begin to respond. Closing my eyes, I feel his tongue probing my mouth and my own tongue touches his tentatively. This is not part of the plan – I feel betrayed by my own body's stirrings.

My surroundings begin diffusing and disappearing into a hazy cloud. I can't believe I am moving with him, arching my body higher to meet him. The ecstatic moans are no longer forced. How can I be enjoying this act that I dreaded doing? I try to remember why I am here but all thought disintegrates. Our pace quickens. My buttocks clench together like welded steel and I stiffen into rigid, mind-numbing ecstasy.

Moments later tremors convulse my body. I stifle a scream but a moan escapes and I taste the mingling of blood and salty sweat on my cut lips as our juices flow together.

We stay motionless until he rolls off me to lie on his back, staring up at the ceiling. The happy glow of the aftermath is short lived for a sense of self loathing begins to creep in. How could I have lost control of this situation?

We are lying on a rug on the floor of his office at the rear of the club. My body is slick from perspiration, my hair plastered across my forehead and I vaguely notice a couple of curly, dark hairs from his chest, stuck between my breasts. He stirs and begins to move away.

"Don't leave." I say.

"Just give me a few moments. Let's have a drink." He stands and disappears into the darkened club but soon returns, holding a bottle of French champagne aloft.

"I keep this to celebrate victories" he says "battle ones I mean, but I like this one better. Sorry there are no champagne glasses."

He hands me a plastic tumbler then takes a swig from the open bottle.

"I'd let you drink from my shoe" I say "but they're only old army boots."

"You know you really turn me on!" He looks me up and down. "Your body would arouse any man." This was not news to me. As a dancer, my body was a big part of the act.

"You're in pretty good shape yourself. Why don't you come closer?" I smile. When he moves beside me I take a mouthful of champagne. Turning, I put my lips to his and slowly let the champagne trickle down his throat.

"That's the best way to drink Dom Perignon. It's too good to drink from the bottle."

He sits up and says "Lie down." Soon the cold champagne is spilling over me and he is licking it off as he kneels across me. My mind and body are in such conflict. I don't know whether to be happy that my plan is working so well or upset that I have enjoyed my part in what was meant to be a charade.

In my wildest dreams I never thought I would enjoy fucking the enemy. Not literally anyway. Justifying the situation I tell myself that if I am prepared to put my business on the line and maybe my life, then why not my body? This crooked gang was already suspicious of me since I had made no secret of the fact I hated paying the kickbacks.

Sex was not a foregone winner to get the results I needed but I could see no other way to infiltrate this mob. There was an over abundance of sex in Vietnam with thousands of Vietnamese bar girls offering their bodies for a few paltry piasters. However, I had the advantage of being a 'round-eye'- a real prize in this country.

If I was convincing – and he was making it easy for me – who knew what I would eventually learn from pillow talk?

I focus back on the moment. Hours have passed and again he is filling me – slow and rhythmic this time. The first desperate hunger has gone. Whereas it seemed we had been dancing a fiery tango – we were now down to a slow and delightful waltz.

And so the night of our first coupling went, on and on until dawn – probing, discovering, pleasing one another in every way. When at last we were sated I lay listening to him breathing softly. Finally he was asleep. I rose to dress and slip away before the army camp came to life.

As I closed the door, an unexpected sadness came over me. I was going to betray this man. Eventually I would destroy him along with all the other club sergeants. That is what they deserved. I hated the lot of them and what they represented – the worst of society's greed which always surfaces during wartime. For some, war meant dying; for others it meant grabbing all the money possible as long as the war raged.

The intimacy with Delaney had confused the issue for I no longer hated him yet he was as guilty as the others. I had to remind myself that I was sacrificing my body for a higher cause. The fact it didn't end up seeming like much of a sacrifice left me feeling just a little bit tawdry.

Did Mata Hari feel like this, I wondered?

CHAPTER 1

WASHINGTON D.C.

October 1969

It was winter when I arrived at Dulles International airport. I had not experienced winter in any country for many years. Living in Vietnam had been hot in every sense.

Although the air terminal was uncomfortably over-heated, I knew I would freeze once I stepped outside. My light summer dress and open toed sandals contrasted sharply with the parka-clad, scarf-wrapped travelers around me.

At least I should be safe here, I thought, no more hiding or worrying about when a bullet or claymore mine is going to get me. Yet, such reassuring thoughts did little to comfort me. I was aware of my conspicuous appearance. Young, curvaceous and improperly dressed, I would certainly stand out if the bad guys were looking for me here.

People bustled around me, heading stern faced for the exits or talking and laughing loudly over the sound of the PA system. I dragged my suitcase along and peered into the waiting crowd, looking for the two senate investigators who were supposed to meet me. I hoped they wouldn't be late. This was my first trip to the U.S.A. and under most unexpected circumstances.

Unsure of which direction to head, I stopped and absently tugged on a long strand of blonde hair.

"Where are those men?" Setting my suitcase down, I leaned anxiously against a wide column. This wasn't quite the exuberant welcome I had imagined. After a long ten minutes, I spotted Fred and

Duffy hurrying towards me. They were as conspicuous as I, in their immaculate dark suits and sunglasses, looking like the forerunners to "The Blues Brothers". Duffy was the larger of the two and he wore his hair in a short crew cut. His moon face was grim and unusually pallid, the result of rare exposure to the outdoors.

Fred, the junior investigator, increased his pace and strode ahead.

"I apologize for being late," he said, grasping my hand in a vigorous shake.

"Traffic was worse than usual, thanks to the fog."

"No apology necessary" I answered, as Duffy caught up and nodded a stiff welcome.

"Grab the luggage Fred," he ordered, indicating my one small suitcase.

What an odd couple they made. Other than their dress, they seemed to have nothing in common. Fred was slender, around six feet tall and much less imposing than his partner. His hair was cut conservatively short in front. When he turned, his rebellion to required conformity was declared in the shape of a pencil-thin strand of braided hair. The last vestiges of a summer tan enhanced his handsome face and a bright red tie only slightly minimized the 'spook' persona. I guessed his age at about thirty.

I had first met the investigators several weeks earlier in Saigon. The Senate Sub Committee into Un-American Activities had sent them to Vietnam to investigate the US army camps' Non Commissioned Officer (NCO) and Enlisted Men's (EM) Clubs System. The acting chairman of that committee, Senator Abraham Ribicoff (D. Connecticut), was determined to find out if there was any truth to the disturbing reports of corruption which had reached Washington.

In Saigon I had welcomed them joyfully, realizing they may represent my escape from the danger I was in. Although I was in hiding, the investigators were brought to me by a Special Forces major and Agent Winthrop, of the CID (Criminal Investigation Division). Winthrop was one of two agents to whom I had first given my damning deposition about the corruption I had encountered whilst booking my

Filipino entertainment shows into the American army clubs.

When the club managers somehow learned I had squcaled, Winthrop felt some responsibility for my safety. Jumping into his jeep, he raced to my apartment and warned me to 'lie low'. Immediately I called a trusted friend, Major Chuck Darnell of The Special Forces (commonly referred to as The Green Berets). I'm sure he broke regulations initially but he quickly installed me in a well guarded Special Forces compound unavailable to regular army, the source of my danger.

Major Darnell arranged for the investigators to safely meet with me on three occasions. I told them of my first-hand experiences with the corrupt sergeants who were running the U.S. Army's Clubs and Messes system. These sergeants were controlling hundreds of millions of dollars with no supervision from their superior officers whose minds were pre-occupied with casualties and body counts. I learned an exorbitant price was placed on my head and overnight I became poison ivy, even among the other entertainment booking agents. Nobody likes a squealer. Nobody wanted to rock the boat. Everyone was making too much money. The unwritten rule had been to close your eyes and keep your mouth shut; even if you did not like what was happening.

Of course my business, supplying Philippine entertainment groups to the US army camps' was destroyed. I had difficulty even returning my entertainers' passports and tickets so they could leave the country.

Tan Son Nhut airport was being watched, Agent Winthrop warned, and I had no idea how I was going to leave. That was the situation when I met the two American Government investigators.

"Why did you put yourself in danger by reporting these things to the CID?" Duffy asked suspiciously on our first meeting. Fred was sitting in the corner, fiddling with the controls of a tape recorder.

"Why wouldn't I? The situation sickened me and of course, I thought no one would discover that I had squealed. I expected the dishonest club custodians to be arrested and replaced by honest men. I thought I would be able to get on with my business and no longer be required to pay kick-backs."

Duffy frowned thoughtfully as he listened.

"I couldn't possibly have known there would be a leak from the

Provost Marshall's office. I was unaware the CID worked in conjunction with the Provost Marshall's office, although that knowledge would have made no difference. I was naïve enough to think that all military cops were the good guys. Thank God agent Winthrop and his partner are honest. If it wasn't for their warning, I don't expect I'd still be here." I paused and reached for a glass of water.

"I'm sure Winthrop suspects the leak could only have come from the Provost Marshall's office. The Provost Marshall himself, General Carl Turner, ordered Winthrop to sanitize my testimony after he read it."

"We've met the general," Fred interjected.

"Can you imagine that, a two star general?" Time had not decreased my incredulity.

"Change is on the way." Duffy spoke grimly.

"One more thing," Fred cut in, "Agent Winthrop said you had a tape recording of some of the illegal transactions. Do you still have it?"

"I certainly do."

"Then could you bring it to our next meeting?"

I nodded as Duffy stood and buttoned his jacket, indicating our meeting was drawing to a close.

"Tomorrow will be our last meeting. Tonight, try to remember if there's anything you've forgotten."

I wondered if Duffy ever smiled or showed emotion.

The following day, Duffy told me they had finished their investigation and were returning to Washington to begin arranging Senate Hearings into the corruption.

"You are going to be our star witness. Just continue to lie low until we send for you," Fred added.

I frowned. "I don't know how I will get safely through the airport; $5000 is a hell of a high price to have on my head. A PFC's (private first class) pay is only $400 a month and there are dozens of desperate deserters out there who would kill their own mother for five thousand."

"We've already spoken to the head of the Special Forces Intel Group and they swear their men can get you safely through the airport and onto a plane." I wasn't convinced.

A blast from the P.A. system almost made me throw myself to the floor. Feeling stupid, I stopped mid-lurch and hoped the investigators had not noticed.

"Let's get out of here." Fred said. "You must be tired and ready to take a shower and rest up."

"Cut the small talk until we're away from here." Duffy interrupted curtly. "You never know who is watching." He grabbed my arm firmly and hustled me towards the exits.

"Does it matter who's watching?" I asked breathlessly.

"Not really, but those guys at The Pentagon have got wind that you're coming. They're not happy, knowing whatever you say is going to make them look bad."

"Serves them right," I mumbled. "I warned them in 'Nam about what was going on. I went to the top brass and they did nothing. All they cared about was body count."

"Yeah, you already told us all that. Come on. Hurry it up." Duffy pulled me unceremoniously through the automatic doors and out onto the sidewalk. A strong gust of freezing wind blasted in from the Potomac River and my hair whipped across my face.

"Hell. Is it always this cold?" I asked through chattering teeth.

Fred took one look at my thin dress flapping about my knees and the goose bumps rising on my arms. Setting my suitcase down, he removed his coat then draped it over my shoulders. I smiled gratefully. Duffy beckoned to the driver of a large black government sedan.

I tried not to gawk as we sped away and I had my first glimpse of the United States of America.

"Thank God this car is heated. I desperately need winter clothes."

"It's not as bad when the wind isn't blowing." Fred assured me.

"Now June," Duffy turned back towards me, his usual pragmatic self, "You're going to have to delay any sightseeing or shopping trips until after the hearings. We've got you booked into a Georgetown hotel and we don't want the army boys to find you."

"Why not? No one's going to harm me after I've already spilled the beans.... Are they?"

"We can't let our guard down. They might send some one over to see you - probably someone you knew in Vietnam. They will want to know exactly what you are going to say so they can prepare a rebuttal."

I glared at him. "Don't insult me. And there is no possible rebuttal."

"Well, you won't have any free time." Fred replied, "We have worked hard preparing the statement you will be reading to the Committee. We need to go over it with you."

"Yes," Duffy agreed, "You must be well prepared. The senators will want to question you after you deliver your statement. Tomorrow morning we'll send a driver to bring you to our office for rehearsal."

"What about my warm clothes?" I wailed.

"Don't worry," Fred replied, "I'll take you shopping on the lunch break." He deferred to Duffy, "Is that alright?"

Duffy's impatient nod annoyed me. Sure, they helped get me out of Vietnam and were enabling me to tell my story, but I was their star witness and I thought he could be a little more courteous. And why did I need a 'prepared' statement? This was a story I knew better than my own name. A story I had risked my life, my body, my business to get!

My anger over what I considered the needless death of so many young GI's had changed me. So many of the young troops shared my disillusionment and drug use was high. Even the patriotic ones who hadn't waited to be called up seemed to regret their decision soon after arrival. Only the regular army guys avowed we had a legitimate reason to be there, and maybe some of them were stifling their true feelings. Battle brought more chance of promotion!

I didn't need a rehearsal to tell my story to the world! I knew I could tell this story from my heart with much greater impact than any prepared statement would have. But, I also knew better than to tell the investigators what I planned to do.

After the investigators left me ensconced in my hotel room I placed a call to my mother in Australia. She must have been worried; I hadn't contacted home in months. Slumped on the bed I waited for the operator to call back. The committee had not sprung for five stars, I noted, but it was okay. After Vietnam, anything looked good. On the bedside table sat a vase of pink carnations with a welcoming note from Fred and Duffy.

In Vietnam, I had really missed the smell of flowers and the delightful sounds of birdsong. I saw almost no birds in Vietnam and I assumed they had wisely fled the sound of war.

Now here I was in a hotel room in a strange city, no family or friends nearby. No lover to hold me. Never had I felt more alone. Shouldn't I be elated? Miraculously I had beaten those sergeants. Where was my triumphant joy?

When the phone rang I grabbed it fast, my heart skipping a beat at the sound of my mother's familiar voice.

"I'm in Washington DC, Mum. I'm sorry I couldn't call before. I've really missed you. How is the family?" It felt so good to speak to someone who cared.

"What are you doing there June? I can't keep up with you. When did you leave Vietnam? I've been so worried. Are you alright?"

"It's a long story Mum. I'll write you a letter. How is everyone?"

"Well, don't forget... You never write anymore. And the family's fine," she paused, "But you won't be happy to learn that Lorraine has moved out of the house you bought for her. I'm afraid it's looking a bit shabby and the agent hasn't rented it."

Lorraine was my young sister by mother's second marriage. When she married as a teenager, she and her husband had little money. Feeling sorry for them, and earning great money in Vietnam, I bought a house in the rural town of Tamworth and let them live there rent free for the first year. Now it was time for them to start paying rent and my brother-in-law's work had suddenly transferred him out of town.

It felt strange to hear of this other 'forgotten world'. I did not need the additional stress of taking care of a mortgage.

"That's fucking great timing." I exploded, too late to bite my tongue.

There was silence. I hadn't meant to curse. No one spoke like that in my family. Before going overseas, I hadn't even said "shut up"!

Now, I cursed as foul as any GI who had been 'in country' too long. Too much shit can do that to you.

"Mum, are you still there?"

"June, your language is disgusting! I never thought I'd hear a daughter of mine use filth like that. I'm ashamed of you."

Her words cut deep.

"I'm sorry, Mum. One day you might understand. Now I must hang up. I'm very tired. I just wanted you to know I'm OK." I hesitated. "And I love you."

"I love you too, June." Her voice had softened. "You write… and take care."

I hung up and sat motionless on the bed. How would I fit back into civilian life? I felt like a Martian, belonging nowhere. I was so uncomfortable around 'normal' people. Their conversations, their whole lives bored me, especially pampered women with their mundane interests of diet, exercise, fashion and gossip. I was only at home now with my Vietnam War military cohorts. We had a different outlook on life which did not include society's shallow judgments. But, I was NOT in Vietnam now, or even Asia and I must try to 'fit in' again. It might be a good start if I cut back on my drinking. But could I harness my anger?

I longed for the adventurous, fun-loving girl I had been in that BV life (before Vietnam). Becoming a whistle blower would have been unimaginable to her. Her motto had been 'live and let live.'

Now I was about to testify against all those middle-aged, beer-bellied, diamond ring and gold, Rolex watch wearing club sergeants with their Swiss bank accounts. They never cared how many young GI's died as long as they were lining their pockets.

Emotionally and physically drained, I pulled my thin dress off and slipped between the crisp, white sheets. For awhile I lay awake, marveling that my tortuous travels had brought me to this. But that's a long story.

CHAPTER 2

SYDNEY AUSTRALIA

1940s

I was sitting around the oak table in the dining room of our home in Kingsgrove, an outer Sydney suburb, playing the board game Snakes and Ladders. Sitting opposite me was my younger sister Clarice. Russell, my youngest sibling, was playing with his Meccano set on the floor. Blonde and tousle haired, at five years of age, he was already showing signs of extraordinary intelligence. Al Jolson was singing "Mamie", his voice transmitted through our large floor wireless. My mother hummed along as she peeled potatoes at the sink in the small, adjoining kitchen. I could see her through the archway and hear the sizzle from the baking dish in the oven. My mouth salivated at the smell of roast lamb permeating the house. I was eleven.

"My turn" I said, picking up the dice and grabbing the dice cup. Then the door opened and my father noisily entered, followed by three of his mates.

He sniffed the air and circled my mother's waist with his strong arms.

"What's cooking, good looking?"

"I thought you were going to the races?" Mum frowned and put the potato down.

"The boys and I thought we would have a few beers here and listen to them on the wireless instead."

I groaned inwardly. That meant we children would have to play outside. Dad always turned the volume to full blast and the whooping and hollering of the men egging on their selections almost drowned out the voice of Cyril Angles, the race caller. Soon the room would be filled with a cloud of stinking cigarette smoke and if we children dared come inside and speak, we would be quickly shunted outside. I wondered why my mother, a meticulous housekeeper who never smoked or drank didn't complain. Dad stepped to the wireless and switched stations.

"Come on kids" I irritably swept up our dice and markers "Let's go outside and play in our cubby house."

My father's gambling addiction had often hurt the family. He once said that if he was starving and had two bob in his pocket, he would put it on a horse before he would buy a pie – meat pies being the popular staple of the Aussie male diet.

My pretty, four foot ten inch tall mother was frequently mistaken as my sister. She usually tied her thick, dark hair back in a velvet bow. I thought my father was good looking too and he was more fun than Mum who filled the role of family disciplinarian. Convinced I was the ugly duckling of the family I compensated by acting the clown to make people laugh. I deplored my skinny legs and knees that stuck out like the gnarls on a tree trunk. Clarice's lovely thick plaits and straight teeth caused me enormous envy. My straight, brown hair was unmanageable and my front teeth were wide-gapped. Inherited from my father, they were the bane of my life and made me so self-conscious that whenever I laughed I covered my mouth with my hand. Dad said because I could fit a two-shilling coin between the front teeth, it meant good luck. I was doubtful until years later when Laura Hutton became a world famous model with the same teeth. She must have received my luck as well because vanity had impelled me to alter my lucky teeth by then.

Our family was working class. A little on the upside of the scale I suppose, for we owned our own home at a time when most people in Sydney were renting. Dad was a supervisor at a factory that made airplane parts. Our home was a typical three bedroom, one bathroom Aussie house, built of red brick with a red tiled roof. There were no garages as most people traveled by bus.

The houses on our street looked almost identical because our grandfather S.J. Harrison, my grandmother's second husband, had built them. Most houses in Kingsgrove and the surrounding suburbs were built by him. When Mum and Dad married, our grandfather, whom we called Pop, gave them our house as a wedding present. He did the same for mum's only sibling, Uncle George, whose house sat just a few doors further up on the same street.

We never owned a car; only the rich could afford one then and there were few rich in Australia immediately after WW11. Pop was an exception.

We should have been quite comfortable with home ownership and Dad's good job but thanks to his gambling, we were not. We were Aussie clones of the day – typical house, typical fare. Mid-week staples were stews or sausages with mashed potato's, pumpkin and beans or peas. Weekends meant roast lamb with gravy, mint sauce and vegetables. Sunday's treat was baked custard with stewed fruit. Like most people, we owned an ice chest, not a refrigerator, so we could never have ice-cream.

Because of Dad's gambling, it was feast or famine. Whenever he gambled the money away, we ate bread and butter with sugar. Or bread with condensed milk. There was bread boiled in milk and as a last resort, there was always bread fried in dripping. When the bread was gone, Mum walked to the red phone box on the street corner where she used her last two pennies to phone Nan to come to our rescue.

Nan soon arrived in her big, shiny green Buick loaded with enough food to keep us eating well until Dad's next payday. Her arrival was always an EVENT. The car itself was a great attraction for the neighborhood children and a pretty, fair haired, female driver was a rarity indeed.

Despite the days when Dad left us short of money, I was a happy, chatty, child who loved school. Good grades catapulted me easily into the role of class leader. After school I often organized the local children for backyard concerts, charging the parents one penny admission. We split the money later and raced to the lolly shop on the corner.

Unfortunately those idyllic days were shattered one Saturday just before my twelfth birthday when Dad went to the races and didn't come home. As the night progressed Mum became increasingly anxious. Whenever she heard a bus approach the corner bus stop, she jumped up and looked out the window to see if Dad was on it. By midnight when the last bus drove by without stopping, Mum closed the window.

I had sat up late, keeping my mother company. Seeing the worry on her face I thought she might cry, but my mother never cried. Not fully understanding the situation, I felt a little flutter of fear.

Weeks later we discovered Dad had sold our house to cover his gambling debts and Mum confirmed he had left us. After losing our home as well as my Dad, we hastily packed up and moved in with Uncle George in his identical house further up the street.

When it comes to marriage, our family has a dismal history. Uncle George's wife had left him only weeks earlier.

The one thing I knew for sure; our mother would NEVER leave us.

Life without Dad had lost its zest but Mum said 'Good riddance', she was sick of his gambling.

School had finished for the day and I was the last one to leave the classroom. After putting my books and the wooden pencil case into the brown, leather bag, I fastened the buckles and slipped the worn straps over my shoulders. Heading for the back gate of the near empty playground, I shuffled along, head down, lost in thought. Why had Dad left us? Why were my legs so skinny? I rode my bike so hard, trying to develop the muscles. I kicked a stone fiercely and it ran along the dirt in front of me, stopping only when blocked by a man's shoe. I jerked my head up and my eyes widened.

"Dad, what are you doing here? I was just thinking about you." Not waiting for an answer I hurled myself into his arms. Oh the thrill of it! I nuzzled into him, smelling that familiar, male smell, not hearing his mumbled reply, just overflowing with joy that he was back.

After a few moments he disengaged himself and held me at arms length. "Let me look at you my beautiful girl." He always called me beautiful. I smiled from ear to ear, not covering my mouth with my hand. After all, I got my gapped teeth from him, didn't I?

"The kids will be so pleased you're back." I babbled "I hope Mum has made extra food for dinner."

His smile faded. "Sorry pumpkin, I won't be coming with you. I only came to say 'Goodbye'. I feel real bad about how I left. I love you kids."

"But why, Dad, why?"

"I've made a few mistakes, Pet, and I take the blame for that but your mother's nagging is difficult to live with."

My joy escaped like the air from a pricked balloon as I digested his words. He then reached into the inside pocket of his sports jacket and pulled out a photograph.

"Look Pet. This is my new girlfriend".

Blindly, I looked at the face of a blonde woman.

"Isn't she a better looking sort than your mother?"

Shock and a strong urge to defend my mother sent the blood rushing to my face, but lost for words I blurted "I have to go Dad, goodbye." And I ran as fast as I could, not stopping until I reached home.

It was many years before I ever saw him again.

Moving up to Uncle George's house, we still had the same bread delivery man. Each day his arrival was heralded by the clip clop of his small brown mare and his lusty voice as he belted out Irish songs. He was a well liked little Irish Aussie whom we children called 'Bake'. Whenever we ran to his cart to collect the bread he regaled us with his repertoire of jokes which we seldom understood. However, his uproarious laughter was infectious so we pretended to understand, giggling and slapping each other boisterously.

After Dad left, Bake insisted on carrying the bread to the house and he spent quite a time chatting with our mother. As time passed, Mum started taking us by train on week-ends to visit him at his home.

Bake's small house in the Sydney suburb of Wiley Park, was dropping flakes of peeling brown paint onto the patch of dying lawn.

Observing my mother's teachings, I made no judgments on this show of poverty.

Mum told us that Bake's wife, a good catholic woman, had died shortly after delivering Billy, her sixth child. Four of these children, three of whom were now working teenagers, lived with Bake. Two other girls boarded with a nearby family and came home on weekends. Billy was a year younger than me.

I enjoyed the visits for they were a cheerful bunch. The older girls painted my nails and curled my hair. Clem's missing finger which he lost while working in a butcher shop fascinated me. He helped me practice my acrobatic entanglements as I secretly dreamed of running away with the circus and I developed my first schoolgirl crush on him.

With the participation of Clarice, Russell and Billy, I continued producing concerts and either we were hilariously funny or the Wiley Park audience was easily amused for they screamed with laughter – week after week after week.

As time passed I grew uneasy over the regularity of these visits, wondering if there was more than bread rising between Mum and Bake.

My Mother with a very young Clarice and Russell in Sydney

CHAPTER 3

PRELUDE TO VIETNAM

Late 1965.

It was fate that took me to Vietnam. But I'm 'jumping the gun'. I have to start with the forerunner, Korea.

My overseas travels started in 1962 when I left Australia to fulfill a contract in the Philippines as an exotic dancer. Traveling abroad for the first time, all alone, I was scared but determined to experience 'life'.

After the Philippine contract expired, I spent three years dancing through the night clubs of Asia. The entertainment circuit in Asia included Manila, Hong Kong, Bangkok, Taipei, Singapore, Kuala Lumpur, and most lucrative of all, Japan in its entirety. Foreign entertainers flocked to Japan for the clubs along the Ginza were bright, modern and plentiful. They did a roaring trade with thousands of affluent Japanese men craving Gaugin (western) entertainers.

Moving from country to country was a cadre of entertainers from the USA, Australia, Britain and Europe. We continually bumped into each other and life was heady as we partied the nights away. In Japan we were highly paid, especially if we removed our bras. I was a skillfully choreographed jazz dancer but I obliged their lustful curiosity by flinging my bra aside at the finale of my act. My friend, a talented American vocalist who was concerned about catching a chest cold, refused, and was paid much less.

Missing from that entertainment circuit was Korea. It was desperately impoverished, not yet rebuilt after the Korean war, and had no night clubs with sufficient money to attract overseas entertainers. Yet, nearing the end of my second six months tour of Japan, I was invited to work in Korea

Commencing in 1910 the Japanese had occupied Korea for thirty years and treated the people abysmally, denying them their own culture or ideology. They stripped the country of its timber and shipped it back to timber poor Japan, leaving Korea with soil erosion. Koreans were forced to learn the Japanese language and forbidden to speak Hangul, their native language. If any were found secretly teaching the children Hangul, they were killed.

This foreign occupation was finally ended during WW11 but too soon it was followed by the five year Korean War. That war left both the North and South reeling and gained neither any significant ground. By war's end, despite the sacrifice of many lives, the demarcation line remains to this day basically at the 48th parallel.

In the 1960's, foreign entertainers still by-passed Korea yet that is where fate led me, with life-changing consequences.

When I arrived at Kimpo airport the Koreans' hatred towards the Japanese still lingered. Aware that most Koreans spoke no English, I anticipated communicating in Nippon Go.

The muscular customs officer gave me a hard look and opened my suitcase. Sitting in full view was my musical arrangement of 'Sakura', an old Japanese folk song. Tucked into one corner was 'watashi no akutcha' - my Japanese doll. The man cleared his throat – or was he speaking? I couldn't tell. He grabbed the doll and glared.

"What's wrong?" I asked after being accosted by a guttural sound from deep within his throat. He shook the doll violently. Was he looking for drugs?

"What is it?" I tried again, dodging the flying spittle as he continued incomprehensibly roaring. Assuming he did not understand English I switched to Japanese.

"Nandeska?"

"Gggrrr." He threw the doll down and grabbed my musical arrangement. With my language skills failing I tried disarming him with a smile.

Half an hour later I left the empty air terminal minus my doll and music. I had learned a lesson. Be careful when speaking in Japanese to a Korean. Maybe next time I would preface it with "Gomenazai, Watashi wa Hungul wacalymasen. Neehon go wacalymaska? Daijobi deska?" Of course, my Japanese is always grammatically incorrect and the spelling is merely a phonetic guess.

The poverty I found in Korea was unlike anything I had previously encountered. Seoul had few paved roads and no electric street lights. Old buildings on either side of the roads were in disrepair.

At night the darkness was filled with flickering, yellow kerosene lanterns. Fumes from charcoal fires tinged the air. The rough, narrow streets overflowed with collapsing vehicles and dirt poor men vied for road space. These hapless males moved, bent double, beneath the loads strapped to their backs on structures that looked like towering A frames. Trudging amid the traffic, inhaling petrol fumes, they did the work of animals.

My six month contract from Walker Hill Resort came at a time when I was tired of hopping on and off planes and constantly changing hotel rooms. Furthermore, I had been in Asia so long that I had worked most clubs at least twice and my solo act was becoming stale. The club managers were looking for fresh acts and my money had begun to drop.

Although Walker Hill Resort offered less money than what I normally earned, the opportunity to sleep in the same bed for months was attractive.

The Resort, a compilation of several buildings and sporting facilities, sat on the banks of the Hun River, seven miles outside of Seoul. It was one of the few places in Korea where visiting dignitaries or the rare tourist could comfortably stay.

I was employed with a dual role; featured dancer in The Walker Hill Show plus English speaking emcee. There was also a Korean emcee. The audience constituted a mix of wealthier Koreans as well as American officers from the nearby military camps. Thirty talented young Korean girls and six young men made up the Honeybee Ballet. I, the only Caucasian, was the star of the show.

The club's stage, an engineering marvel with hydraulically manipulated floor sections, could rise or lower, turn slowly in circles or transport the dancers sideways at strategic moments. Back drops, props, and costumes were first class, as was the white coated orchestra in the pits. The Honeybee dancers, under the demanding eye of their choreographer, practiced arduously each day until their precision equaled that of New York's famous Radio City Music Hall Rockettes.

I was dancing vigorously, maintaining my position centre stage and smiling fixedly at the audience. My two piece costume was a masterpiece of sparkling Swarovski crystals as good as anything found in The Follies Bergere. Fortunately, my strenuous solo did not require I wear the cumbersome, pink, feather head dress worn by the chorus girls. We danced to the tune 'Steam Heat' and appropriately, dry ice and wind machines caused huge clouds of 'steam' to billow up from the stage floor around us. When the music reached a crescendo, four of the male dancers hoisted me aloft where I posed grandly amid a final, volcanic, burst of steam. The heavy curtains came down to a less than deafening burst of applause. I did not take the lack of appreciation personally for it was mid week and the crowd was sparse.

"Tae Dun Hee Kunnnns shumneedah" I spoke gratefully to the young men as they set me down. They spoke no English and I had learned only a few words of Hangul. Nevertheless, I got on well with the entire troupe for I had quickly warmed to the Koreans.

Dressing hastily in the unisex dressing room, I pulled on a gray woolen coat with a fur collar and pushed my feet into calf high, white boots. Waving goodnight to the few Honeybees looking my way, I stepped out into the snow. My contract at Walker Hill included accommodation at one of the resort's two hotels. I lived in the 'civilian' hotel. The second hotel was leased by the Korean Government, who owned the resort, to the American military. They used it as an 'in-country, mini R and R for their officers. The American's still maintained a military presence in Korea. Peace was precarious, and the North Koreans along the DMZ (demilitarized zone) remained dangerously confrontational.

The grounds were well lit as I crunched through the icy snow. My warm breath formed little clouds of mist in the night air and soon my nose felt like a small nub of ice. My journey took me past the Hilltop bar which closed later than the night club. It was a small round building, elevated from the ground by a curving staircase. Deciding to stop for a quick hot toddy, I climbed the stairs and pushed open the heavy, gilded door. Peering into the dim interior I saw that it was even emptier than the nightclub. Monique Monet, a brash, blonde New York stripper I had met years before when we worked together in Manila, was sitting on a banque in the corner. She was passionately kissing a young, slender-bodied Korean who looked at least ten years her junior. He was lapping it up like a little puppy.

The room wasn't much warmer than the weather outside. I pulled my fur collar closer and climbed onto a bar stool. Choi, the congenial bartender hurried towards me "Having the usual, Miss June?" he inquired.

"No thanks Choi. Give me a hot cup of coffee if it's not stale. It's damned freezing tonight."

"I make you fresh pot" he offered.

"And pour a shot of Courvoisier on the side" I called after him.

Monique, recognizing my voice, came up for air. "June Collins" she called "Is that you, you old whore?"

I winced at her words but took them for what they were worth. She had lost her shock effect on me long ago when we worked at Kings Theatre in Manila. Kings was undoubtedly the worst flea bag of a joint in Asia and I shuddered at the memory of how I had been tricked into working there. That was the initial contract which brought me from Australia but that's another story.

Monique dragged the innocent looking young man from the seat and led him over to where I was sitting.

"Meet Pak" she said "He's my boyfriend and, believe it or not, we're getting married next week before heading to Japan."

I couldn't believe my ears. Monique getting married? To a young Korean? She was Jewish and stunning looking. She was also the most hard-boiled, foul mouthed woman I had ever met. When I first met her, still quite naive, she had completely shocked me. It took me awhile to realize the more I re-acted to her crudeness, the worse she became. Once I learned to shrug it off, she toned it down.

"It has been years" I said "What on earth are you doing in Korea? Besides Walker Hill, there's no clubs hiring over here and Walker Hill doesn't hire strippers."

Choi placed my drinks on the bar. I thanked him and signed the tab.

"Oh, there are a few underground joints," she grinned and I didn't dare ask for details.

"I thought you'd gone back to the States years ago. You're not serious about marrying this young boy are you? Does he speak English? He looks like a child."

"I've taught him a few words" her lips curved in a feline smile." And yes, I am marrying him. He's a musician..... I've got a gig in Japan and I'll try to get him work. He's never left Korea before." She turned to her young lover and commanded "Say hullo to my friend."

I had swallowed a mouthful of the Courvoisier and was about to wash it down with some coffee.

The young man smiled at me from his sweet, hairless face and said "Very happy and fuck you, Miss." My mouthful of brandy splattered all over him and he recoiled in shock. Monique all but rolled on the floor with laughter. Confused, but taking his cue from her mirth, he regained his composure and giggled.

"I told you I taught him a few words" she said through her tears. "The look on your face was priceless."

"You can't really marry this innocent" I said "It would be leading a lamb to slaughter."

"You bet I will," she replied. "What sort of a life has he got here? I have enough money for both of us."

"But why? He's so young."

"Yeah! He's a great fuck. He can go all night."

I shook my head and finished my drink.

"You're too much for me Monique. I'm going to bed."

"Please don't go." She became serious. "Like you said, none of the entertainers come this way. It's been ages since I've spoken English. I need to talk to someone." This plea was unlike Monique.

"I know how it feels," I said, thinking of the Honeybees. None of them spoke more than a few words of English, even though I had been trying to teach them. But I had the advantage of the Americans who visited Walker Hill, as well as Kwon Duk Choo, our general manager.

"My wedding's next Wednesday. You must come." She sounded desperate. "There will be dozens of his relatives there and not a soul for me to speak to."

I could just visualize the scene. The ladies would be wearing their voluminous, traditional Korean dresses and the men, their black, lacquered, high crowned horse hair hats.

"It's just as well they can't understand English. But no doubt, you will find some other way to shock them."

"Don't be like that. I really could use a friend."

"Oh alright," I said, rising from my stool "I'll come. I'm sure it will be one to tell the grandkids some day."

CHAPTER 4

AUSTRALIA

1940's

Australia is a country of renowned beer drinkers and the brewery strike was seen as a national disaster. Mum was still taking us to visit Bake on week-ends and like half the men of Australia, he had begun brewing his own beer. I stared curiously at the bathtub which was filled with the greenish/ brown liquid and wondered where everyone bathed. The strong fumes of yeast, barley and hops were enough to inebriate me.

I was helping Bake's daughters shell peas when a sudden series of loud popping noises made me knock the colander of peas onto the floor. I watched as several bottles blew their corks, spraying beer foam almost to the ceiling. It spewed down the bottles and dripped onto the linoleum, floating peas away in little streams of beer.

I do not recall Australians using deodorants at that time and with bath tubs being used as brewing vats, the entire nation must have been rather smelly. Ladies had not started shaving their armpits and it was common to see stains on their garments where the under-arm dress pads had been ineffectual. Of course, air conditioning was widely unknown.

Soon after the beer strike ended, poverty forced my mother to look for work. Most women had rudimentary education and no job skills. My father seemed to have forgotten us completely and he never paid child support. I don't know if the government offered welfare at that time but if it did, my mother would have been too proud to take it.

Once again our patriarch, Pop Harrison took control. He arranged for Mum to work as a barmaid at the Belmore hotel, which was owned by his friend Joe Van Dyke. In the 1940's, society had not entirely divested itself of Victorian values and barmaids were considered loose women. Mum insisted I not tell my friends where she worked.

She settled into the job quickly. "I don't allow the men to swear or tell off color jokes around me," she told me primly "I'm not like some of the other women."

At night she came home exhausted and reeking with the revolting odors of stale beer and cigarette smoke. Our lives were turned upside down. I now had the responsibility of supervising the younger children and helping with the housework and cooking. Soon my school grades began faltering.

We struggled along, each one trying to shoulder our share of the load. Gradually, Clarice and I became concerned that something was wrong with our mother. She had lost her appetite. Without warning her head would fall forward onto the dinner table. Before long she started dropping to the floor in a dead faint.

"Is she dead?" Clarice would cry, scaring Russell into crying as well.

"Buck up" I commanded "She's just overtired. Here! Help me carry her into bed." We struggled to lift her and carry her into the bedroom, even though she now weighed less than ninety pounds.

As I removed her shoes and threw a blanket over her, I hid my trembling hands from the younger children. When Uncle George arrived home early one evening and saw our nightly drama, he hurried to the public phone box and called Nan and Pop.

The next day Nan drove Mum to see the doctor who diagnosed her as having a nervous break down. Pop again took control and arrived at our house on Sunday afternoon a week later.

"Here's the plan, Joyce," he said "I'm sending you and the two youngest children to my cousin Tom's dairy farm in Orbost."

"What? Where is Orbost?" Mum had never been beyond Sydney.

"It's in Victoria. The country air will be good for you. You will work in the dairy to earn your keep while you recuperate."

Mum looked stunned. "I wouldn't know one end of a cow from the other. And what's going to happen to June?"

"She will remain behind and live with me and your mother. She will soon be starting high school and you must not hold her back. Marrickville Girls High is a good school, and there is only a one roomed school in Orbost."

Mum looked a little uncertain but I couldn't believe my ears. I was going to live with my wonderful grandparents in their beautiful, spacious home with its manicured grounds. There was a tennis court, stables for Pop's racing horses and a huge separate billiard room. Gigantic oil paintings in ornate gilt frames lined the walls in the billiard room. I had studied them closely, hoping I could become an artist one day.

Whenever I slept over, Nan always brought hot milk or Milo to my bed, declaring it would make me sleep well. She baked my favorite cakes and made vanilla ice cream. Pop made me feel important, allowing me to do my homework at his big roll top desk in the office. I could even use the telephone although I had only one friend whose parents owned a phone. Most people still used the public street phones.

Pop took me everywhere, proudly introducing me to his horse trainers-his tenants- his friends.

As I contemplated my upcoming, privileged lifestyle, I tried to hide my joy for Mum was looking at me and I didn't want to hurt her.

She would now be separated from our bread delivery man by hundreds of miles so I expected that would be the last we would see of Bake. I wondered if that was part of Pop's strategy.

Months later I was sitting on the verandah of Nan and Pop's red brick house.

"How many legs has a hoss, June?" asked Uncle John, in his rich, deeply accented Scots brogue. I could see his ten year old black, roadster car, shining like a new penny in the driveway. Everyone made fun of Nan's cousin for the way he pampered that car. He was not a rich man and his car was his pride and joy.

"Don't be silly, Uncle John. A house doesn't have any legs." My response elicited a chuckle.

"Here girl" he replied, reaching into his pocket "Here's two shillings for you."

I liked Uncle John even though he was hard to understand. Nan did not have that strong accent for she, the youngest of ten siblings, was the only one born in Australia.

In 1889 her family had owned a timber mill in Kirkinner, Scotland. At that time many British were migrating to America, Canada and Australia. After her father read in the newspaper about Jarra and other fine timbers to be found in Australia, he sold the timber mill and their cottage. The family then set sail from Liverpool on a clipper bound for Sydney. After 130 days at sea they reached Australia and settled on several acres of land in Penrith. Located not far from Sydney, Penrith was still mostly bush land and Nan was born there, four years later.

When my grandmother became a teenager, she controversially married a rough and ready larrikin who worked as her family's stable hand. He was a tough little Cockney who had jumped ship in Sydney. Undoubtedly her parents were displeased with their genteel daughter's choice for a husband. When I thought about it years later, I wondered did she have to get married for she was a soft person who would have a hard time saying no. But it was not a question one would have the temerity to ask.

Nan and my biological grandfather moved to the rumbustious, Sydney suburb of Balmain where Nan kept a spotless house and bore two children in quick succession. Meanwhile her husband found work on a meat lorry, hauling the split carcasses of beef to the Sydney butcher shops. After a hard days work he habitually stopped off at the local pubs to drink beer with his mates. Week-ends found him at the rugby league matches where he became a fanatical supporter of the Balmain Tigers. His mates were a hard drinking mob who paid homage to his pugilistic talents. Brawling was a favorite pastime in those days and earned a man respect. After the Italians started migrating to Sydney in droves, his frequent lament was "You can't trust a wop. They don't fight with their fists, they carry knives."

Nan was unimpressed with her husband's penchant for booze and brawling. She never accompanied him to either the pub or the football field. Nice ladies avoided such places.

It is not surprising that by the time my mother was ten years of age, Nan found her husband with another woman. I learned only sketchy details of the scandal. Sufficient to say that shocked and humiliated, Nan fled the family home in a flood of tears, finding refuge with an older sister whose husband owned a small Sydney petrol station. Eventually they employed Nan as a book keeper. It was there that Pop, a regular customer, discovered her, and I assume, was smitten by her beauty and fell in love. He was a widow, probably on the look-out for a wife. His first wife had died young, as they did in those days, leaving him with four young children.

Pop was the exact opposite of Nan's first husband. I'm certain he never engaged in any fist fights. He had no interest in football. Preferring a glass of Scotch in the comfort of his home, he never hung out in pubs except for an occasional drink with his construction workers. His speech was refined and a good night out meant sitting in the owners stand at Harold Park, watching his horses race. Coincidentally, as well as being a building contractor, he too was in the timber business, being the proud owner of Harrison's Timber Yard on Canterbury Road in the suburb of Campsie.

Much of Pop's money was made during the war years. At night, after the trams stopped running, he would take a team of men into Sydney to demolish the old buildings. They hauled the bricks back to the timber yard, cleaned the unbroken ones and used them again in his new houses.

For years I was unaware he was not my biological grandfather. I met my real one only a handful of times and his connection to me was always vague. No-one spoke openly about divorce for they were rare and considered a sign of failure. I re-iterate -- my family has an appalling history when it comes to divorce.

It felt fantastic being the richest kid in school. Most days I took a tram to my new high school but if I slept late, Nan drove me in the Buick. She never packed lunches. I was given money to buy mine and there was always plenty of change left to buy lollies and milk shakes for my suddenly numerous friends.

My bedroom was furnished with fine antiques and I slept in a luxurious double bed with many pillows. Nan tried to turn me into a 'lady' - meaning any prospective friends were rigidly screened. I was forbidden to whistle or climb the paling fence or run with the neighborhood boys. I could out race every one of them but my bike was given away with a stern reminder of past accidents. Until then, becoming a professional bike racer had been another dream and I rode as if fleeing Satan. One time I hit a rock, flew over the handlebars and landed headfirst on the road, lying there unconscious until the hot sun woke me. When I limped home, pushing my crumpled bike, my mother screamed "Go look at your face in the mirror. The neighbors warned me this would happen!"

I could have qualified for a part in a horror movie. Broken, loose teeth had cut through my swollen, bleeding lips. Skin was completely gone from one side of my face and neck. Small pieces of grit had embedded in my bloody flesh which soon scabbed into an enormous gravel rash.

Life had become sweet! Dinner was always a highlight for Nan was a fantastic cook. Week-ends meant gay tennis parties which ended at night with everyone singing around the Pianola.

Mum wrote weekly letters which I dutifully responded to. She constantly urged me to grab the opportunity to take piano lessons but pushing the pedals of the Pianola was so much easier and I scorned her suggestion.

Best of all were week-ends when we stayed at Nan and Pop's second home. This was built over the ocean at Cronulla, an outer seaside area of Sydney.

Pop parked his car along the cliff crest where stately Norfolk pines grew. We carefully climbed down steep, sandstone steps, crushing pungent Pine needles beneath our feet as we carried our suitcases and boxes of groceries. Sweet smelling flannel flowers with velvety, white petals, sprouted from the sand around the steps. The air was splendidly fragrant with the scent of gum trees, Pines and ocean spray.

Supported on huge pilings, our holiday house sat alone at the bottom of the cliff. I slept beneath a mosquito net on a glass enclosed verandah. The sliding windows allowed the sea breezes in and I could look straight down into the ocean. Pop loved to fish from the deck which led to our saltwater swimming pool; a small section of enclosed ocean. At high tide the waves crashed over the rock walls which were topped by heavy, rusted cable chain. At low tide they ebbed away, leaving the sand temporarily exposed outside the wall. During low tide Pop and I would climb down into the wet sand. With it squelching between our toes, Pop pried oysters from the rock wall. Opening the shells with his pocket knife, he carefully stabbed the oysters and popped the juicy, sea-salt fresh morsels into my salivating mouth.

School holidays came around and I traveled to visit my family in country Victoria. It was my first trip outside Sydney and it took me all day by train and bus. Nan later claimed she was worried sick until Uncle Tom called to tell her I had arrived safely.

Meeting my older country cousins, June and Sylvia, and learning about life on a dairy farm was challenging. I helped bring in the cows and wash their udders with a rag kept in a big, silver bucket of cold water. Crouching low I tentatively cleaned their milk engorged teats, feeling the warmth of their flesh against my face as I reached for the farthest teats. I hated it when they showed their disdain by lifting their tail and splattering me with warm cow dung.

My fear of the massive, heavily muscled bulls must have shown for Mum pulled me aside one day. "June," she said "All animals can smell fear. You must learn to control it." I nodded mutely. A day later I was put to the test.

It was growing dark as I returned to the farmhouse and soon the bats came out. There were millions of them and their swooping and screaming terrified me. I took a shortcut through what looked like an empty field. Half way across I discovered one of those dreaded bulls heading my way. I eyed the distances between it and me and the nearest fence. I wanted to run but at that inopportune moment, my cousin Sylvia rode up on the far side of the fence. I could not give her another opportunity to ridicule me. Staring straight ahead I forced myself to continue nonchalantly. Sylvia had reined in now and I could see she was smirking. Where was that bull now? Was it pounding towards me? I refused to turn my head to look. My brain screamed run, run, run but I plodded on, heart racing. At last I reached the fence and my breath burst free as I climbed the rails. Looking back I saw the brute had its head down, grazing.

It was good to see Clarice and Russell again but we had grown apart. They were country kids now, competent at rounding up cows, hosing out the dairy and shoveling cow dung. My mother's health had obviously improved and surprisingly, she had developed into quite the skilled horse woman.

The holiday had been a happy re-union and a new experience, yet I wasn't too sad when it was time to say goodbye and return to my pampered life in Sydney.

CHAPTER 5

KOREA

My mother had always instilled in me that 'all men are equal.' I believed her even though Australia had that 'White Australia Policy'. She used to read me stories from the newspaper about atrocities the white Americans committed against the Negroes. Sometimes I cried. One time she said "June, when you grow up, any man you marry is welcome here as long as he is a decent person. But it would be easier if you stick to a man of your own race. Society is too hard on mixed marriages and I don't want you to have a difficult life." I nodded mutely, thinking I didn't know any non-whites.

This liberal outlook served me well on my travels through Asia and I never adopted the role of the arrogant white tourist as so many travelers unconsciously or consciously did. Indeed, I immersed myself in the cultures among which I traveled, taking delight in the people. I absolutely loved the Koreans, admiring their hard work, their strength, their courage, their fierceness, their strong, white teeth and their loyalty to family and friends. However, I instinctively knew I wouldn't want one as an enemy.

It is not surprising therefore, that I developed quite a crush on Mr. Kwon Duk Choo, the general manager of Walker Hill. He spoke fluent English, was well traveled, elegantly dressed, unusually tall, and deeply tanned.

During the winter months the resort's tennis courts were hosed down, transforming them into skating rinks. I learned that Mr. Kwon had represented his country internationally in speed skating competitions. Many mornings I rose early to watch him practice.

He flashed past in a blur, flying ice chips stinging my face as I drooled. After discovering he was a married man I was heart broken for months.

The comfort and small luxuries of the resort were a far cry from the rest of the country and I must admit I seldom left those pleasant surrounds. Most people know that Japan is called 'The Land of the Rising Sun'. Few know that Korea is called 'The Land of the Morning Calm'. At Walker Hill I found that description apt. During winter, the mornings were grey and white and misty, ageless and ethereal. It always woke me with a sense of calm; so different from the flaming, red sky, bird shrieking, mornings of Australia.

On the few occasions when I visited downtown Seoul I found no serenity. There were too many people, too much hustle and bustle, too much noise. Wandering street vendors hollered for people to bring their knives and scissors out to be sharpened. Children with dirty faces were dressed in rags. The poverty depressed me.

This nation that I had grown to love had many problems. I read somewhere that American economic aid that year was US $200,000,000 yet there was nothing to show for it. Because of the continual threat from North Korea, the South Korean government maintained a strong, highly trained army of 600,000 men. Even with ridiculously low salaries, this was a huge government expense and rumor had it that the soldiers sometimes went unpaid. Ten years after the war ended, the Americans still had 50,000 troops in Korea. A lesser number of Turkish troops also remained along the border at Panmunjon. It was a sorry situation.

My love affair with the country included their hot, spicy food. On one of my rare trips to Seoul I decided to drop into a local restaurant for lunch.

The manager sat me at a table up front, beside a plate glass window which overlooked the main street. I ordered a meal of Bulgogi, rice and Kimchee. Kimchee is a hot fermented cabbage liberally spiced with chilli and garlic and it's guaranteed to leave an unpleasant breath. All Koreans consume large quantities of it so only 'outsiders' notice the breath. I had gustily taken to it myself, attributing the superbly strong, white teeth of most Koreans, to this sugar free diet.

During the sixties, hordes of tourists were not traveling the world as they are today. Few could afford it. In out-of-the-way places I was sometimes the first white woman the locals had seen and I grew accustomed to being stared at. Therefore I was not too concerned when a crowd began to gather outside the restaurant, staring at me through the glass.

The crowd grew but I tried to ignore them. The Kimchee was extraordinarily hot. I was gulping water, blowing my nose and wiping tears from my eyes when I became aware of a commotion. Looking up I saw a muscular young Korean striding towards me with a smaller man wrapped round his back. The man's hand was outstretched and as they drew closer I saw the young man being carried had only half a torso. Before I could move, there came an angry roar from the rear of the restaurant and the manager charged out like a raging bull. Chairs crashing in his wake, he reached my table at the same time as the two beggars. Grabbing the upright beggar by his arms, he dragged him across the floor and hurled him through the doorway. I gasped as the men crashed onto the rough pavement, and fell apart. The paraplegic rolled over the ground until coming to rest in a stream of dirty gutter water.

Awakening from my stupor I jumped up and ran outside. The manager reached the pair ahead of me, screaming and arm waving. The swelling crowd stood staring stonily. No-one tried to help and I couldn't fathom their lack of sympathy.

The two men pushed and shoved each other. Spittle and obvious curses flew. The legless youth moaned helplessly. When the manager drew his fist back, I jumped forward and grabbed his arm. He spun around, transferring his anger to me.

"Leave them alone you bully." I yelled. He shoved me aside. I staggered backwards, trying not to fall. We shouted at each other in two different languages. Unzipping my money belt, I angrily thrust a handful of won at him. Undoubtedly it was more than what my meal cost but it ended the situation. He stamped inside, slamming the door. The able-bodied beggar raced to the gutter, scooped his companion up and jogged away. Pulling the remaining won from my money belt, I gave chase. They barely paused as I pressed the money on them.

I had been in Asia long enough to learn a few things. Maybe those beggars were family or friends. Maybe it was a business arrangement. It was common practice for healthy 'entrepreneurs' to pay to take handicapped people or sickly babies into the street to beg. Mothers rented out their children; and if they were sick and dirty they were worth more.

Once again, as I had done so often since leaving Australia, I thought sadly of the inequities of the world. Nobody could choose the country, the parents, and the circumstances they were born into. I thanked my lucky stars for Australia and my good health.

Monique's wedding was held at noon on the outskirts of Seoul. The exotic venue was a semi open pavilion with the typical Korean, curved roof, fading red paint and worn gilding. Tables were set, piled high with all types of unfamiliar delicacies. When I arrived, slightly late, a group of small children was singing "Arirang, Arirang," a popular, old Korean folk song." Monique joined in, singing her own smutty version in a high pitched, off key voice. I gawked as she moved about, greeting the formally dressed wedding guests. Ignoring the climate, she was wearing a pair of purple latex pants, cowboy boots, and a sequined bra top which barely protected her nipples. She had scrounged up a white wedding veil from somewhere and wind gusts continually blew it high into the air. As each guest bowed low before her, she refrained from bowing back, which was fortunate, considering the conservative nature of her guests and the brevity of her bra. She welcomed the guests with a few words of Hangul which I had hastily taught her the previous night.

"How do I say 'Thank you for coming in Korean?" she had asked

"Don't ask me," I replied.

"Oh, come on woman. I've heard you speak in Korean. Help me out. I've got to say something."

"Honest. The only Hangul I know is thank you, you're welcome, service please waiter and hullo."

"You're no help. I know that much myself." She sounded disgusted.

"Wait!" I said "I had to learn how to say "Happy New Year' when I emceed the New Year's Eve show. Do you think March is too late in the year to use that salutation?"

"Hell no! That will work just fine." She seemed satisfied.

My tuition had not gone to waste. Monique tripped among her guests, wishing them all A Happy New Year. She clung to young Pak with one hand and clutched a bottle of scotch in the other. The Korean language is a guttural sound and so many exuberant greetings no doubt parched her throat because she kept taking a swig from the bottle before loudly belching then issuing her next Happy New Year. Pak declined her offers to share the scotch but he couldn't stop grinning proudly. I didn't understand why she needed me there for she seemed to have forgotten my presence except for a few occasions when she noticed me and hollered "Hey you old whore, aren't you glad you came?"

For awhile, I munched on rice and black beans with a few varieties of Kimchee but I was cold and becoming bored. About the time I saw Pak try to give her a marital kiss I was ready to go. She responded to his kiss with a humping movement and as they lost their balance and fell into an oversized bowl of eel jelly, I took my leave.

CHAPTER 6

I never did like cold weather and the spring was taking its sweet time arriving. Monique was gone. I had a new routine to learn and although I still loved Korea, I was bored with serenity and craving action.

Another show was finished and, true to my habit, I stopped off at The Hilltop Bar. Passing through the gilded doorway the first person I saw was O'Halloran, the American liquor salesman. He sat puffing on a cigar and blowing smoke rings into the air. O'Halloran liked to boast about his lucrative work selling liquor to the U.S. army clubs. He traveled the camps from Germany to Okinawa, Korea to the Philippines.

After I seated myself at the bar, Choi hurried towards me.

"Gin and tonic Miss June?" he smiled.

I nodded and glanced around. The bar was almost deserted- again. O'Halloran immediately stood, smoothed back his receding hair and pulled his stool closer to mine.

"How was the crowd in the club tonight?"

Not waiting for my answer, he took a slug from the can of Budweiser he was holding.

"Dead like every Tuesday night. Only a handful of Koreans! None of your countrymen are out and about mid week. It should pick up when the weather improves."

Choi set my gin and tonic down. O'Halloran belched. The smell of regurgitated beer mixed with cigar smoke was nauseating. I decided to finish my drink and leave. He was as attractive as a baboon's butt.

"Nice manners" I said, shaking my head. He let my remark pass, wiping his mouth on his shirt sleeve.

"I came out here especially to talk to you tonight."

"Better make it quick then. They keep it too damned cold in here and I need an early night."

He was another past his prime expatriate living the good life in Asia. I'd seen plenty of these men. They strutted about, deluding themselves they were a real catch and not just a meal ticket to the young, good looking Asian girls who invariably clung adoringly to them. But in a community where there were few Westerners, we all knew and tolerated, even sometimes liked each other.

"How long you been kickin' up your heels in this joint now?" he asked.

"Five, six months – . I forget."

"Don't you wanna get back to making real money again? You can't be makin' much here."

"After working non stop these last few years I've enjoyed this break."

"Well, if ya ready to get your ass in gear again I've gotta business proposition that will knock your britches off."

I stared stonily.

"You might find it interesting. I do believe ya are some sort of expert on jewelry. Right?"

"I wouldn't call myself an expert. However, over the last five years I have gained some knowledge."

For the previous two years I had invested my money in gemstone quality jewelry, learning all I could from a Chinese jeweler friend in Hong Kong.

"Well I need someone like you to manage a string of jewelry concessions. I dunno enough myself."

"Are you planning to open a shop here in Korea?"

"Hell no! I'm joining the crowd moving to Vietnam."

"Vietnam? Where the hell's that?"

"Where have you been lady? There's a war going on down there. It's in S.E. Asia. Your neck of the woods."

"Well I've rarely heard of it and I'm certainly not interested in any war zone."

"How much ya making here? It ain't much, I'll wager." He sucked on his cigar then blew a stream of smoke in my direction. I twisted away.

"That's none of your damn business."

"Well if ya wanna be like that I'll go to someone else. I'm making ya an offer that could make ya a rich woman. Anyway, I've gotta go piss. When I get back ya tell me if you're interested." He slid from the stool and left the room trailing a spiral of smoke.

The mention of money had pricked my interest. I was beginning to miss it.

O'Halloran returned and gestured for another beer. "I'll pay for hers too," he said.

"Thanks but I run a weekly tab." I didn't want to be indebted to him. "Now tell me more about your proposition –if it's not a scam."

"This is strictly legit." He paused to gulp his fresh Budweiser. "You musta heard we Yanks are sending troops into Vietnam?"

"Not really."

"You have connections where ya can buy jewelry wholesale in Hong Kong, right?"

"Sure. But anyone can find wholesalers if they've got the money."

"Yeah, and the knowledge. Anyway, this war is gonna escalate and Uncle Sam will be sending beaucoup troops. Those men will require PX's and commissaries where they can buy stuff, ya know?"

"I'm listening."

"PX stands for Post Exchange and the troops can buy any Goddamn thing they want there. Because of my contacts, I'm gonna put a jewelry concession in the one on Long Binh base.... Shit," he became excited "that will be the biggest supply base in the whole of Vietnam and the potential is limitless. Every fuckin' GI in Vietnam will pass through there at some time or another. Ya know?"

"I know nothing except I'm taking exception to your disrespectful language."

He spluttered, "God almighty. Come down off your high horse. You run around Asia with half your tits hangin' out and ya sound like a Salvation Army broad."

I conceded he had a point and let it drop.

"Exactly what would my role be in this Lung Bin place then and just how dangerous is it?"

"Your job, if you take it, will be to purchase the stock and supervise the Vietnamese broads who sell it. You will fly regularly into Hong Kong on buying trips."

Now he had my attention. Hong Kong was my favorite city on earth. I had many friends there. The only reason I didn't live there was because a solo dancer could rarely stay indefinitely at any given place.

"And how dangerous is this Lung Bin?"

"If the gooks ever got that close it would be all over. Don't worry. It's only a few miles down the road from Saigon. There's no fighting around there."

I absently swallowed some gin tonic as I thought about this.

"Two more questions – how much would I be paid and where would I live?"

"I'll give you a thou a month and you will make commission on volume. The sky's the limit. We'll start with the main location and maybe branch out. Believe me, we will walk out of there set for life."

We sat momentarily silent, each with our thoughts. Finishing his drink he ordered another round. I didn't stop him. We were the only remaining customers.

"Are we keeping you from closing Choi?" I asked.

"He don't mind" O'Halloran interrupted. "I tip him real good. Don't I Choi?" he paused, "So, what's your answer?"

"It's a big step." I was hesitant but intrigued.

"Well with you or without ya, I'm off to Vietnam in the next few weeks, along with half of Korea. Saigon is where it's gonna be happening now."

"Why is half of Korea going?" I frowned.

"Same as anyone - money!" He rubbed his fingers together, grinning.

"I still don't get it!"

"Uncle Sam don't wanna look like he's goin this war alone. He's trying to drum up allies so the world won't think it's just an American war. The Korean government has agreed to send ROK troops down there – for a price."

"ROK?" I frowned.

"Republic of Korea. Everyone calls the Korean troops ROK's. They're damned tough. Since the Korean war ended and with North Korea just over the border at Panmunjon, they are trained as some of the best Goddamn soldiers in the world now."""

"I understand" I said, "The Turkish Charge D'affaire's took me up to the DMZ to visit the Turkish camp. Those North Koreans look scary."

"Well this is a great opportunity for South Korea. The government pays them a pittance so they're lining up for the privilege of goin to Vietnam."

"Privilege?"

"Money- woman! Uncle Sam is gonna pay every ROK the equivalent pay as an American of the same rank. For a Korean that is a fortune. Add to that the American PX and commissary benefits. They will be sending home cheaply bought refrigerators and television sets by the plane load."

"Well, I don't blame them."

"Yeah, the black market is gonna be flourishing in Vietnam and Korea. The money lenders here are raking it in."

"How's that O'Halloran?" I frowned again.

"For God's sake woman, call me Hal like everyone else." He emptied his beer, squashed the metal can in his meaty hand and continued. "Everyone's gotta make a buck. The ROK assignment officers are demanding a helluva kickback from each man placed in units shipping out. The troops are selling their souls to the moneylenders to pay for this opportunity. They'll HAVE to deal on the black market to pay back their loans at fifty percent interest rates."

"It's disgusting." I said, "Somebody's always squeezing the little guy."

"Well are ya in?"

"I'm definitely interested. It's getting boring around here."

It was a new adventure, I thought, but, was it one I really wanted?

"And accommodation? Is it in this Lung Bin place?"

"That's part of the package. I'll go ahead and find us both a place in Saigon. And I wish you'd get the damned name right. Long Binh. L O N G B I N H. Got it?"

"Sorry! And you're sure you've got this deal sewn up Hal. I don't want to quit here and have it fall through down there." I felt uncomfortable, lowering my barriers by using his nick name.

"As certain as I can be…. Like the saying goes, 'It's not whattcha know. It's who ya know.' And I'm good buddies with Bill Woolridge, the top enlisted man in the whole goddamn United States Army. Sergeant Major Woolridge has more power than most of the officers put together, and he pulls strings."

"Doesn't an officer outrank a sergeant major?"

"Not this one. Each division has several sergeant majors one per battalion. My buddy Bill is above the lot. He is the highest ranking enlisted man in the entire army, answering directly to the Commanding General himself. That's real power." He shot me a smug look.

"Are you sure I'll have my own place to stay?"

"You bettcha! It may not be fancy but it will be adequate."

"And there are no strings attached?"

"Aw come off it. I'm a married man. Besides, if I wanted a bit of pussy there'd be more than a man could handle in Saigon."

"You have an explicit way of expressing yourself, Hal."

He guffawed and looked at his Seiko watch. "I'll soon trade this one for a gold Rolex, but speaking of wives, I've gotta get home. Are ya in or not?"

"Looks like I'm in." I said, silencing the little voice inside.

Back in my room, I took a shower to remove the stench of cigar smoke. What exactly was I getting into? I didn't trust O'Halloran. Yet I'd heard it said he was a rough diamond but 'straight'.

I dried my hair and pulled on my flannel pajamas. Better get some sleep, I thought. Tomorrow I have to tell Kwon Duk Choo I'm leaving.

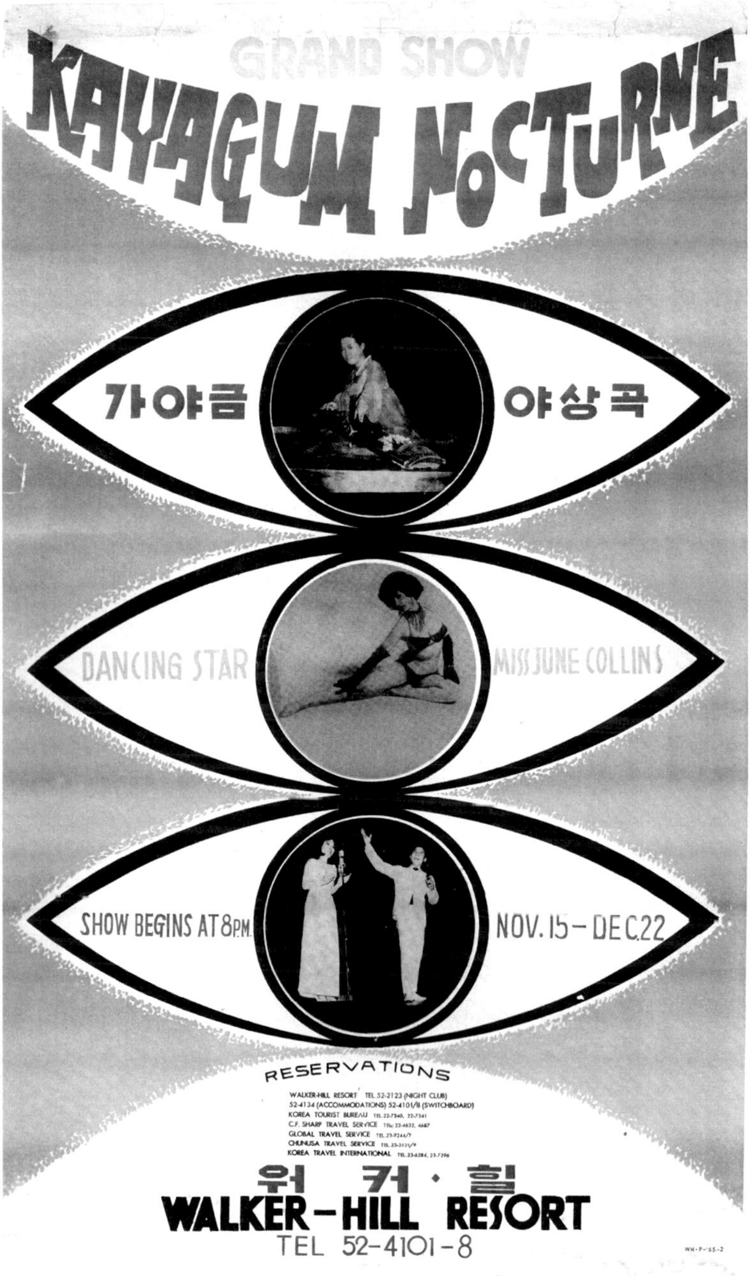
GRAND SHOW
KAYAGUM NOCTURNE
가야금
야상곡
DANCING STAR
MISS JUNE COLLINS
SHOW BEGINS AT 8P.M.
NOV. 15 – DEC.22
RESERVATIONS
WALKER-HILL RESORT TEL. 52-2123 (NIGHT CLUB)
52-4134 (ACCOMMODATIONS) 52-4101/8 (SWITCHBOARD)
KOREA TOURIST BUREAU TEL. 22-7340, 22-7341
C.F. SHARP TRAVEL SERVICE
GLOBAL TRAVEL SERVICE
CHUNUSA TRAVEL SERVICE
KOREA TRAVEL INTERNATIONAL
워 커 · 힐
WALKER-HILL RESORT
TEL 52-4101-8

CHAPTER 7

SAIGON APRIL

1966.

After so many years of dancing through Asia, I should have become street smart, yet I occasionally disgusted myself with naiveté. Now I was anxious over my commitment to work with O'Halloran.

I was disillusioned with men. My father had run off and my grandfather's love cooled after I grew old enough to develop a mind of my own. My high-school crush, Dennis, turned out to be a despicable braggart. Last of all was my husband Peter who was weak when I needed him. After leaving him I vowed I would never rely on any man again.

It was a time when independent women were a rare species but I was determined to blaze my own trail. However, that trail blazing did not stop me from enjoying male company. On the contrary, I preferred male company and was prone to share my bed if I found someone irresistibly attractive. And I was a scrupulously faithful, temporary mate. But the keyword was definitely TEMPORARY.

O'Halloran certainly was not irresistibly attractive and I had doubts about relying on his word when a working relationship meant propinquity.

The Air France, 707 plane landed at Tan Son Nhut airport on a steamy April day in 1966. Air France was the primary commercial carrier between Hong Kong and Saigon and I was then unaware that the ex patriots in Saigon caustically referred to it as Air Chance.

I prepared to disembark, a mixture of apprehension and curiosity.

Descending the steps in my four-inch heels, I did my best to appear nonchalant while wondering if bullets would start whizzing past at any moment. But all was calm as I strode towards the shabby terminal building. Oppressively hot air caused beads of sweat to cover my face after only seconds. My stilt heels sank deep into the sizzling bitumen of the tarmac, becoming imprisoned by the sticky tar which pulled one shoe from my foot. The hot ground burned my foot as I pulled the shoe free, the pointed heel trailing thin strands of black tar. Hopping about, I slipped it on my foot and continued on my way. 'This is not a spectacular entrance to the next chapter of my life,' I thought, sighing heavily.

Inside the terminal there was no air conditioning and no relief from the stifling heat. I surveyed the unimaginable bedlam and any remnant of confidence quickly evaporated along with my makeup. The crowds stood shoulder to shoulder, pushing and jostling their sweat soaked bodies forward in the stagnant air. Claustrophobic under any circumstances, I was overwhelmed. Deodorants were not a high demand item in those days and body odors made me almost retch. Grabbing a lace edged handkerchief from my bag, I held it to my nose as the throng of chaotic humanity shoved me towards the immigration officers. At last, I stood before a frazzled officer. The little man in his crumpled, damp uniform glared at me before challenging "Why you here?"

Good question. Why indeed? Every instinct told me to turn and run like hell. But gutless and out of my comfort zone I suffered the interrogation until he stamped my passport and shoved it at me with a few unintelligible words.

Beyond the immigration desks, civilians and military men of many nationalities sat, lay, leaned in every available space. Very small, black-toothed people, in conical, straw hats, pushed and spat among the soldiers. American GI's (government issue) carried duffle bags almost as big as themselves. The ROK's, ramrod straight and starched, were intimidating, and towered over the clusters of small soldiers who slouched about holding hands. I guessed that these smaller soldiers were the Vietnamese whom the Americans were there to help. They looked beaten already with their slumped posture and crumpled uniforms and I questioned their sexuality, confused by their hand holding. By that time I was sure I looked pretty beaten myself and it was with immense relief that I heard O'Halloran's voice.

"June, June, this way. Over here, come on."

I never thought I would be so pleased to hear his voice. At last I saw him towering like a hairy bear above a group of Vietnamese civilians.

"Welcome pardner" he grinned.

"Hal, get me out of this hell hole." I gasped. "This place stinks."

"Yeah!" He agreed, "It's that stinkin Nuoc Mam fish sauce they eat. Welcome to Saigon." He grabbed a suitcase in each hand. I lifted the third one and puffing, (it was the days before suitcases had wheels) I followed him from the building.

Outside, a slight breeze stirred the tropical air and I inhaled deeply.

An old sedan pulled alongside and O'Halloran proudly said, "This is my car and driver. I've got a permit to bring them on base." In my ignorance, his momentous achievement was lost and I merely shrugged. The withered Vietnamese driver leaned from his window at that moment and squirted a mouthful of dark red betel nut onto the road. I jumped back, repulsed as O'Halloran commented, "Better get used to it. The older ones here go for that stuff." I wondered what kind of drug it was, certain it needed some helluva kick to compensate for the ugly black mouth and teeth it produced.

We settled into the back seat of the old non-air-conditioned Ford sedan.

"Caravelle Hotel, Huey," Hal ordered.

"Is that where I'm staying?"

"No. I thought ya might like to have a cool drink and see the town first."

"A cool gin and tonic would indeed clear the dust from my throat. The town can wait."

We drove out of Tan Son Nhut, passing the American armed guards at the gate of the terminal, which doubled as a military air base. I fell back against the seat as we edged into the fume-spitting, heaving traffic. Clouds of dust and exhaust gas floated through the open window. We lurched from pothole to pothole, dodging the thousands of small Honda scooters that zipped all around us. I was astounded to see the scooters carried as many as four people each. Hundreds of little blue and yellow Renault taxis tooted their tinny horns, but were totally ignored by the masters of the road, the lumbering khaki colored army trucks. I could see, squashed into the open backs of these trucks, groups of fresh faced American soldiers. They sat with their rifles pressed between their knees and bemused expressions upon their faces.

The only bright sight in this drab, dirty scene was the youthful Vietnamese girls who clung nonchalantly on the backs of the crowded Honda's. Their black hair hung long and shiny down their spotlessly white ao-dai's (white cotton dresses, split up each side) and I marveled that they could remain so clean.

"You'd better be right about making some money here," I said, "This God forsaken place looks like hell and these Vietnamese are the most undernourished, bedraggled people I've ever seen and you know I've been in Asia awhile."

"Don't be so negative. You'll get used to it." I doubted his words, noticing we had pulled onto a slightly wider, smoother road. This street was tree lined and the two storied, white buildings were an improvement over those we had previously passed. Colonial in style, they uniformly sported black, barred windows.

"Ah, civilization is it? These must be the villas the French used to live in."

"You're probably right. This is Hai Ba Trung. But how do you know about the French? You said you'd never heard of Vietnam?"

"Big boobs and blonde hair doesn't make me an airhead, O'Halloran. Once I decided to come here of course, I read up on it. A Frenchman named Bernard Fall wrote a terrific book called 'Street Without Joy'. Have you read it?"

"I'm too busy making money to find time to read." He grumbled.

"Well I read this one twice and it makes you wonder why America wants to get involved here. There probably wouldn't be a war if your country, along with the British, hadn't broken a promise made by one of your ex-Presidents to these people. They were promised liberation from the French after you kicked the Japanese out in WW11. That promise was not kept and you handed them back to the French. No wonder they're mad."

"Don't blame me! Anyhow, I'm not interested in politics. Look here," He pointed, "See those villas – the outer walls are topped with barbed wire and broken glass."

I shrugged.

Fifteen minutes later, we moved into a circular roundabout and I could see we had reached the city. Dominating the centre of the busy roundabout was a massive black statue of a crouching soldier grasping a rifle at the ready.

The driver eased the car over in front of a colonial style building with the name The Caravelle Hotel.

"Straight ahead is Tu Do, the main drag." Hal said, pointing to a bar lined street overloaded with flashing, neon lights. "Anyway, jump out so Huey can go park."

I followed him into the Caravelle Hotel. He stopped before a table in a wide, open-air section overlooking the busy corner traffic. Hiding my anxiety, I wondered how safe we were in such an exposed position. The place was thronged with Caucasian men wearing civilian clothes. They seemed unconcerned by the vulnerable location so I relaxed. Few Vietnamese or military people were present.

"This is a journo's hang-out." Had O'Halloran read my thoughts? "Television crews, journalists, the lot of them hang here when not chasing the action. And for those too lazy to chase the action, there are always the 5 o'clock follies."

"Speak a language I can understand O'Halloran."

"Hal's the name. Remember?" He beckoned a white coated Vietnamese waiter over and ordered drinks.

"The Follies are the military's daily update of battles and body count. It's all bullshit of course."

I took my handkerchief and powder compact from my purse and tried to repair the damage to my make up.

"I'm gonna take a leak. Be back in a minute." Hal rose and left but I noticed he didn't get far before stopping on the opposite side of the room to talk to a group of men. They looked in my direction and one slapped him over the shoulder. I wondered was he bragging, making some proprietary claim to me. The drinks arrived. My throat felt like a blocked sewer. Grabbing a glass, I finished half my drink in one huge swallow.

"Couldn't wait, huh?" Hal returned and sat down, lifting his own drink.

"Scholl"

"Camp pye" I smart-assed in Japanese "Anyway, tell me Hal, where are you and your wife staying?"

"Are you shittin me? Why on earth would I bring her here? She's got our kid to look after. I sent them to the States. This ain't no place for any woman. Not my wife, anyway."

I let his remark pass.

"How about you? Ya ever been married?"

"Yes."

"What happened?.......... Ya got any kids?"

"Let's drop that subject if you don't mind. Leave the past in the past..." I drained my glass. "Anyway, tell me, where am I staying?"

He cleared his throat and took another swallow before answering.

"Well honey, there's been a bit of a snag. I've had a helluva time finding a place for either of us."

I had a sinking feeling and frowned at his familiar use of the endearment 'honey'.

"But you have found me a place, right?"

"I've found one place. If ya like it, it's yours. If not, I'll keep it for myself. But meantime we will have to bunk together until I find a second place."

I could feel my temper rising. He read my expression.

"What you've gotta realize little lady, is that this place is going through a shit-load of upheaval. Troops and businessmen are flocking in here from everywhere. Apartments are as scarce as whores in a cathedral. People are paying top dollar to snap up any rat-infested dump. There's just not enough to go around.

It's the same with everything. Look at my car for instance. I paid as much for that ten-year-old clunker as I'd pay for a brand new machine back home. You take what you can get and be grateful ya beat the next guy to it." He reached for his drink and finished it in one giant swallow then waved irritably to our waiter to bring refills. My mind raced. "What the hell have I got myself into?"

CHAPTER 8

AUSTRALIA

Arriving home from school I stopped by the kitchen and gave Nan a peck on the cheek.

"Had a good day Junie Moon?" she called me Junie Moon sometimes and I quite liked it. "I've made your favorite sponge. Would you like a glass of milk or a cup of tea with it?"

I eyed the fat sponge dripping pink icing onto a crystal plate. It presided over the long, aluminum counter top.

"I'll change my uniform first, Nan, and then a cup of tea would be lovely."

Hurrying soundlessly along the thick, Axminster carpet in the wide hallway, I passed through ornate glass doors and glanced at the seven foot high Roman soldier in full metal armor. The bronze statue held aloft a glass torch which, at night, emitted a soft yellow light. Grinning, I recalled how, as a younger child I was scared of that statue and ran by as fast as possible.

After changing and washing my hands I returned to where Nan waited with a big slab of cake and a steaming cup of tea.

"By the way, June" she said "a letter came from your mother today. It's over there on the side board."

I retrieved the letter, tore it open and read while eating.

Orbost Wednesday

Dear June,

We were all pleased to read your last letter and learn everyone is well. I am happy with the results of your last physics exam but disappointed with your attempts at the French language.

But enough of that! I have big news! This time next month we are returning to Sydney. We will only stay long enough to collect you and then we are taking a long train journey. You see, I have decided to leave Orbost and make a new life for us in a country town in New South Wales called Tamworth. The good news is that we will all be together again like a proper family. Please make sure that all your clothes are packed and do collect your school records so that you can enroll in your new school…………………

I stopped reading, crumpled the paper and threw it across the table.

"Why, what's wrong, dear?" Nan's eyes searched my face.

"Mum's taking me away." I blurted.

"What? She wouldn't. Here, let me read that." She retrieved the letter and smoothed it out.

"Pop and I will try and talk some sense into her dear." Nan said frowning "You will be much better off finishing school here."

Mum's news devastated me. Why did my life continually change? I wished I was old enough to control my own destiny, if such a thing was possible.

The month passed too quickly. I had never heard of Tamworth. Mum may as well have said we were going to the moon. How dare she uproot me this way! I would not leave and go with her. I would not! I wandered into the sun room where I found Nan sitting, a skein of navy wool in her lap as she knitted a jumper for Pop.

"Why are we going to this place?" I asked "She seemed happy in Orbost. Something's wrong!"

Nan kept on clacking the tortoise shell needles, not looking up.

We had already exhausted this subject. "No doubt we will find out when she arrives tomorrow…..Try not to worry, dear."

"Well I won't pack." I said truculently as I left the room, recalling the days when I lived at Uncle George's house. There had seldom been time to do homework, or to read or paint…… And I was so happy here. How could my mother do this to me?

The next day, when I returned from school, I found Mum had already arrived. My sister and brother were no-where in sight and I wondered where they were. Standing unnoticed in the sun room, I saw Mum and Pop in the dining room, having a heated argument. Pop seldom raised his voice and their loud, angry voices brought grim foreboding. Creeping closer, I heard Nan sobbing in the kitchen. I stepped into the room and stopped in confusion. My mother certainly looked well. Gone was that little ninety pound weakling. In fact she looked rather robust. Almost fat! Then it hit me! My mother was pregnant! But why? How? Who?

Dad had been gone a long time and this was the woman who had constantly preached to me about maintaining high moral standards and saving myself, a virgin, until after marriage. She had never told me exactly how one lost their virginity but she had alluded to it in self conscious little bursts ever since my thirteenth birthday. Sex education was not then part of any school curriculum and adults apparently couldn't bring themselves to talk about it. The whole process was a bit of a mystery to me. But I could recognize a pregnant woman when I saw one and I knew the process took nine months. Seething with anger I wondered how she could practice such a double standard. This woman who constantly preached respectability - when did she abandon her principles and to whom?

"Have you no decency? And he's a catholic to boot." Pop, a Mason who disliked Catholics, was yelling. "Your daughter has a future here. Think of her."

"Yes Mum" I interjected, causing them both to spin around "And I won't go with you. You can't make me."

"You will do what you're told young lady. I'm your mother and you are not old enough to make your own decisions. Go get your bag."

"I will not." I hollered, surprising myself for I had never spoken to my mother like that. Her eyes blazed.

"Listen to you. You've changed" she said "You've become just like him" she nodded in Pop's direction. "He's turned you into a snob. You're not staying here another minute."

Nan entered the room, tears running down her cheeks. "Calm down everyone" she sobbed "This is not getting us anywhere."

I ran over and threw my arms around her. "You tell her Nan. She can't take me."

Mum lowered her voice, seeing her mother's tears, but when she spoke again she was cold and unyielding "Get your bags June. It's my life, you're my daughter and if I have to call the police to take you I will."

Devastated, I left the room as Pop had the last word "You're finished here. You've brought shame to all of us. When you walk through that door don't ever come back. Your mother and I will have nothing more to do with you."

My mother and I rode the red, double-decker bus in silence. She told the bus conductor we were going to Central Railway Station. Arriving, I followed her off, each of us struggling with a suitcase.

Another shock awaited me at the country train platform. Clarice and Russell were there. My eyes opened wide. So were Bake and his youngest son Billy.

So this was the score! She had never mentioned in her letters that he had been making trips to Victoria to see her. I was speechless, wondering how I could live with the stigma of an unwed mother.

Looking back upon that day years later, I tried to put myself in my mother's shoes. She had become basically a social outcast. Nevertheless, I thought she should have left me behind.

My anger now included Bake and I was surly with everyone, concluding they were conspirators. Remembering that Bake was a poor, uneducated man only fuelled my anger.

We boarded the train and stowed our luggage on the overhead racks. I sulked throughout the long, dark night, straining to hear the adults' conversation. I gathered that our new life would commence with a share farming job on a dairy located a few miles outside of town. The prospect of living every day surrounded by cows did not lift my spirits.

CHAPTER 9

VIETNAM

It took only one night to realize this project between me and O'Halloran was not going to get off the ground. Despite his assurances, I had spent a rough night rebuffing his advances and early the next morning I checked into the Caravelle Hotel. This was quite an accomplishment but a last minute cancellation enabled my lucky break.

Trying not to make an enemy of O'Halloran, I had let him think our working arrangement was still in place, and I had moved out only to find a place of my own. But, I knew it would never work with him and I was now in a desperate situation with no Plan B.

Once again I sat in the open air lounge of the Caravelle Hotel, this time drinking a strong, chicory filled coffee and reading The Stars and Stripes. I assumed the last customer had left the American military newspaper on the table.

I was surrounded by an alien world. Horns tooted discordantly, engines roared and aircraft flew noisily overhead. American Army jeeps, troop trucks, small blue and yellow Renault cabs and hordes of overloaded, Honda scooters circled the round-about. Waiting for customers, on the side of the road was a gaggle of identical cyclo drivers. They squatted beside their bicycles on sinewy, muscled legs, flashing black teeth under straw hats. Most smoked hand rolled cigarettes or chewed betel nut, spitting often into the hazy cloud of exhaust fog encompassing all.

Caucasian women were conspicuous by their absence. It wouldn't be the destination of choice for most women and I wondered how I had landed there against my better judgment.

As lunchtime approached I ordered a chicken sandwich but before I could take a bite, a man's voice distracted me.

"I don't suppose I could share your table could I? All the tables are taken and I would like to eat some lunch." The voice was obviously American.

I looked up to see a short, freckle faced, red headed man with pasty white skin. He looked out of place and I concluded he was a newcomer like me. Shoving his blue sunglasses on top of his head he reached out his hand "Steve Baker's the name."

"Go ahead" I indicated the opposite seat. "I'm June Collins."

"An Aussie?"

"Isn't it obvious?"

"Well you could have been English."

The waiter took his order. "Can I get you a drink?" Steve asked.

"It's a bit early for me and I'm leaving now."

"Don't let me run you off. I hate eating alone."

Bored, and with nothing better to do, I relented. The waiter soon returned with a steak and salad for my table mate.

"That's probably buffalo meat you're eating." I said.

He took a mouthful and chewed solidly in silence for five minutes. After swallowing, he wiped his eyes and asked, "How did you know?"

"A lucky guess! I've lived in Asia a long time. Anyway, what brings you to Vietnam? You don't look like military?"

"Neither do you" he smiled, eyeing me brazenly.

"My presence here is a mistake. I expect I'll fly out to Hong Kong in two days… Now, how about you?"

He doused his steak with more ketchup, causing me to ponder the American love of the stuff.

"I'm here to do my patriotic duty." He said placing the now dripping bottle back on the table.

His pomposity rankled me.

"Actually I'm an entertainer."

"Really? I'm also an entertainer and I've never seen you on the Asian Entertainment Circuit."

"I hope not. Strictly American audiences for me. Back home I do a lot of television."

My first opinion was re-enforced.

"I'm a magician. And I picked you as show biz immediately. Do you sing or dance?"

"Afro-Jazz dancing."

"Working the camps are you?"

"I wouldn't know how. Besides, as a solo artist my routine only lasts for ten minutes. I'm not part of any show."

He set his fork down "Talk about fate. That's about to change, June Collins. Here I was, looking for a Vietnamese broad to hire as an assistant while I hit the camps for a few weeks. What luck, to run into you on my very first day in town. So how's about we team up?"

"I don't think so. I've already got a bad taste in my mouth."

"Pleeeaase, stay. I could teach you what to do in a couple of hours and I promise there are no strings. Your main concern will be looking after Cedric."

"Cedric?" I frowned absently while thinking 'the no strings bit sounded familiar.

"Yeah, Cedric." And within a flash he produced a cute white rabbit from God-knows-where and set it on the table where it hopped about and nibbled at his salad. We laughed and my defenses crumbled.

To this day I blame that damned rabbit that I became a magician's assistant in Vietnam.

By the end of the day I had rehearsed sufficiently to handle the job. My costumes were suitable for the role. When we returned to the lounge, a couple of the journalists recognized Steve from his television appearances and joined us. They gave helpful advice about how to best reach the camps.

As darkness fell and the neon lights outside sparkled even brighter, I rose from the table.

"Time for a shower!" I said "If we are heading out to the airport at six a.m. I plan on getting an early night."

"What about dinner?"

"I'll settle for room service."

One of the journo's spoke. "Not going now are you?"

I nodded.

"You'll miss the fireworks. You're going to join us, aren't you, Steve?"

"What fireworks?" Steve looked worried.

"Everyone takes their drinks up to the roof top deck. There's a great view from there. The Viet Cong put on their evening show a few miles out of town, around Binh Hoa."

"I'm up for it." Steve grabbed his drink and stood.

"I'd better see this too." I said, changing my mind and following the men as they headed for the stairs.

The dark rooftop was abuzz with the hum of conversation and the sound of tinkling glasses. Waiters ran back and forth amid shadowy groups of men. There was an undercurrent of excitement as people anticipated the evening spectacle. Before long the darkened sky lit up. Explosions flashed then faded –bursting in a kaleidoscope of color and brilliant white light, producing oohs and ahhs from the spectators.

"How long does this last?" I asked one of the cameramen after ten minutes.

"It will end any time now. Either our artillery will find them or the VC will dee de mau before they get caught."

"Dee de mau?"

"Run away!"

"Ah. In that case, I will dee de mau myself. Good night gentlemen....See you bright and early Steve!"

While showering in lukewarm water I speculated on what wretched soul may have just lost their home or maybe their life. War had provided macabre entertainment for some. I couldn't quite get my head around it.

CHAPTER 10

1966

When Steve and I set out in April 1966, there were very few entertainers in Vietnam and the total number of American troops numbered just over 250,000. Those numbers would eventually swell to 500,000 and by that time, entertainers would be flocking in, mostly in group shows. Because initially, entertainers were so few, no arrangements had been made to assist us in any manner. It was only after the troop build up that MACV (Military Assistance Command, Vietnam) set up an office to regulate and assist entertainers.

Steve and I took a small blue and yellow Renault taxi to Tan Son Nhut airport which doubled as an American Air Force base, making entry difficult for civilians. The cabbie let us out a few yards short of two solemn faced, American MP's (military police) guarding the gate. We clambered out of the ridiculously small vehicle and began unloading our gear, which was crammed to the roof. Steve stared at the pile of boxes and paraphernalia sitting in the dusty road and scratched his head.

"Son of a bitch! How on earth are we supposed to move this lot out to a plane?"

"Don't worry" I said "One of your obliging young countrymen is sure to offer help. But first, we have to get past those guards. Give me your driver's license or your passport."

"What?"

"We need to show I.D when we tell the guards why we are here."

"Oh, of course! Well I'm the American here so I should talk to them while you watch our stuff. Don't let Cedric out of your sight."

As if recognizing the sound of his name, Cedric gave a little squirm against my chest. He was diapered and tucked inside my shirt.

By the time Steve reached the gate, a jeep had already screeched to a halt beside me.

"Can we help you ma'am?" A skinny, black kid in the passenger's seat yelled over the sound of two, low flying helicopters.

"That would be lovely Thanks a lot." I yelled back.

The driver, a white kid with bad skin grinned, "Oh boy, a round eye," he said, jumping eagerly from the Jeep. The two of them had the stuff stowed by the time Steve returned with permission to enter.

"Thanks guys." Steve shook hands and struck up a conversation with the GI's as they drove us towards the military aircraft loading area.

An hour later we managed to board a C130 Hercules heading for Cam Ranh Bay. The enormous cavity of the plane was crowded with sweating, uniformed soldiers. Seats had been removed from the big transport and, we were obliged to join the men on the floor. I sat, rubbing shoulders with young Americans the age of my half brother, Stephen. I thought of Stephen as I looked about and was pleased he was a farmer unlikely to be conscripted. How recently had these youngsters graduated school and how many of them would survive the next year?

No seats, meant no seat belts but a strong yellow tape, similar to those now used at crime scenes, stretched from side to side every few yards. Presumably they were to prevent us from tumbling backwards or forwards on take off and landing. I dared not think about what would happen in severe turbulence.

We soared into the air with the four Lockheed turboprop engines roaring. I flopped heavily against the GI behind me. Cedric poked his head out of my shirt, to see what was happening. He certainly was a good conversation starter. The nearby soldiers kept Steve and I busy answering questions until my throat grew hoarse.

The stuffy interior of that sun-scorched, metal bird was bacterial. For most of us, it was our first trip in country and none of us knew what lay ahead. One sweaty GI bumped my shoulder as he awkwardly climbed over us, heading towards the rear of the plane. I wondered what induced him to make such a precarious move and I turned to follow his progress. Reaching his destination he unzipped his fly and I jerked my head forward, embarrassed as he peed into a tube.

In those early days, few camps had yet replaced tents with more permanent structures and some never did. In the dry weather the helicopters, on take off and landing, kept a continual hurricane of red, powdery dust blowing over all. It filled your mouth, blocked your nostrils, stung your eyes and caked onto eyelashes like pale, lumpy mascara. The monsoonal season was anxiously awaited but too soon, slogging through ankle deep mud also grew old. Rain soaked uniforms clung to bodies until the relentless sun steamed them dry again. Then they stunk as sweat soaked them a second time, leaving soggy patches. Most EM's (enlisted men) spent their free time in camp shirtless.

Clubs were yet to be built and many early shows were performed in the open with poor lighting and even poorer acoustics. For the first year at least, I never heard of any such group as The Clubs and Messes System.

Steve and I performed our first show in a large tent. As night fell, the air had cooled slightly but still we sweated. Steve wore a blue and gold lame tuxedo and my clingy dark green strapless gown stirred the boisterous crowd. Steve was a good magician, quickly winning the men's approval. My contribution, apart from smiling and handing him props was to perform three simple tricks. One entailed plucking a series of paper flowers from the air. The second mystified the audience with ropes containing hidden magnets. My last trick was performed with a series of silk scarves. These were simple, Magic 101 tricks, that any child could do, but from the men's thunderous applause, you would have thought I was the next Houdini. Steve was furious.

I assume the men passed the hat around because after the show they handed us a handful of Military Payment Script. Receiving MPC upset Steve as it was worthless outside of Vietnam.

"If you are here strictly for patriotic reasons, the money shouldn't bother you." I goaded.

The next morning we hitched a ride out of there on a helicopter and for weeks we flew from camp to camp, moving on almost daily. At night, we ate in the officer's mess and the food was surprisingly decent. I wanted to eat with the enlisted men but the one time I tried; my presence almost started a riot.

Our sleeping arrangements were flexible. On rare occasions when we were in a headquarters camp which contained donut dollies (Red Cross girls) I could bunk in their quarters. More often though, Steve and I scrounged up army cots and squeezed in wherever we could find any measure of privacy.

Mini skirts, the fashion then, were obviously unsuitable for climbing on and off helicopters. We stayed at one American camp which had an ARVN detachment (Army of Republic of Vietnam). These men were more my size and I managed to scrounge a pair of fatigue pants and army boots that fit. My new American friends made a belt from a parachute strap with a brass buckle which cinched my waist in more effectively than any Victorian corset.

Now suitably dressed for travel, I had only my hair to worry about. Traveling by chopper was like sitting in a wind tunnel. The doors were kept open, allowing the door gunners quick response to enemy action. It is not surprising that on my arrival I was often mistaken for Phyllis Diller. Wising up, I braided my hair.

After our first month of shows, Steve suggested we incorporate my dancing into the act. I purchased a tape recorder from the PX and taped my music, ready to go.

There is an expression called 'bringing down the house'. That literally happened the first time I danced. The remote camp's commanding officer, a major, and a couple of his junior officers, were showing us where we would perform that night.

"This is it" said one young Captain proudly. "We built it ourselves. What do you think?"

The small, square building had a thatched grass roof and waist high walls of unpainted plywood. Blinds of rolled-up canvas kept out the rain when unfurled, undoubtedly turning the interior into a sweat box. The entire structure was elevated on bamboo poles.

I half expected to see a sarong clad Rita Hayworth wander out onto the surrounding deck.

"It's very nice" I complimented "but is it strong enough to hold a crowd?"

"Is the Pope a Catholic?" The captain quipped "There aren't many of us and those who can't fit inside can watch from the deck."

We were the first, and probably the only show, to ever visit the camp. Later that night I was in the middle of my dance number and the crowd was insanely stamping and whistling. Some danced on the bar, others jumped on table tops. Steve stood off to one side holding Cedric and actually smiling. The men's exuberance was infectious and, I spun and gyrated like a dervish.

Suddenly the floor dropped away beneath me and I was spinning through space. Flailing bodies accompanied me on the way down. Surprisingly unscathed, I crawled out from under a piece of plywood and plucked a sheaf of grass from my hair. The club was destroyed, the show ended but still the troops celebrated, staggering from the wreckage, hollering and whooping.

In all the bedlam, Cedric suddenly found freedom, sending Steve into a paroxysm of panic. He ran about, calling for volunteers to help find his errant performer. Dozens of testosterone stymied young men staggered among the tents, calling Cedric's name and adding a few unflattering epithets. He was soon found shivering and dirty, huddled beside an empty beer can.

As the weeks passed the relationship between Steve and I deteriorated. Propinquity began rearing its ugly head plus it appeared Steve now regretted including my dance act in the show.

"What can you expect, Steve?" I said after one show "It wouldn't matter if I was the worst dancer in the world and you were the very best magician, I would still get more applause. Stop taking it personally. These men are starved for women."

He spun on his heel and left, grumbling under his breath. His moodiness was depressing. Whenever a GI flirted with me, Steve hugged me, incorrectly indicating we were a couple. Sometimes I didn't object but if I liked the guy, it was annoying.

We received three hundred dollars for each show of which he pocketed two hundred and gave me a hundred with a sneering reminder that he was the star of the show. I wondered why he was jealous when he seemed to hate me and I started counting the days until he left. By now I knew I wanted to stay. After breaking the ice with him, I believed I could continue as a solo act when he returned to the USA.

This experience was an ego booster like no other but there was more to it. In my travels I had pursued both adventure and money. There was adventure and money aplenty here but the big draw-card was the appreciation of the young men. It had dawned on me that I was doing something worthwhile by lifting their morale. With each passing day my empathy grew.

A show needed to last for an hour to justify gathering a large group together. My entire dance act lasted ten or fifteen minutes. But I could easily stretch my act to an hour by including a bit of humorous patter and some audience participation with the dancing. Extraverts in the crowd loved nothing better than a chance to leap on stage and show off. I would soon become an independent woman again.

CHAPTER 11

AUSTRALIA

Nothing could have prepared me for that share farming cottage. I don't think anyone had lived in it for a hundred years. Located ten miles out of town on Calala Lane, it sat drunkenly upon wooden stumps. The wood planked walls were so weathered that cracks had opened up between the shrunken planks, allowing the wind to blow through. The yard was encircled by barbed wire for no apparent reason as it contained only a few drought hardy weeds and a collapsing out house. A slack black wire linked the roof of the house to a pole, indicating the dump had electricity. The only running water came through the roof when it rained but we were yet to discover that. Sitting against one wall was an old metal tank that looked as if someone had attacked it with a bee-bee gun. The lower holes trailed ribbons of green slime.

The interior was no better. The floors sloped and linoleum was worn so thin that patches of wood showed through. The kitchen stove looked as if it came from a museum and I mentally compared it with Nan's beautiful big enamel stove and spotless kitchen. This dismal kitchen would become my domain for I always had to cook for the family when Mum worked. Pregnant or not, I knew she would be in the dairy every day. The only thing that could fix this monstrosity, I thought, would be some kerosene and a box of matches.

Noticing my look of horror Mum said "Look on the bright side June. There's nothing a bit of elbow crease can't fix."

She was surely putting on a brave front.

Within days, the three younger children were enrolled in a one-roomed country school within walking distance of the farm. I was enrolled at Tamworth High School. Mum purchased a bicycle so I could ride the long distance each day. I hated the school. I hated my life. This was entirely my mother's fault.

When the dry, hot summer months arrived, there were torrential storms most afternoons and drenched, I rode blindly through them as there was no shelter along the way and my time was too precious for me to stop. My heavy serge uniform collected puddles of water in my lap. With each downward thrust of the pedal, the collected rain ran down my legs into my shoes. The brim of my hat hung limp as water cascaded down my face, blurring my vision and passing automobiles splashed fountains of water over me. Too often, thorns called 'cat heads' pierced my tires, forcing me to push the bike for miles, wasting more of my time. Of course, arriving home, I had to repair the tyre.

With little time to study and my motivation gone, my grades suffered. No longer was I a leader among my peers. I sought no friends for I was ashamed for anyone to see how we lived.

Bake bought an old jeep which had only two bucket seats up front. We children sat in the back on a wooden stool. Bake had never driven before and he always took off like a mechanical bull. These erratic starts toppled the stool over, throwing us onto the floor. We lay with our feet up over the fallen stool, screaming with laughter. It was one of the few things I found to laugh about but the more we laughed the angrier Bake became. Embarrassed by his driving, he was still more comfortable with a horse.

Whenever Bake drove us into town I asked to be let out before we reached the town center. I'd rather walk than let anyone see me in that rattle trap, so maybe my mother's frequent accusations of snobbery were true. I longed for the day I turned fifteen when I planned to leave.

We all had to get up early and work in the dairy or the house before going to school. After a few months, Bake increased his income by buying a milk run. This meant additional work for Billy and Russell who had to accompany Bake into town. They ran from house to house, pouring the milk into the billy-cans which the customers left on the door steps. They did a day's work before going to school and it was back to the dairy again in the afternoon. The teachers continually complained to Mum that Russell was so tired, he often fell asleep during classes.

Regardless of the hard work we remained poor. There were countless tribulations. One of my previous enjoyments had been bathing in Nan's gleaming white bathtub in the steam filled room. Now I took my turn in a tin tub set out on the back verandah, not always getting first turn in the water. And the outhouse stunk no matter how much Phenyl Mum poured down that hole. A poisonous brown snake frequently took refuge there making my hasty visits even hastier. We couldn't even afford toilet paper and one of my chores was to cut newspaper into squares and hang it on a rusted hook within arms reach. The day a Willy Nilly blew the out house down I cheered. My sister Clarice however, was inside at the time and did not join my celebration.

Despite the hard work and lack of study, Russell still excelled at school. He was the smartest of all of us and we later discovered he had a mensa level I.Q. Mum said he got his brains from our father – that bloody no-hoper.

One day Russell came home from school with a black eye. We were shocked and tried to find out what had happened. He wouldn't answer, running straight to the room he shared with Billy and slamming the door. Days later we discovered the truth. A kid had screamed at him "Your mother's a whore. She's having a baby and she's not married." I doubt Russell was aware they weren't married and I'm certain he didn't know the meaning of whore. But he flew to Mum's defense against the much larger boys.

How the neighbors learned Mum and Bake weren't married is a mystery but that incident started to turn Russell against our mother, much as I had. Only Clarice seemed non-judgmental. The marriage situation was not of Mum's choosing but at that time she could not find our father to start the divorce.

We were a product of our time – sharing our mother's shame.

Today unwed mothers go through life with government assistance, free from aspersions. Back then, it was considered so disgraceful that young women committed suicide or died from having illegal backyard abortions.

Even the celebrated Swedish actress, Ingrid Bergman, temporarily ruined her career in 1950 when she had a baby by the producer Roberto Rossellini, while still married to Dr. Peter Lindstrom. Overnight she became a Pariah in America where she was denounced on the Senate floor. Her movies were blackballed and it was years before she was forgiven and hired to make another American movie. Mum carried her illegitimate child during that same unforgiving period. I regret that in ignorance I judged her so harshly and trust I made up for it later.

Understandably, I was a conflicted teenager. I don't like remembering the times I screamed "I hate you" at Mum or her stinging slaps to my face. Occasionally love for her and pity touched me, but those moments were few and far between. I hated seeing her slaving outside under the hot sun. Chopping wood had developed her biceps as large as those of any weightlifter. She had clearly inherited her biological father's toughness. I remembered how beautiful she had been when we lived in Sydney. Now the exposure to the harsh, Australian sun and the heavy work was taking its toll.

We had been in Tamworth for two or three months when Stephen was born. Mum did not work in the dairy that evening but she refused to stay overnight in hospital. By the next morning she was back milking cows.

"You will have to help care for the baby now June." She said.

Each Christmas Mum had given me and Clarice dolls. I was a tomboy and never cared for mine. Clarice always ended up with both.

When I lifted baby Stephen from the clothes basket which doubled as his bed, I was stunned by a maternal surge of love.

CHAPTER 12

Vietnam

I had lost the bloody rabbit and Steve was beside himself. It must have got out of its portable cage somehow and Steve held me responsible. Trying to calm him I had asked one of the Green Beret sergeants from the Special Forces camp in NhaTrang to drive me into town. I had to try to buy a replacement and it was as easy as finding a vegetarian in a butcher shop. After hours of searching, we found a brown rabbit at a farm on the outskirts of town.

"It's a bit big to fit into the Top Hat" I said, eyeing it doubtfully.

The sergeant cocked an eyebrow. "You can always eat the damned thing if he doesn't like it."

I wrinkled my nose "And its color is all wrong."

"Just be grateful you found one at all." He answered philosophically.

An hour later I presented it to Steve. He hated it.

"What do you expect me to do with a fucking, fat, fucking brown rabbit?" he snarled.

"A rabbit is a rabbit. What difference does it make? Are you a bloody rabbit racist or something?" I had always abhorred women cussing yet the habit was growing on me

"You stupid bitch," he glared, "Whoever saw a magician with a brown rabbit? You know nothing about show business. You'd starve back in the USA."

He had never spoken to me this harshly before. I bit my tongue, determined to finish our time together

We hitched a ride on a C123 to Quin Nhon, one of the larger camps. Quin Nhon was a well established camp, luxurious compared to some we had worked in. Located along the coast north of Saigon, the compound included an American military hospital. Nearby was a Korean camp with a Korean military hospital. The American general commanding the troops in Quin Nhon, was dating a nurse from the Korean hospital. After our first show in Quin Nhon, while we were socializing with the general and some of his officers, he suggested we give the Koreans a show.

During the daytime, we visited the patients in the American hospital and tried, with some success, to lift their spirits. The more seriously injured were always airlifted as soon as possible to hospitals in Japan or to Walter Reed, back in the States.

One morning I asked Steve to accompany me to visit the Korean patients and he agreed. It was his final week before returning to the States and he was in a good mood. The two hospitals were worlds apart. The Korean troops spoke no English so there was little we could say and they roused my pity.

Many of the patients lay in iron beds on the verandah of the over crowded French villa. A roof protected them from the sun but there were no outer walls to protect them from driving rain or wind. I saw no magazines or books to occupy them. No glasses of juice sat on bedside tables, no fruit or candy, only water. However, everything was scrupulously clean with not even a discarded cigarette butt anywhere.

The camp commander, Major General Choe Dae Myong, was the Deputy Commander of all Korean troops in Vietnam. After learning I had lived in Korea, and we were giving a free show for his troops, he invited us to be his dinner guests. Steve struggled through the hot Korean cuisine and he balked at the Kim Chee.

Our show was visual so it was unimportant that the audience understood no English. Steve had taught me a new trick that day and I was a little nervous. The sturdy Korean warriors filled the room to capacity. Among them were ambulatory patients, nurses, doctors, wards men, and technicians.

When Steve handed me the black, plywood box I put on my stage smile, peered into the audience and selected a volunteer. My chosen man bounded onto the platform, impressive in his immaculate uniform and bowed sharply. I placed the open section of the box over his head. An excited murmur rose from the audience when I grabbed a handful of large, shiny daggers. Twirling the first dagger with theatrical flair, I plunged it through a slot in the box, into my volunteer's head – or so it was meant to look. "Aaahhh," murmured the crowd and each time I repeated this process my confidence grew. Several daggers now protruded from the box, all apparently stuck in my volunteer's head. Grabbing the last dagger I grinned triumphantly, gave an enthusiastic flourish and plunged it deep into the box. Instantly there came a muffled yell of "Apo. Apo", which translates to "Ow, Ow" or "Shit, Shit". Flustered, I ripped the dagger out as Steve burst onto the stage and removed the remaining weapons. Obviously I had angled the dagger incorrectly, missing the protective, inside lining. Steve lifted the black box and my volunteer emerged with blood trickling from his ear. He snapped his heels together and saluted smartly before leaving the stage. The audience applauded politely; unaware the finale had gone awry.

When we bowed, Steve pulled my arm behind my back and pinched a chunk of flesh from my wrist, drawing blood. My eyes watered. We straightened up. I blew the audience a kiss and ran from the stage.

The following day my partner and I were not speaking. However, the sun was shining brighrly and we had great plans, which I thought would thaw the ice. Four young American officers had arranged a day out on the water in one of the camp's recreational speedboats. We met up with them as they carried an icebox filled with cold beer across the sandy beach. The brilliant blue ocean was a tremendous respite after the dusty, inland camps we were accustomed too.

A few off duty hospital staff lay sun baking. I waved gaily to them before clambering aboard the speed boat. Steve followed and seated himself on a bench as the officers pushed off.

I stood in the bow of the boat, hanging onto a side rail as the boat gained speed. The wind whipped my hair across my face and I laughed with pleasure, forgetting about the previous night. The boat hit a large swell, thumping down hard and my can of beer flew from my hand and struck Steve on the head.

"You stupid bitch!" He snarled, jumping up "Look what you've done."

"It was an accident," one of the officers shot back "Watch it buddy."

"It was no accident. Just like last night when she deliberately screwed up my show."

"You know that's not true Steve." I said, knowing it was the officers' attention towards me that aroused his anger.

He glared and we quickly forgot the incident, succumbing to the sunshine and salt air while the war seemed very far away.

"Ready for another?" a captain asked, placing his arm around me. Steve's face darkened.

"She's had enough." He barked. "We've got a show to do tonight and I don't need a drunken assistant stabbing half the audience."

"Oh come off it. I wasn't drunk and I can handle two beers."

"It's my reputation on the line," he harped, "Put that drink down right now."

"Lighten up buddy" the major ordered. "We don't get many days like this so don't screw it up."

"Screw it up?" Steve squawked "You're like a pack of dogs after a bitch in heat."

"You're an asshole," another said. "You need to cool off."

"Go fuck yourself."

I gasped "You need to apologize Steve."

"Apologize my ass." His face, already burnt from the sun, turned a shade darker. The Major gave the Captain a nod and seconds later I heard a loud splash.

"That should teach him to respect a lady," One of them said as the driver gunned the engine. I saw Steve screaming and waving his arms. The men laughed and I joined in nervously.

"Please guys. We can't leave him out here. It's too far from shore."

"You don't really care about that son of a bitch, do you?"

"Well, no. But if this ocean is anything like back home, there are sharks."

"Bringing him along was a real cluster fuck." Someone said.

Steve bobbed in the ocean, still frantically waving.

"Please. Turn around."

"Well you're a spoil sport but if that's what you want.......... and anymore shit and out he goes again."

That night's show was cancelled, and Steve and I never performed together again. It was a sour note to end on but I thanked God I was independent again and this time for good.

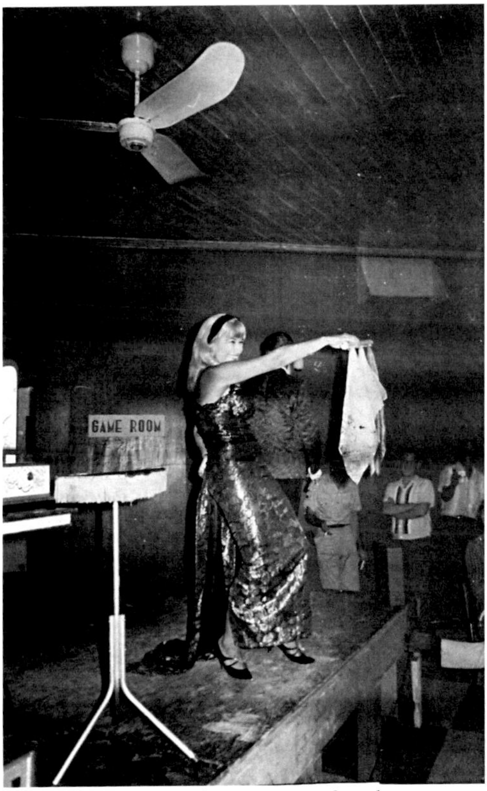

Here I am, doing my scarf trick in an NCO club near Saigon

CHAPTER 13

AUSTRALIA

How does one climb out of poverty? Today it can be done through higher education. The Australian government offers loans under the H.E.C.S program and there have always been scholarships for the exceptionally talented. But back then there were very few scholarships and I never heard of any loans. Few students indeed could afford college. College students were so rare that I looked upon them with awe.

My childish dreams of becoming a circus acrobat, a bike racer, or a famous artist had all faded. All I wanted to do now was escape and support myself somehow.

Approaching our second year in Tamworth, Mum gave birth to baby number two, (or five if you counted the first lot). She named her Lorraine. This continual pregnancy perplexed me. Mum and Bake seemed to be always fighting. But the babies did add a touch of sweetness.

Mum was fanatically honest and my step-brother Billy made the unforgivable mistake of stealing money from her purse. No longer trusting him, she complained about him to Bake constantly. To appease her, I suppose, Bake rode him hard. Billy had had enough. One night he stole a neighbor's horse and rode away. He was fourteen.

Mum had finally located my father and divorced him. She and Bake, quickly married. I was calling Bake 'Dad' by then but not to confuse the issue, I shall still refer to him as Bake.

The marriage was a turning point and some months later, Pop Harrison relented. He and Nan began periodically driving up from Sydney to visit us. These visits were cause for great excitement. We cleaned everything to perfection and I tried to camouflage the dump by picking huge armfuls of pungent Eucalyptus leaves and flowering wild wattle, placing them in dairy buckets throughout the house.

Our situation must have shocked Nan. By this time, much to my disgust, Mum was pregnant for a third time. I don't know if Pop was moved by pity or if he was impressed with all the hard work they were doing. He had always admired good workers, even Catholics. Whatever the reason, he loaned Bake money so he could quit share farming and buy a small dairy farm a few miles closer to town. .

The move to the new farm meant I had less distance to ride to school and money became slightly more plentiful. We built a simple, four roomed fibro cottage with a long, covered verandah. It was new and clean, a huge improvement over the dump.

The new property fronted onto Scotts Lane, a dirt road. During wet weather it became a muddy quagmire. The mud was impossible to ride my bike through so Mum bought me a pair of rubber gum boots just like hers. Whenever it rained I slogged through the mud into town, changing into my school shoes once I reached the hard top road. My gumboots were hidden beneath a bush until my return journey.

Occasionally the creeks flooded, cutting Scotts Lane in two places and trapping me between them. I then had to wait until they subsided before I could continue home. Sometimes it became dark but as soon as the milking was finished, either Mum or Bake would ride down carrying an old hurricane lamp. I climbed on the horse behind them and we waded through to safety.

Along one side of the farm, a creek created a boundary between us and our neighbor. It was wide and deep but a time came when we had no rain and the creek almost dried up. Our cows, which previously could not cross the water, now walked up the opposite creek bank and entered the neighbor's fields then ate his crops. One afternoon our gigantic neighbor rushed to the opposite bank waving a rifle and yelling. Hearing the commotion, Mum and I hurried to our side of the embankment.

"I'll shoot these bastards if you don't keep them on your side" he screamed across the open divide, indicating our grazing cows with his rifle.

"Like hell you will." Mum screamed back "You touch any one of them and you'll be dealing with me."

"Don't threaten me, you stupid little woman." He emphasized his words by firing his rifle into the air. Mum pulled herself up to her full four feet ten inches.

"That's it!" she hollered "Come over here you mongrel and face me like a man." She teetered on the creek bank, her fists clenched in fighting stance. She had told me once, that to defend herself when she was a child, she had learned boxing

I watched in alarm as the angry neighbor lay down his rifle and lumbered down the creek bank. He splashed through the trickle of water muttering curses then clambered onto our side. Towering above Mum, he raised his fists.

Mum was bouncing back and forth, practicing little jabs "Not scared of a woman, Huh? You coward! Come on, strike the first blow."

I watched helplessly, wishing my mother would back off but grudgingly admiring her spirit. The neighbor spat into the dirt, pulled his huge fist back then lunged forward ------hitting the air. He spun on his heel and headed home, yelling over his shoulder "Damn you. I can't hit a woman, even you."

"Geez Mum" I said, running up to her, "Can't you pick on someone your own size? Are you crazy?"

"June, learn this lesson. You must never show fear. But thank God he changed his mind. My knees were shaking in my gumboots."

Unfortunately more money did not mean fewer fights. I could not understand how they fought so much yet kept making babies.

It was seven o'clock at night when Mum, Clarice, Russell and I were sitting around the kitchen table eating dinner in the new house. The two little ones were sleeping. Bake was late getting back from town and we hadn't waited for him. I was almost finished eating my sausages and mashed potato when I heard the old Jeep pull up outside. Bake entered the kitchen with a dopey smile on his face and the smell of beer on his breath.

"You've been drinking again," Mum accused, slamming his dinner down on the table "Now your food's all dried out."

Bake's smile disappeared instantly "I work bloody hard all day. I'm entitled to a bloody drink."

"Shut up! I do most of the hard work around here. Me and the kids. You spend half the day gossiping with your customers or drinking beer in the pub."

It was true that since moving closer to town, Bake was spending more and more time away. It seemed to me that Mum was correct about doing most of the work but I also remembered my father saying she was a nag.

Soon the familiar screaming started. Clarice and Russell hunched lower in their seats, food forgotten. Again I wished I was back in Nan's home. Russell looked at the two of them with disgust and I expected Clarice to cry at any moment.

Bake's face turned crimson as the fight escalated. Why did Mum goad him that way? She was smarter than he so my sympathies were often with him, viewing him as the underdog. He shouted and blustered but she stung with icy, stinging barbs.

Screaming, Bake snatched up his dinner plate and hurled it at the brick wall. The plate smashed into pieces and fell to the floor, sausages tumbling amid the shards of broken crockery. Mashed potato and gravy clung awhile longer before losing grip and sliding down, leaving a greasy, brown trail. My hands began to tremble. Clarice had covered her ears with her hands.

Leaping to the kitchen cabinet, Mum flung the door open "Two can play at that game!" she screamed, dragging out our only decent china cups and smashing them one by one. The children cowered lower in their seats.

As each cup hit the floor, Bake's rage increased. Reaching across the table he grasped the bread knife off the cutting board, clumsily dragging the cloth and half the things on the table onto the floor. The sugar, bread, and milk, lay in a mess at our feet.

His face the color of pooling blood, eyes blazing, he held the saw-toothed knife to his throat, screaming, "I'll end it now. I swear I will. Is that what you want?"

"Yeah, I dare you."

I jumped up, grabbing Russell by the arm. "Run Russell, run!" I yelled. "Clarice, help me grab the little ones."

Within seconds we were out of there, leaving the shouting behind as we stumbled in the dark towards the shelter of the diary.

"Don't worry kids; I'll take care of you." I panted "Let's just sit here until we see the lights go out."

"Do you think they'll kill each other?" Clarice whimpered.

"Probably not" I answered "They never do."

The cement floor was cold. The dairy was dark and the time dragged. After what seemed an eternity we saw the house was in darkness. All was quiet as we crept inside and, as usual, we found no dead bodies. They must have been back in bed together. It was all a terrifying bluff.

As I grew older I became quite philosophical. Mum had always taught us to judge people by their character, not by their power, position or wealth and certainly not by their color, religion or race. Yet it seemed to me that few people thought that way. I noticed that money and acquisitions contaminated many people's judgment. I remembered how proud I felt, whilst living with Nan and Pop. Now I felt shame.

My favorite writer back then was Robert Rourke and I had read "Poor No More". I decided that title would characterize me one day.

I was no longer popular. My only friend Norma, an overweight girl, also came from a poor family and was unpopular. Yet, I had not changed. Only my circumstances which I had no control over had changed. The world seemed unfair and I was determined to take control of my life as soon as possible.

Despite being poor, we were always well dressed. Elva, mum's wealthy stepsister and Pop's only daughter, was my Godmother. She bought so many clothes that many of them were never worn. These she gave (still with price tags attached) to Mum who cut them down, making stylish dresses for all of us.

Marrickville High School was, and is, a school for girls only. Tamworth High School was co-educational. As I passed the groups of ogling louts each day, they snickered and made obnoxious comments. I believed I behaved like a 'young lady'. Was their unpleasant attention because my breasts kept growing? I hated the boys and I hated my breasts.

The end of the school year approached and the students were excited about an end-of-year ball, to be held in the Tamworth Town Hall. I was not anxious to attend but Mum insisted I go.

For several nights she sat at the sewing machine, creating a magnificent blue ball gown for me. This dress was not made from Aunty Elva's 'hand-me-downs'. That week our meals were almost meatless. Mum must have juggled the food budget to pay for the expensive new fabric.

I awoke one morning to hear loud voices in the kitchen while it was still dark outside.

"We're bloody late," Bake grumbled "Forget the cup of tea. You'll be no bloody use today after sitting up sewing all night."

"My daughter deserves it." Mum replied, "Don't you worry about me."

When I heard the door close, I crept into the lounge room and saw, hanging on a wooden coat hanger, the most beautiful dress I had ever owned. Pale blue lace over taffeta tapered tightly in at the waist above a billowy skirt of frothy blue tulle.

Later that day I held my breath as Mum zipped me into it. Running to the full length mirror in her bedroom I gasped when I saw my reflection. The girl staring back at me was almost pretty and she had the curvy figure of a movie star. Surely it wasn't me?

I turned and looked into Mum's weary eyes. Over recent weeks my resentment had been dissipating, replaced by a growing ripple of soft, warm love. Spontaneously, I grabbed her and held her tight. She stood stiffly, more shocked than I by the embrace.

"Thank you Mum. I love you." The unfamiliar words washed over us, pulsating through the room. Mum allowed one ecstatic moment in time before breaking away. As she turned to leave, with her back towards me she replied, "I love you too Junc." Her voice sounded strange.

The day of the ball arrived and I awoke horrified to discover I was menstruating. My menstruations were always heavy in the beginning and I considered staying home. Remember, these were the days before such feminine aids as Tampax.

"You must go June." Mum said. "You look so pretty. Just sit out the fast dances." Her words, coupled with a crush I had developed on a student named Dennis, persuaded me. Dennis was in a class a year above mine. One time, when the boys had made rude comments as I passed by, he told them to shut up. I was grateful and I thought he was incredibly handsome. Now I dreamed of wearing the blue dress and twirling around the dance floor in his arms. Stupid, girlish dreams!

Opening the drawer, I took out one of the flannelette napkins Mum had made when I first started to menstruate. I looked at it with disgust. I had never heard of such things as disposable pads and if they were available, we were too poor to buy them. These matters, like anything to do with the human body, were never discussed. Even after washing such unmentionables, they had to he hung out to dry in hidden places, in denial that such unpleasant bodily functions occurred. Nobody would have believed that some years into the future, female hygiene products would be advertised in minute detail on television commercials. But of course, television was still unheard of.

CHAPTER 14

VIETNAM

It was June 1966 and I was starting out on my own as a solo act for the American troops. The weeks spent touring with Steve Baker had built my confidence. There were few entertainers in country and those who came later, after MACV (Military Assistance Command Vietnam) set up an office to organize entertainment, came in packaged shows – usually groups of six or more. It took courage for a female to go out alone.

I traveled light; a change of uniform for traveling during the day, a dress to change into after my show, my dance costumes, which were miniscule, and my tape recorder.

My very first show was in a small camp, far out in the boonies. The men had just returned to camp after weeks out in the field and were pretty excited to be getting a show. They rigged a truck flatbed as my stage, and as night fell, illuminated it by the headlights of several Jeeps.

Covered by an army poncho I waited nervously backstage (behind the trailer) for my cue from the taped music. The music sounded thin and reedy, lost in the open space of night air. I had never performed solo for a full hour before and I was apprehensive. Time to throw off the poncho! I nodded to the two soldiers assisting me and they lifted me onto the stage. The crowd's roar was deafening. I commenced dancing to the strains of "Harlem Nocturne" then followed it up with my choreographed routine of Peter Gunn. Some years earlier, I had paid extravagantly to have Keith Bane, Australia's most well known choreographer at that time, work up some routines for me. I never regretted the price as I danced these same routines for several years in many countries, returning the cost over and over.

The Vietnam air was humid, coating my skin with a sheen of perspiration. As the last strains of the music drifted away I grabbed a microphone and yelled "Are you men ready for fun?" The reply was deafening! From then it was easy. Twenty minutes later, young soldiers bounded on and off the stage; showing off and working up a sweat as we danced the latest craze called the twist. Their buddies cheered noisily, sometimes laughing, occasionally booing. Spirits were exuberant as GI's competed to get up on stage. I allowed them their fun while maintaining control by instinctively selecting partners I felt were manageable.

One young soldier looked no more than eighteen. I was a good ten years older than him and I smiled encouragingly as we danced. He was an awkward dancer and the audience jeered. My dance movements were sensual but well within restraint. Gradually I heard an audible stir arising from the men up front. The murmur swelled, becoming a roar of laughter. Looking for the cause of their merriment, I was embarrassed to see that my sweet, shy partner had ejaculated, leaving a wet patch on the front of his uniform trousers. He crumpled under the ignominy of his buddies ridicule, stirring my compassion. I grabbed him, giving him a big hug and a kiss which ended his humiliation by arousing his buddies envy. He left the stage, clasping his fists overhead in a winner's gesture, his dignity restored.

Being from Australia I had not had much contact with African American's, but I quickly learned that they were terrific dancers with phenomenal agility. My next volunteer was a tall, slender black man who could writhe like a snake. The audience was going wild and with my best efforts, he outshone me. I was sweating and breathing hard. He hadn't broken a sweat. A sudden clap of thunder rent the air and lightning flashed so brightly there was no longer need for jeep lights. Blinding rain instantly followed, soaking everyone. My partner kept gyrating all over the stage, not deterred but seemingly invigorated by the deluge. The storm raged fiercely but nobody left. I followed my partner's lead with my hair clinging wet against my face. Raindrops filled my eyes, yet I kept on dancing as water streamed over my body. In fact it felt much better than the sweat and my spirits soared, matching the wildness of nature. Carried away by the moment, my partner ripped off his drenched shirt and threw it into the audience. Following his example, one by one the men jumped up and started dancing in the mud, ripping their shirts off and twirling them in the air. One smart-ass found a cake of soap somewhere and threw it onto the stage where my partner deftly caught it and lathered up his chest, never missing a beat. Not that we could hear much music for now it competed with the racket all around and was muffled by the poncho someone had been quick thinking enough to throw over the tape player.

We certainly looked like a bunch of crazies, roaring with laughter and dancing frenziedly in the storm. When the soap was thrown at me, I followed my dance partner's example before tossing it back. He caught it, did a quick double pirouette into the air, hit the deck and with a loud 'Yahoo' began to unbuckle his trousers. Acting fast, I brought the show to a close before the exuberance required the intervention of the MP's. Besides, nothing could top that rain dance for a finale. The storm ended as quickly as it began. Stars came out and the damp air filled with laughter as the men straggled away. My first solo show was a raging success and I felt terrific.

With each show, my affinity for the young troops grew stronger and I became proficient at handling a crowd. It didn't take me long to determine the difference between the support troops, and the grunts who were out in the field.

Certainly not to diminish their contribution but the men in the camps around Long Binh, or any camp close to Saigon, had it not only safer but better in every way. Those big camps were the first to be built up – replacing tents with more permanent structures. The troops soon had clubhouses and the pick of whatever entertainment came in country. They had easier access to the big PX and commissaries, and they ate better. Some of the Long Binh camp's improvements became mind boggling over time. Topping the list was a huge massage parlor. Decorating the front of that building was a long row of tall naked women; statues, of course! Two hundred attractive Vietnamese 'masseuses' took care of the men's needs inside. A large Chinese restaurant provided a change of diet and an ice cream parlor served up twenty seven flavors. Think of any money making venture and one most likely found it there. Outrageous as it seems, the GI's could purchase new cars, diamond rings, fur coats, hair spray and panty hose. And do remember, we did not have women in the military as we do now. Far removed from the men in the field, these troops rarely came under mortar attack and certainly were never over-run by the enemy.

For the grunts (the infantrymen) out in the field it was a different story entirely. Tramping through the jungle, often for long periods of time, they ate only cold C rations. They slept on the ground and in the rain. These were the ones with leaches sucking their blood and with feet blistered from walking all day. These were the ones fighting diarrhea and foot rot. These were ones losing their buddies, and wondering if they would be next. These were the ones most likely to die. These were the ones I gave my heart to and chose to entertain.

It would have been much easier for me logistically to work close to Saigon where there were more clubs, bigger clubs and they were close together. Working there meant I did not have to stand for hours choking in the swirling dust and heat of the airfield, waiting for a ride to my destination. Working there meant I never had to spend time sweating in the stagnant air of a bunker, dodging spiders and fighting claustrophobia while listening to bursting mortars. Working there meant I could relax and feel safe. As O'Halloran once told me –"If they ever get to Long Binh it's all over."

But, the appreciation and satisfaction would not have been the same. And I would not have become so emotionally involved, my passion aroused the way it eventually was.

CHAPTER 15

AUSTRALIA

With this forgiveness and rekindling love for my mother, I was finding a small glimmer of inner peace.

It was impossible for me not to compare Nan and Mum and I felt guilty about loving Nan so much. One is supposed to love their mother above all others, aren't they? I was strong willed and whenever my mother and I clashed she was prone to say "You've got the bad Weatherstone (my father's name) blood." Words can puncture the heart a lifetime.

One would never guess my mother and grandmother were mother and daughter. I tried putting the history of my family into some perspective.

Nan was fair skinned, fair haired and blue eyed. She laughed softly, cried easily and was plentiful with kisses and cuddles. Pop was the protector she needed. She spoiled her grandchildren outrageously yet I doubted she would be capable of protecting us.

Mum was dark haired, brown eyed and olive skinned. She never cried. She needed no protector. She rarely kissed or cuddled. She nurtured in a different way, urging all of us to be independent and strive do our best. "The world is a tough place" she would say "You have to know how to survive."

I wished I was soft and angelic like Nan but I realized I was made of sterner stuff like my mother. Maybe that came from the responsibilities of being the eldest child. Maybe it came from my biological grandfather's genes. Who knows!

And there was one great mystery about my Grandmother. She had deserted her two children; something my mother would never do.

"Why did you do it Nan?" I asked impertinently one afternoon while I was living with her.

"It was a mistake, June." She avoided my eyes. "After I found your grandfather with that woman I just went crazy. He was drunk when he brought her into our home. I hadn't suspected a thing until then, yet it had been going on forever and everyone knew. Overnight, he installed that woman and her three daughters in my house. He wouldn't allow me back in and he forbid me to see your mother and George. Of course I started court proceedings as soon as I had money."

"Why didn't the judge return them to you?" I frowned.

"He said I had abandoned them and as I had no income and no home for them he awarded custody to your grandfather."

I mulled over this information, wondering if Nan had already met Pop Harrison by the time the case went to court and if so, had pleasing Pop influenced Nan not to pursue it. Her explanation bothered me. I did not want to acknowledge a flaw in the most perfect person I ever knew.

The story told from my mother's perspective was a little different.

"I will never forget that night as long as I live, June." Her voice cracked. "Mum packed some clothes into a suitcase and ran sobbing into the street. It was dark and I ran after her, yelling 'Don't leave us Mum' but she didn't seem to hear. I can still picture her running away with the bag she had hastily packed banging against her leg. A corset strap was dangling out one side, flapping. She jumped onto a bus before I could reach her." My mother's voice dwindled and she looked away.

"What happened next Mum?"

"Cinderella could have been written about me. I suppose I was a bit of a brat. Nan was never very strict, you know. My new stepmother made trouble between me and my father. He became so angry one night that he hurled a cup of boiling tea across the table at me. I ducked just as his best mate opened the door. He copped the lot and they almost came to blows"

"No wonder you don't see him much."

"They were tough times and he had his good points. He never shirked work and he was spotlessly clean and scrupulously honest. Mum and he were just unsuited."

I pondered my far from illustrious background but like all children, I wanted to know more about those 'olden days' as we referred to them.

"When did you see Nan again?"

"Not for awhile but then she moved in with Pop, initially as his housekeeper, and learned to drive. After that she started to visit. We would sit outside in the car and talk and she always brought gifts."

"And Uncle George?"

"He started working at thirteen but occasionally he joined us. Unfortunately the gifts made my step-sisters jealous. They ate my chocolates while I was at school and left the empty box of wrappers. Bottles of scent were emptied down the sink and re-filled with water. A lovely beige woolen coat had the buttons ripped out, leaving huge holes."

"Couldn't your Grandmother rescue you?"

"She died when I was five. I don't remember meeting her."

This insight into my mother's past helped me to understand and forgive.

The night of the big school dance arrived and I excitedly spun around in the lounge room, causing my skirts to fly out as Mum looked on admiringly.

"Thank you Mum. I feel like a Princess. Are we ready to go?"

"Dad's nearly ready. We'll let you out at the town hall. We're going to see a movie with that actress, Doris Day! Be sure to be waiting out the front for us by eleven."

Usually, I became irritated with this arrangement for it meant I had to leave the dance before it ended, but this time I was too happy to care.

Bake entered the room "Holy cow girl. You'll be the prettiest one there." I smiled, pleased at his flattery. He and I always got along just fine. Even when he was angry, it was all noise and he never hit any of us. When he was in a good mood he could be really funny.

Thirty minutes later, I nervously entered the Town Hall alone. As usual, the girls sat self-consciously along the wall on one side while the boys stood in clusters against the opposite wall.

It was soon apparent I was a wall flower and my spirits wilted. When I saw Dennis dance past with a girl from fourth grade I was further dejected. Norma, the overweight girl who always sought my company, was chatting in my ear again. "Does she ever stop talking?" I wondered, wishing she would find somewhere else to sit, mentally blaming her proximity for my lack of popularity and then immediately hating myself for such disloyalty. I began to wish it was eleven o'clock already.

A short while later I looked up and saw Dennis heading in my direction! He looked really handsome in his brown, pin-striped suit. Maybe he was coming for someone else. I tried not to get my hopes up but then he smiled at me and I began to shake. Clumsily, I stood and stumbled into his arms. He guided me around the floor and I tried not to step on his toes.

When he escorted me back to my seat, his lips 'accidentally' brushed my cheek as I sat. Fifteen minutes later I spotted him heading towards me again. My heart pounded. Asking me for two dances must mean something!

The band was playing "You stepped Out of a Dream" which seemed dizzyingly romantic! Dennis held me closer than I had ever been held before and I felt the warmth of his breath on my face. We were swaying towards the main entrance when he whispered, "I want to kiss you but my science teacher is watching. Quick! Come outside."

Mum had given me plenty of warnings about never leaving the hall. But, with barely a hesitation I followed him outside and down two blocks to the park. His hand was firm as he led me past the rose garden. It was the first time I ever felt desirable and wanted.

The night was magical; the moon emerging from a softly illuminated cloud. Our first kiss made me physically weak. His soft lips were gentle, his breath peppermint sweet. My lips responded shyly. This, the most intimate moment of my life, was fulfilling my romantic dreams. His kisses became more passionate. A few moments later, I felt his hand slip inside the bodice of my dress and cup my breast. My nipples hardened beneath his warm fingers. I knew I must stop right then but I lingered a moment longer. Alarm bells rang when his kisses were fiercely demanding and I began to nervously pull away. Removing his hand from my breast, he fumbled with my skirt.

"Stop!" I spluttered against his lips but he gripped me tighter, bending me back further and now his kisses hurt. His breathing grew loud and his hands groped at my pants. Desperately, I wrenched my head sideways, gasping, "Stop it! I can't, I mean it." The more I tried to escape the more inflamed he became. Still lip-locked, he leaned me so far back that we fell to the ground. I struggled but his body pinned me down and he had his hand inside my pants. Hadn't he felt the sanitary napkin? The thought was gross and I felt debased! Once he realized my condition, I was certain he would stop. Any man would. Wouldn't they?

"Stop! Stop! I've got my period." I cried, humiliated to make such a disgusting admission. My plea went unheeded as somehow he managed to one handedly get his pants down a ways. My writhing efforts to escape landed me on a rose bush and the thorns hurt as they pierced my buttocks. Dennis moved up and down on top of me and I heard people walking by not far away. I considered calling out but I was too ashamed to let anyone see me in such a situation. We were bathed in moonlight but the magic had gone. Soon it was over but I found no pleasure - only shame and betrayal in my first sexual encounter.

He rolled off me and stood up. There was a moment of awkward silence before he whispered, "I'm sorry," then disappeared into the dark. I heard running water from a nearby garden tap and I assumed he was cleaning himself. I sat up, filled with self loathing and emotional chaos. How could I have been so gullible? This was not the romantic love I had read about in Georgette Heyer's novels. Finally, I whispered aloud "Snap out of it girl. Mum warned you the world's a rough place. Toughen up."

I found my small beaded purse on the ground nearby then went looking for that tap in a hope of cleaning up myself. By the moonlight, I could see a dark patch of blood on my dress and I felt a ten-inch tear in the tulle skirt. My beautiful dress which Mum had slaved over was now desecrated. For a moment I almost cried. No-one must ever know about this night. I ran the water over the dark patch on my skirt and scrubbed it fiercely. I tried my best to fix my hair and make up then sat on a park bench, willing my skirt to dry quickly.

When it was almost eleven o'clock I walked back towards the town hall and waited in the shadows outside. It wasn't long until the Jeep pulled up. Quickly I ran across the pavement and jumped into the back, talking excitedly about the dance, pretending I'd had a good time. They suspected nothing and I thanked God that my skirt was so full it hid any tell tale signs.

Safely home, I made a beeline for the privacy of my bedroom and lay in the dark, dry-eyed. My hurt had turned to steel-cold anger. I would finish with both school and Tamworth and I would never be so gullible again. Did this event (the term date-rape had not been coined yet and because of the stigma, such events were rarely reported) count as losing my virginity? I didn't know. As for sex, I still knew little about it but I recognized its power. From now on it would be my weapon, to be used only when I was ready and only to my advantage.

CHAPTER 16

VIETNAM

For a year I flew from one end of Vietnam to the other, entertaining the troops, visiting the wounded in hospitals, making friends and experiencing life, good and bad.

The G.I's had an expression that went; "War is long periods of boredom, punctuated by moments of sheer terror." I never experienced too many boring moments but I did share in a few of the sheer terror ones.

One of those occurred whilst I was flying in a small spotter plane from Pleiku to Nha Trang. By the end of my first year, there was not an aircraft I had not flown in – from the big C130's and C123's to the Australian military's Caribou's, the Otters "Low and Slow", the big Chinook helicopters, the Hueys, the small LOH (Light observation Helicopters) or Bubbles, and to General Westmoreland's personal Beechcraft (he was not in it and unaware I was – I knew his pilot).

It was mid afternoon. The weather looked ominous as I thanked the young pilot and climbed into the spotter plane, a two-seater Cessna L19 (referred to as a Bird Dog by the men.)

"Look's like a storm is brewing." I observed.

"That's normal this time of the year," the young Lieutenant replied, "We'll beat it."

It was the monsoonal season and brief, violent storms blew in and out most evenings.

The pilot pushed his seat forward, allowing me to climb in over it and settle myself in the back. For about thirty minutes we flew high over the jungle, out of gunshot range, in relative calm. Almost without warning, the storm broke all around us and we were bucking and jerking about amid the lightning strikes. The pilot twisted his head and yelled something, but I couldn't hear above the thunder. The rain lashed us as we pressed on and visibility became nil.

I was normally a good passenger as I had flown extensively in light aircraft piloted by my brother Russell, and I was never scared. However as the weather deteriorated, fear began churning my stomach.

"No use turning back." The Lieutenant yelled above the roar, "Before my radio cut out I heard that all flights are grounded, even the big C130's." He then turned his full attention back to keeping us in the air and never spoke again.

"Just great!" I mouthed.

The little plane was taking a battering, and the sky was rolling grey and black around us. Streaks of crimson lightning flashed in every direction, splitting the heavy black cloud cover. Unable to see at all, we quickly dropped below the dense cloud smothering us until we could make out the bends of a river below. The pilot used that river as our guide, jerking along, keeping it in sight as it snaked through the mist-shrouded jungle. I had flown in Bird dogs before and I knew how dangerous our low altitude was. Even our view of the dark green jungle was almost obliterated by rain and mist. I tried to calm myself by thinking "Not even Charlie is fanatical enough to be out in this".

We were doing our low altitude devil's dance and I sat shaking and sweating, glad no-one could see me. Nature was toying with us, jerking us like a yo-yo when suddenly I saw another flash of red. This did not come from above, it came from below. Instantly the pilot did a hundred-and-eighty-degree turn and we headed out towards the mist shrouded ocean. I was wrong about that fanatical VC! There was no way he would let weather rob him of the glory of killing an American; or an Ouc da loi (Australian) for that matter.

By now I was speechless with fear and praying madly, making all kinds of rash promises of how I would change if I survived.

We made it out of gunshot range and I slowly exhaled, unclenching my muscles whilst silently mouthing a big 'thank you'. But no sooner had one danger passed when another loomed, rising out of the fog. I gasped and my stomach lurched into my throat as the small island rose out of the ocean, only feet in front of us. The pilot pointed the nose upwards and the valiant little aircraft barely scraped over the rocky pinnacle, climbing so steeply that I thought we would stall. Vietnam had a myriad of those sharp, small mounds of land along the coastline; not a hazard if you could see or had enough altitude.

We leveled out and I was wishing the nightmare would end when I noticed the sound around us had changed. The wind and thunder still roared but something was not the same. "Oh my God!" I realized the engine had stopped. Panic! Panic! We were falling. That ocean which had saved us once now looked like becoming our grave. As we fell closer and closer, the waves looked increasingly angry and I could see the spray blowing above the bubbling white caps. I no longer prayed and nor did my life flash before my eyes. There was no time for that. I was thinking of survival. I waited for impact, frantically measuring the distance to shore and wishing I was a better swimmer. I wondered if the plane would break up when we hit or if it would float. I wondered if we would still be conscious. I wondered how I would get over the front seat and out the door if the pilot was unconscious or dead. I wondered could I get him out and hang onto him. I wondered if we could float in on a piece of a wing. I wondered… I wondered…

We were ten feet from the waves when the plane suddenly shuddered and coughed to life. Time stood still as we spluttered and crept, ever so slowly, back into the sky. Somehow, we managed to get back on course and even though the storm still raged, it was anti-climactic as we limped into Nha Trang.

We landed in Nha Trang and I climbed shakily onto the ground and rested my arm against the side of the plane, just above a row of bullet holes. I was unable to speak for a while. The pilot opened a stick of gum and popped it into his mouth. His hands were shaking.

"That was pretty hairy." He finally croaked.

"Yeah."

"Let's go get a brandy in the officers club. We need something stronger than beer."

"Yeah."

We made our way on shaky legs into the clubhouse. A few grounded pilots were standing about in their blue-grey flight suits. We sat on bar stools and ordered our drinks.

One of the pilots detached himself from a small group and ambled over.

"Hi guys. Where did you come in from?" I could see him looking at the Lieutenant's insignia and wings, trying to place his unit.

"Pleiku."

"No way. Everything is grounded between here and there."

"Well thank God we made it. My Bird Dog's out on the tarmac. Go see, if you don't believe me. She's the one that looks like a sieve."

"Hell man. Let me pay for these drinks."

After he left to tell the story to his buddies, I gulped my brandy. Only after the heat of the liquor hit my stomach did I find my voice.

"I have one question Lieutenant. What made the engine start up again after we almost hit the water?"

He looked sheepish. "Well. I switched fuel tanks."

"What do you mean? You switched tanks?"

"An L19 has two fuel tanks. With all the shit that was going on I temporarily forgot to switch over. I'm sorry I gave you a scare."

"Hell. It was only one scare of many. But, I guess I'll forgive you. You got us here.......Here's to survival" And we clinked our glasses together in a toast.

"I'll drink to that." He said.

After a year of dancing I had saved quite a bit of money. For years I had planned what I would do once I had enough money. Step one was to return to Manilla and legally adopt one of those little girls off the street. (I will return to that subject later) With that taken care of, I planned to continue onto Australia and open a club.

The delay with the child sometimes caused me guilt. I had been having too much fun to settle down. Whenever I did accumulate money, I continually blew it on diamonds and pearls. That probably sounds a bit shallow. I suppose it was but my heart was in the right place. Now I again had the money but I wasn't ready to leave Vietnam. I felt I was needed and I enjoyed both that need as well as the excitement.

It was now 1967 and the troop build-up was in full swing. With it came increasing numbers of entertainers. I asked myself "Why not forget dancing and open that club you've always wanted. Open it right here in Vietnam."

God knows every town and village in Vietnam had a string of bars. They were dilapidated hangouts for herpes and gonorrhea riddled prostitutes, thieves and spies. They sold the hapless soldiers watered down "Saigon Tea" at high prices in dirty glasses. If venereal disease didn't get the men, Hepatitis did. (Fortunately they were the days before Aids)

My club would be a reminder of 'back home', clean and attractive. There would be no bar girls or Saigon Teas. The men would not be robbed or cheated.

Nha Trang would be the perfect location with several military installations providing me the customers. So far Charlie had left Nha Trang in relative peace, focusing on the country more to the north. And the biggest attraction of all; Nha Trang sat on a beautiful, white, sandy beach.

CHAPTER 17

TAMWORTH, NSW, AUSTRALIA

15th May 1954

There was a clear blue autumn sky with just the slightest chill in the air when I married Peter Skewes. I was eighteen.

Holding hands and laughing we ran down the steps of the little Methodist church and out into the bright sunshine. "Husband and wife," Peter whispered, hugging me close.

We had been dating for a year and were deeply in love. The week long separations had been excruciating and I watched the clock, willing my life away until we were back together. Our parents said we were too young to marry so we had threatened to elope until, possibly guessing our activities on the seat of Peter's ute, they acquiesced.

Peter lived on a sheep station two hour's drive from Tamworth and we could only meet on the occasional week-end. Of course our hormones were on fire and the dread of pregnancy was always with us! These were the days before the "morning after pill," and contraceptives were impossible for a single man to obtain in a country town without starting tongues wagging. Back then, the pleasure of intercourse between unmarried couples was always overshadowed by fears of pregnancy. Unable to resist the indisputable power of sex, there were a great many marriages among teenagers who had little alternative if the girl became pregnant. One outcome of unwed motherhood was to leave on an 'extended holiday' financed by the mortified parents. After relinquishing the baby and returning home, the girl was susceptible to community suspicion and scorn. Young girls, too fearful to tell their parents were sometimes butchered in illegal, back-yard abortions. Only the bravest souls kept their babies, and became social outcasts.

Not testing fate further, Peter and I rushed into marriage as fast as possible and we never joined in the condemnation of girls less fortunate.

Peter was unaware of my so-called date-rape. Certain that Dennis had ruined my reputation; I left school soon after the event and took a job as a salesgirl, abandoning my dreams of becoming a circus acrobat-a famous artist- a bike racer.

Meg Skewes, a fellow salesgirl my own age, boarded in town during the week. On week-ends, she returned to her parents' cottage in the small village called Watson's Creek. I jumped at the chance to escape Tamworth when she invited me home one weekend. Her mother, Aunty Ida, was warm and nurturing like Nan. When she pulled me close and hugged me to her ample bosom she smelled like raspberry jam. Her large, friendly family soon became my refuge.

Watson's Creek had sprung up in the early 1900's when tin was discovered. It was not quaint and a hamlet would probably be a better way to describe it.

Over the years, families moved away as the ore was mined out and cottages were left to rot. A few remained, eking out an existence mining what was left of the tin. These diehards clustered around a small country store which sold a handful of basic goods. On the edge of the village, a corrugated iron woolshed was used for social functions.

Aunty Ida's family enjoyed simple pleasures; a game of cricket on the harsh, dry grass, a sing-a-long or game of cards on the front porch and food, food- fabulous food. Indeed, every room in the small house was lined with shelves, ceiling to floor, and every shelf was crammed with jars of colorful preserved fruit and vegetables. The house always smelled of baking bread and scones or stewed fruit.

One Saturday night while attending a country dance in the woolshed, I met Meg's Cousin Peter. The moment I saw him I knew he was the one. I loved his crooked smile, his drawling voice, his wide shoulders and narrow waist. It was not the beginning of a smooth romance however, for during the next few months he came on strong one minute, ignored me the next. This strategy worked well. Past vows flew out the window and I became the proverbial 'lovesick fool.'

By marrying Peter, I wasn't moving far from Tamworth, but it felt like another planet. Glen Barra was a 17,000 acre sheep and cattle property managed by his father. Peter and his two brothers plus another worker, helped run the property. Peter lived with his parents and his sister Judith in a spacious homestead. At twenty-two, he was the youngest of the boys and the last son to marry. Judith was my age.

His mother Stella Skewes was not exactly thrilled at her son's choice of a wife. Maybe it was simply because I was a city girl. She was heard lamenting that country boys should not marry useless city girls.

After the church service we joined our guests at the hotel for the small reception. The cost customarily fell to the bride's parents which in our case actually meant me as Mum had no money. Peter was paying for the honeymoon and my money had mostly been spent on clothes. Therefore we had no music no entertainment and no sit down wedding feast – only drinks and finger food.

Following an age-old tradition, the men stood together in a group drinking beer, uncomfortable in their best suits. The ladies sat on hard chairs politely sipping whatever was offered. The waitress was not delivering the food fast enough to please my mother. Mum tried to supervise things from the chair she was forced to remain on since, as usual, she had a baby in her arms. This was Della, baby number six. Lorraine, the previous year's pretty blonde addition was standing shyly at her elbow in a lovely pink dress which mother had embroidered with silk roses.

"June," Mum called "Your guests are hungry. Go and help the waitress carry the trays around."

"I beg your pardon?" "These arrangements are yours and they are inadequate. You help."

"It's my wedding day Mum. I don't think I should be serving food."

I felt annoyed and wished Peter and I had eloped as planned. Popping into the 'Ladies', I looked at myself in the mirror. Bowing to tradition, I was wearing a white lace dress. Breaking with tradition, it came only to my ankles so had no train and I wore no veil. My lace hat had a red rose pinned beneath the wide brim. Red roses were my favorite flowers and I carried a basket of them instead of the customary, trailing white bouquet. This probably sounds like a trivial detail but the point is that I was beginning to assert myself when I broke with tradition which EVERYONE stuck to back then.

I touched up my lipstick and decided to please Mum by carrying the food around.

Back with the guests again, I cringed, seeing my mother breast feeding the baby, even though her breast and the baby's head were modestly covered beneath a big white nappy. Recalling my embarrassment as I write, I marvel at how one can change.

Peter stood with a group of men in one corner and was obviously getting drunk. Not only was I peeved with my overly fertile mother but with my new husband as well. We had to drive part way to Sydney that night. The fixed smile began slipping as I picked up a tray of sausage rolls and hurried around the room.

A week later, Peter and I returned from our honeymoon. When we pulled up in front of his parent's home late in the afternoon, his mother, wearing a floppy straw hat, was out front hosing her precious roses. I wondered whether I would be watering roses when I reached her age. I recalled Nan too spent most afternoons watering her rose garden.

Seeing us, Mrs. Skewes turned off the hose, removed her gloves and hurried out to the car. "Welcome back." She said, "Come in for a cup of tea. How was your trip?"

"Good," Peter replied rather sheepishly. Neither of us felt like admitting we had been out of our comfort zone in the expensive, waterfront hotel where most of the patrons were middle aged and looked wealthy. When they smiled at us we felt self conscious. Young couples rarely checked into hotels unless they were on their honeymoon. In fact, it was customary for the desk clerks to ask for identification from young people, proving their marital status. If this was not forthcoming, neither was the room. So that explains why most pre-marriage love-making occurred in vehicles at isolated town look-out or country lanes.

We additionally felt conspicuous by Peter's wide brimmed Akubra hat. It advertised that we were 'country folk' and not one of 'them'.

In the hotel dining room we felt at a loss, staring at the extensive array of cutlery, unsure which piece to lift first. After the first day, we ate at a nearby café serving greasy pies and fish and chips. So I was happy to be home and I hoped Mrs. Skewes had cooked a roast dinner.

"You look tired, June." Stella said as she led us into the house "Why don't you sleep in Peter's old room tonight and move down to your place in the morning?"

Glen Barra is steeped in history. The homestead sits on a small hill surrounded by rose gardens, a tennis court, and an ornately fenced cemetery which holds the remains of the original owners, the Mungo Parkes family. They were pioneers and sufficiently prestigious to be mentioned in the Australian history books.

The large property was located too far from town to have electricity; however, the homestead had its own generator power. Hot running water was piped from a massive, cream-enameled, combustion stove in the gigantic kitchen. All the rooms had high ceilings for hot summers. Ornate Rosewood mantels surrounded the open fireplaces which kept the house warm in winter.

By contrast, in a hollow at the bottom of the hill, three small cottages sat in the shadow of a corrugated iron shearing shed with the shearer's dormitory nearby.

Peter occasionally played a game of tennis with his father before dinner and this first night back was no exception. A pair of Kookaburra's laughed hysterically as I looked down towards the enclave of little cottages. The next day I would begin my married life in one of those modest houses. Then I would make my mother-in-law eat her words about city girls not making good wives for country boys.

CHAPTER 18

NHA TRANG

1967

No foreigner could just waltz into Vietnam and start up a business. Fortunately, I had developed friendships with a few good Vietnamese people and one of those was Colonel Vu Van Uoc, the commander of the Nha Trang air field. He in turn was friends with the local Chief of Police who, on Colonel Uoc's recommendation, issued me a business license, no strings attached.

As a patriotic Australian, I was compelled to name my club The Waltzing Matilda. The concrete, three story building sat a couple of blocks back from the picturesque Nha Trang beach. My landlord was a Chinese herbalist with his apothecary in an adjoining building. Shelves held hundreds of bottles containing preserved snakes, lizards, pickled eyeballs and other unidentifiable 'things'. Although he kindly offered a cure whenever I was afflicted with a cold or hangover, I always politely declined.

The drawback to my location was its proximity to the sprawling, local markets. When the vendors departed each evening, taking their unsold birds, snakes and un-refrigerated meat with them, they left behind mounds of rotting produce. This attracted rats as big as cats and a stiff breeze could blow the stench towards my beer garden.

I discovered a small furniture factory and ordered upholstered Bamboo furniture. Large velvet paintings copied from Playboy centerfolds were framed and hung on the club walls. (Every G.I. hooch in Vietnam had a centerfold pinned up somewhere.) Soft lighting and a sound system were installed. A bar was built and I was ready to go.

By designating the club membership, and hand picking mature members only, meaning NCO's and Officers, I avoided trouble. Rank was left at the door; however, members had to respect each other's space and privacy, not intruding where they were not wanted.

Off-duty, Vietnamese bartenders and waitresses were hired from the U.S. camps. These had already undergone CID background checks. There was no check on the two Vietnamese women who cleaned the club each morning. They seemed innocuous enough but I was a little uneasy about no checks.

The flat roof of the third level became a beer garden, overlooking the street and smelly market. The Vietcong were fond of riding their Honda's past American hang-outs and lobbing in a grenade or two so I fully enclosed the upper level within thick, mesh wire.

The second floor held the bar and the main lounge. My living quarters could be reached only through a locked door beside the bar.

Nha Trang was home to The 5th Special Forces Headquarters (The Green Berets) as well as 1st Army Field Headquarters, and a large American hospital plus an Air Force detachment. This was more than enough troops to assure me of success.

Opening hours were midday until curfew, seven nights a week. From the beginning, it was hugely successful and running that club is among some of my happiest memories. Gone were the wasted hours spent waiting in the dust and heat of the airfields. Gone were the uncomfortable nights sleeping on narrow army cots with no privacy. Gone were the communal showers with the 'Donut Dollies.' And gone were the mortar attacks.

Mortar attacks on Nha Trang were rare. Spooky (a cumbersome American cargo plane with an armory of guns) patrolled overhead each night, looking for bad guys. Occasionally I saw Spooky spew his red tracers to the ground but I seldom felt danger in NhaTrang. A massive white statue of Buddha overlooked the town from a nearby hill. Possibly, he was protecting us but he did nothing for the antiquated city power plant which continually collapsed.

At one end of the white sandy beach, a ramshackle restaurant sold the world's juiciest lobsters. It belonged to Francois, an ex-patriot Frenchman who had not fled the war. In that small town shopping was a challenge but I quietly finagled some of my supplies through the American military (Meat, liquor etc.) On occasion I slipped away from the club and quietly gave a show, using the barter system and taking payment in liquor. Otherwise I could only buy on the black-market at exorbitant prices. Basics such as bread, sugar and flour were available from the local vendors. Fresh produce was in short supply everywhere.

Early one morning I left the club to buy a few office supplies. Nha Trang was small enough that I could walk everywhere. Several shops were still closed as I wandered along the 'main' street.

I hadn't gone far when one of Vietnam's many street urchins caught up with me. Not all were victims of war. Many were pickpockets or pimps. Some were shoe-shine boys, others sold smut. They were street wise, adept at surviving and best avoided. It was hard to pity them when they were so brazen and persistent.

Years before, in the Philippines, I had become acquainted with some little beggar girls. They were different – so sweet and funny, they broke my heart.

"You want to eat good Chinese chow Missee?" the boy asked.

"No." I said, increasing my pace.

"I know good place Missee. I take you there."

"It's too early for Chinese chow."

"Not too early. He serve good Chinese soup. You Like?" he tugged on my arm.

Jerking my arm away I spun around "I said no. You Dee de mau. You hear me?"

"I no Dee de mau. You pretty lady. Why you number ten?"

The street boys designated the number ten to anyone bad. Of course number one was someone who gave them money.

I looked at the annoying boy and noted that he was about eleven years old and unattractive. It was unusual for Vietnamese to have freckles and his dry hair stuck out in choppy tufts. He stared boldly at me from eyes too worldly for his age.

"What's your name?" I asked

"Me, Dong."

"Well Dong, I am not hungry. Why do you want me to eat?"

"Because I'm hungry now." He grinned "When I bring GI for food, the Chinese he feeds me out the back."

"Don't you eat at home?"

"No home. No family only me. My village up North get many bomb. I walk many days to Nhatrang."

"Where do you sleep?" Compassion stirred although he seemed to require no pity.

"Anywhere. My life Ok. GI's treat me pretty good."

"Look Dong, I am hungry after all. You take me to this Chinese place. Later, you find me shop. I buy these things." I showed him a handful of paper clips.

"You eat, I go buy." He said "You give me money."

'What a sucker you are, I thought, following him to the small Chinese restaurant. Once he gets the money I will never see him again. I shrugged. It was only a few cents.

Fifteen minutes later, I was eating a bowl of chicken and corn soup when Dong ran in. He spread his hand proudly, displaying a dozen or so loose, wire clips. The withered Chinese proprietor bustled in, his voice angry as he pointed at Dong, gesturing for him to leave.

"No!" I argued, surprised that Dong had returned, and feeling a need to defend him. "He's with me. Bring him food." I pointed to my bowl as I spoke.

The Chinese man grimaced.

"No can do. He beggar boy. He eat out back."

I shook my head "You give me food. I take it home"

He glared at Dong before shuffling to the kitchen to get the soup

"He number ten" Dong said "You number one."

"Don't try to butter me up" I said "Anyway, we take this food and you come home with me to eat it. Would you like a place to sleep every night?" My invitation was spontaneous and surprised me.

"Where?" he looked at me suspiciously "I no boom boom boy."

"Of course not. You can come and live with me. I will feed you every day but if you come, you must go to school."

He backed off warily "I no like school. Teachers is bad. They throw me away."

"Maybe with good reason" I said. "But you can come with me now and take a look before deciding."

Dong carried his soup, following me back to the Waltzing Matilda with little enthusiasm. He was clearly weighing the odds.

That night he slept in a makeshift bed on the floor of the main lounge, but not before we had our first argument over him taking a shower. I knew it would be an uphill battle but it was worth a try.

The Waltzing Matilda was fast developing an excellent reputation and I reveled in my role as the Hostess with the Mostess. Each day I cooked a large meal, providing no menu. The customers either ate whatever I made or else they could have Francois' lobster or Chinese food delivered. Most chose my home-cooked meal.

Soon I began discreetly receiving some illustrious visitors for private parties. Whenever a high-ranking American commander was due to arrive, the street out front was filled with Military police and, depending on just how high the rank was, The Waltzing Matilda premises themselves were sometimes searched from top to bottom for security purposes.

On the rare occasions when high -ranking Vietnamese were in house we had jeep loads of White Mice (Vietnamese Police) patrolling outside. A rare social gathering involving both Vietnamese and American commanders meant the street was closed off with barriers at either end. At such times, both the American and Vietnamese police groups took over in countless jeeps, glaring suspiciously at each other.

My Vietnamese neighbors were clearly nonplussed. Colonel Vu Van Uoc said he had never previously met his American counterpart under social circumstances. He claimed they came to more agreement in one night at the Waltzing Matilda than in any more formal meetings.

Dalat was known as Vietnam's garden city and grew most of the country's vegetables. Occasionally when Uoc had to fly in that direction he would stop off at the club to see what I needed. His airmen must have wondered what sort of a mission he'd flown when he returned with his airplane stuffed full of vegetables.

Dong was giving me plenty of headaches. He had not settled into school well and the teachers told me they were close to expelling him.

"Why can't you try and get along with the other children?" I asked him one day when he was sent home early.

He kicked the rattan matting "They make laugh at me" he said "They say me dirty street boy."

"Well I'll talk to the teachers again." I answered "Things should settle down after awhile."

"I more happy on street" he said, "GI no talk bad to me."

"But the war will end one day and if you stay on the streets you will not be able to get a job and have a good life."

He cleared his throat and spat on the floor.

"For God's sake Dong. How many times do I have to tell you, you can't spit inside. Get a rag and wipe that up."

Grudgingly, he did as told then ambled over to the large refrigerator behind the bar and helped himself to a coke.

"I no worry for after war. Maybe it no end. Maybe I no get old. Maybe one day they kill you – me -, same same they did my village."

That was hard to answer. Maybe I should have left him on the street. My private quarters had only one bedroom. He still slept in the main lounge after the club closed. And I had to be careful to leave no money lying about. He was a petty thief. The two black-toothed housemaids hated him. They felt superior to him and yet, as my protégée, I had unintentionally elevated him above them. They complained that he stole soft drinks and sold them on the streets. Maybe I had bitten off more than I could handle but I felt I had to try.

"By the way," Uoc said to me one morning as we shared a pot of coffee in my private courtyard, "A close friend of mine will be in town tomorrow. We went through flight school together. I would like to bring him and his wife to meet you. Is that alright?"

"Certainly Uoc. What time shall I expect you?"

"My friends will arrive early, before you open for business. Please have the housemaids come in early to clean then leave. I'll send some fresh flowers."

"Goodness me!" I exclaimed, "Who am I expecting?"

"Our Premier, Nguyen Cao Ky and his wife. They want to meet you. He will have security, of course. And later, you might join us for a picnic and some snorkeling over on Hon Tre Island."

"I'd be proud to meet them. His wife looks beautiful and I love the tranquility of Hon Tre Island. It's such an escape".

CHAPTER 19

AUSTRALIA

Peter and I spent our first full day back at Glen Barra, settling into our small cottage. Solidly built of timber, it comprised a bedroom, living room with open fireplace and a large eat-in kitchen. At the rear was the typical, enclosed verandah containing the usual cement laundry tubs, a bathroom with a tin bath-tub and chip heater. The outhouse sat beside a black copper, which was used for boiling clothes. Two rope clotheslines and a prop, fashioned from a slender tree branch completed the picture.

To the right of our little love nest lived Peter's brother Bill and his wife Marj. On our left was the tall, thin station hand named Herbert with his 300 pound wife and their five children. These were the days before television and I blamed lack of entertainment for the reason women had so many children. I was anxious to join their ranks.

Peter and Bill finished carrying my new, bedroom suite inside. Buying it had blown our budget.

"Sorry I can't make you a cup of tea Bill." I glanced unhappily at the big, wood burning kitchen stove. The house had no gas or electricity. "I haven't yet learned to make a fire."

"Another time," Bill replied. "Besides, if I don't get back to work Dad will be out with the whip."

As Bill took his leave, Peter said "It's time to start your education. Without fire we can do nothing," and grabbing an old newspaper, he scrunched it up.

"Now you take kindling and criss-cross it above the paper. Then place a larger piece of wood on top. Throw a little Kerosene in and Voila, you've got it. See!"

I dutifully watched the bright flame lick the kindling.

"Always keep the kettle on the stove. Visitors out in the bush have traveled for miles so have tea ready."

He indicated the largest, blackest kettle I had ever seen and I doubted I could lift it if it was full.

"You will also need to light a fire under the copper to do the laundry and again, light the chip heater to take a bath." I hid my alarm, never having lit a fire in my life.

"After we have tea, I'll show you how to light the Tilly lamp." He continued cheerfully.

Thirty minutes later, while Peter vigorously pumped up the gas in the Tilly lamp, I hid my fears that it might explode.

"That's it," Peter said as the white cotton bag in the centre of the glass spread a nice bright glow.

"Now you'll be able to do the laundry and cook my dinner while I'm away working tomorrow."

I nodded mutely.

"To wash our clothes you must fill the copper from a bucket then light a fire the way I've shown you."

He pulled a silver iron from a kitchen cabinet. "Best you do the ironing with this metho iron. It's cleaner than the flat black ones on the stove." He gave me a demo which included burning metho and more pumping.

"If you forget how to do this, just use the flat irons but remember the stove top gets dirty so wipe their bottoms with a rag."

I sighed heavily, knowing I wouldn't dare pump that metho thing.

"And my mother likes my good, long-sleeved shirts starched."

The following morning I was sleeping soundly in my pretty bed when Peter roughly shook me awake.

"Get up sleepy head. The day's half over." He was leaning over me, neatly dressed in a khaki shirt and riding pants. I groggily noted it was still dark outside and even the Kookaburra's hadn't yet awakened.

"I've already lit the kitchen fire and milked the cow. Go make my breakfast while I saddle up." His spurs clinked as he walked away.

The honeymoon was over! Tottering to the bathroom, I washed in the bracing cold water then headed for the kitchen. Twigs crackled cheerfully and I inhaled their aromatic bush-land perfume while lowering the volume of the battery operated radio. It was too early for me to suffer the warbling sounds of Slim Dusty, every farmer's favorite country singer.

I cooked the gigantic steak and six eggs which Peter had set out. A starving dog couldn't have devoured it all. The smell of lard and frying meat was making me nauseous.

The moment my husband kissed me goodbye and leaped into the saddle, I ran to change the dreadful music. Soothed by the sounds of Glen Miller, I sat down with a cup of tea and surveyed our little love nest. The smell of my husband lingered on my flesh and already I was missing him.

All morning I worked hard, scrubbing the house from top to bottom until even the Magpies sang their approval.

As the noon-day sun made the kitchen stifling hot I let the fire go out. Peter had taken a Spam sandwich for lunch, telling me he was riding too far away to return before dark.

After eating bread and peanut butter, I carried several buckets of water to the copper before throwing up. Amazingly, I then lit the fire on my first try.

Two hours later the water was still bubbling like a witch's cauldron when I grabbed the wooden copper stick and struggled to untangle a twisted sheet. At last one end burst hysterically free and shot snake-like through the air into my face. Ignoring the burning pain, I dropped the sheet into the round metal tub.

Half the steaming brown water came out with the clothes and sloshed about in the bottom of the tub as I groaned to lift it. Somehow I managed to stagger up the steps without dislocating my back.

"I'll show Mrs. Skewes," I kept reminding myself as I wiped the sweat from my brow.

My fingers burned as I turned the handle of the wringer with one hand and guided the steaming clothes between the rollers with the other. At last

I finished rinsing the 'whites' in Rickett's blue and starching the shirts. Triumphantly I gazed at them hanging on the line.

As the day ebbed to a close I prepared dinner. Placing the peeled potatoes and pumpkin into a saucepan of cold water, I sat them uncovered on the stove. Already I had successfully lit one fire. The second time should be a breeze.

Then I discovered I had used up most of the kindling. The three or four remaining sticks burned up quickly without igniting the large chunks of wood. In desperation I threw a pint of kerosene into the firebox. It hit a few red coals and the ensuing fireball exploded into my face. Glancing up through singed eyelashes, I watched little pieces of black charred newspaper drift in slow motion through the air like fragile butterflies. They landed, ever so gently, on my uncovered vegetables. I knew when I was beat and made a couple of cheese sandwiches.

Nervousness delayed me from lighting the tilly lamp but darkness left me no choice. Groping for matches, I removed the glass shade by feel. Soon the little white cotton bag shed its welcome light and I sighed with relief. Alas, I must have given it too much gas for before long; an ugly black spot appeared. Dismayed, I watched it grow steadily larger until the bag turned black, then disintegrated, plunging me into darkness.

Peter found me sitting in the dark, swatting mosquitoes and crying. Fortunately, he understood and after washing down his cheese sandwich with a glass of tepid tap water, he took me to bed and tried to console me.

The next morning, before Peter rode away he reassured me by leaving an extra supply of kindling. Regardless, I kept the stove going all day, even though I almost fainted from the heat. I needed that fire for ironing Peter's shirts. Like hell, I was going to pump that metho thing.

These were the days when a woman's merit was measured by her prowess at both the laundry tub and the ironing board, not to mention the 'dreaded white glove' test.

After stoking the fire and thoroughly wiping the bottoms of the flat irons I held their hot handles with a pot mitt. The miniscule kitchen window kept any breeze at bay and I did my best to stop the rivulets of sweat from soiling Peter's good white shirts. The first shirt turned out perfect. Placing the iron back to reheat, I lifted another. My vision had become blurred by sweat which required constant wiping on my apron. Finished at last and seeing clearly, I was devastated to discover black streaks down several shirt fronts.

The days passed quickly and although it seemed I was proving Mrs. Skewes words correct, Peter still loved me. However, I was feeling unwell and he drove me into Tamworth to see Doctor Stanley who congratulated us. I was pregnant! It must have happened on our honeymoon, fulfilling the assumptions of those older hotel guests. We were elated.

The weeks flew by but my endless 'morning sickness' failed to recognize the noon hour! Even the overpowering smell of a peeled potato made me vomit violently. My mother never reacted like this as she sailed through her numerous pregnancies, I thought bitterly.

Peter, like all farmers, wanted a son. His brothers, Frank and Bill, already had fathered sons. I secretly yearned for a girl.

One morning, after Peter rode off to work, I felt particularly nauseous and returned to bed.

Since arriving at Glen Barra, I had received no visitors. My beautiful china tea set sat unused in the cupboard. We lived too far from town for my family to travel out in the old jeep and neither my in-laws nor my neighbors ever dropped by. I wondered if they were avoiding me because I was a 'city girl'.

Murphy's Law! The one time I decided to go back to bed, I was woken by a persistent hammering on the door. It was nine a.m., the middle of the day for farm folk. I pulled on my blue chenille dressing gown, oblivious to the blob of dried vomit. My hair looked like the stuffing from a rag doll and my brush had vanished. I waddled to the door, patting my hair down and wiping sleep from my eyes.

Standing on the door step was Herbert's wife. Observing my bedraggled appearance she barely concealed a disapproving sniff. I apologized for my disarray and invited her in for the customary cup of tea. She looked around the messy kitchen then dropped, with what I considered thoughtless abandon, onto a frail kitchen chair. The fire was almost out and the kettle had gone off the boil. Flustered, I flitted about, sparking up the fire while simultaneously hurling dirty dishes off the table and into the sink. Trying to cover my embarrassment, I made small talk about the weather forecast. We had little in common and conversation was stilted. I dropped burned toast onto the floor and while retrieving it, noticed the linoleum was ankle deep in dirt and chunks of dried mud from Peter's riding boots. I grabbed a broom, still droning on about how we needed rain.

Now, the only way to feed Peter's twelve working dogs, was by killing kangaroos. He did this with an old World War Two, 303 rifle. This huge weapon scared me and I kept my distance but I did vaguely recognize a few long, thin bullets among the dirt.

Still struggling to converse with my neighbor, I absently swept the dirt into a dustpan and heaved it into the open fire box. I was placing a handful of loose tea into the teapot when a huge explosion and a shrill scream from Mrs. Herbert spun me around. Dropping the tea, I was astounded to see this three hundred pound woman leap into the air with the agility of the Russian ballet dancer, Rudolf Nureyev. She grabbed her neck and crumpled into a heap on the floor with blood trickling between her fingers.

Fortunately, the bullet I'd thrown into the fire had only grazed her without penetration but it gave us both a start. Panting, I strived to raise her and as she wobbled to her feet, the exertion sent me rushing outside to vomit. Upon returning to the kitchen, I discovered that although the kettle had finally boiled, she had not waited for tea.

CHAPTER 20

NHA TRANG

It was 8 a.m. I yawned, finished tying the cord to my kimono and opened the door into the club. This was my favorite time of the day, before it became too hot. I looked forward to making myself a cup of tea and relaxing with yesterdays Stars and Stripes newspaper in the courtyard. But first, I had to make sure that Dong left for school. Sunlight was streaming through the long, vertical windows at the far end of the main lounge as I entered. The air had a slightly stuffy, alcohol tinge to it. I would have to make sure the house maids opened the windows and gave the place a good airing out once they arrived.

"Dong, wake up," I called "You will be late for school."

There was no answer. I called again, hurried around the bar and looked over to the spot where he normally made his bed. No bedding! No Dong! He hadn't slept here last night. I didn't know whether to be upset or angry. Maybe he had just stayed out; having a good time with some generous GI's and he didn't want to go to school. But I had warned him not to do this.

"Damn that kid." I thought. "Now I will have to get dressed and go look for him."

As I dressed I tried to analyze my feelings towards him. I didn't love him. He was hard to love; showing no affection or gratitude either. He certainly could not be called obedient. Nevertheless, I was fond of him and I admired his independent spirit and survival instincts. But as streetwise as he was, he was still a child and I feared he would fall into the wrong hands.

A little later I walked around the back of the Chinese restaurant.

I found Mr. Wong squatting, plucking a chicken, his purple veined hands covered in small white feathers.

"Was Dong here last night?" I queried.

Mr. Wong kept his eye on the dead fowl. "He not here many days. You no worry. He one smart boy."

I looked at my watch. It was almost ten o'clock. I had to get back to let the housemaids in. 'Maybe I've been too strict,' I thought. Having no boundaries for so long, he had balked at my rather liberal restrictions. But the problem was I had forced him to go to school. There was little I could do now. I would just continue looking and making inquiries, hoping he would return when he was hungry.

It seemed motherhood was never meant for me. I tried not to think about those early attempts in Australia. That was another life.

Dong had not returned by eleven o'clock, when the last customer left. I locked the club and went to bed, trying not to imagine the worst. There was no chance he would come back after curfew.

It must have been about 1 am when a noise disturbed my sleep. I felt too groggy to get up but all nightly noise needed investigation. And it might be Dong. I pulled my Kimono on and stumbled across the courtyard and into the club. Spotlights were playing over the large front windows and American voices could be heard yelling outside. What the hell? With my Kimono untied and flapping, I hurried to the window. Four MP jeeps were parked on the road in front of The Waltzing Matilda beside a cluster of Military Police.

"What is going on?" I yelled unheard then ran up the stairs to the beer garden where I could get a better view of the street below. Unlocking the door, I burst onto the deck and gasped. Facing me were three shadowy figures clinging to the wire enclosure. I jumped back and slammed the door, grateful the MP's were on the job. Cautiously I peeped through a window. The lights continued flashing over the intruders as the MP's screamed at them to come down. I was safe as long as they didn't have wire cutters. The roving spotlight pinpointed the lead figure and again I gasped. Surely I was seeing things! It could not be Brigadier General Oscar Davis. I ran back onto the deck calling "Is that you Oscar? What on earth are you doing?"

"Go back inside, Ma am," One of the MP's yelled. "We've got this under control." I ran inside and down two flights of stairs. Running out onto the street I stopped abruptly when I noticed several of the MP's had drawn their guns. One strode towards me. "It's not safe out here ma am. I must order you back inside."

"But I know one of them." I said

"That doesn't matter. They have broken curfew and we are taking them in."

"Er, er. That lead man is Brigadier General Oscar Davis, the deputy commander of the First Cavalry Division. I don't know what he's doing here though."

The soldier's eyes widened "What? Excuse me." He hurried over to where two other MP's were climbing the wire, trying to grab the kicking legs of the officer closest to the ground.

"That top one is a General Davis." He yelled up to his buddies.

"Don't fall for that story" the M.P. furthest up the wire called down.

"Oscar, tell them who you are." I urged.

Oscar only climbed a little higher, infuriating the lead MP. who managed to grab him by the foot, lost his balance and both of them tumbled to the ground. With their leader so ingloriously captured, the subordinate officers came down to check if he was alright.

I rushed forward as Oscar clambered to his feet, grinning inanely. His captor stood up more slowly then limped over, pulling handcuffs from his belt.

"Can't we talk about this?" A young officer asked. "You are about to arrest a general officer. He's been out with his men for weeks on operation Pershing. We just got into town."

"Yeah, and I'm President Johnson. Put your hands behind you."

At that moment, one of the other military police swept his flashlight over Oscar's insignia. The Silver Star blinked back at him.

"Shit!" I heard him say before the MPs went into a huddle. Seconds later they turned back and awkwardly saluted Oscar. "Sorry for the misunderstanding Sir," the limping one said "We were only doing our duty and there is a curfew here in Nha Trang you know."

"And doing it shwell, soldier." Oscar said, slurring his words only slightly. "Maybe we can just forgesh about this little incident, huh?"

"Certainly sir" replied the MP, replacing his handcuffs and stepping back.

"And have the hoshpital look at thash foot soldier. Looks like you'sh sprained it."

"Yes sir, right after we escort you to camp. It is after curfew."

"The three of them can stay at my place tonight sergeant" I cut in "Obviously this was their destination. I'll see they don't leave before curfew is lifted." I couldn't miss the sly grins the MP's exchanged.

"Alright then, that's settled!" They climbed back into their jeeps and drove off, no longer stifling peels of laughter.

"You must be desperate for a drink Oscar," I said sarcastically as he followed me inside "There's no way you would have ever got inside once I closed."

The three officers sat themselves at the bar as Oscar ordered 'After Burners' all round.

"I've been telling theesh very fine officers of mine aboush your place for months," the general said as I poured the cognac. "They didn't believe there wash a place like thish in Vietnam. I jush had to show them. Yoush close damned early."

"Don't tell me this was your first port of call" I replied "It's clear you've had a pretty good liquid dinner elsewhere."

Oscar looked sheepish "Bit of a cluster fuck, I guesh..... Okay men, reashy to drink up."

I picked up a cigarette lighter and sent the flames leaping on the four After Burners.

"Down the hatch men," I said "and fast."

After first exhaling into the fire, extinguishing the flames before the glass became too hot to handle, we inhaled the drinks in the required single gulp.

All except Oscar! His earlier alcohol intake had slowed his reflexes and his fire burned too long. He was the last one to set his empty glass on the bar and I noticed a chunk of flesh from his lower lip clinging to the hot glass, leaving his mouth a bloody mess. These drinks were so named after the fire that shoots out from the rear exhausts of fighter planes on take-off. They were not for the faint of heart. Oscar didn't appear to be feeling any pain; in fact, he found the injured lip quite hilarious.

As dawn set the roosters crowing, I made scrambled eggs, toast and coffee. My guests ate, took a quick shower, and as the sun rose, staggered bleary-eyed to their jeep. They were officers and gentlemen, ready for the pomp and ceremony of the parade ground. But more importantly, they were soldiers!

Later that day I passed Oscar on the nearby 1st Field Headquarters base. Troops were dispersing as a ceremony concluded. General Davis was hurrying to board a waiting helicopter and return up North, a row of medals gleaming on his chest. His bearing was proud, straight, dignified. The only trace of the previous night's escapade was his blistered lip.

"Another war wound is it General?" I couldn't resist.

He raised his eyebrow and nodded coolly, then winked. I watched him climb aboard his chopper and fly back to the war.

Several days passed and Dong never did get hungry enough to return home. I looked for him in all his old haunts without success and concluded he must have continued his journey further south. I heard a rumor that the two housemaids had beaten him but I was unable to verify it and did not fire them. I wondered what would become of him and all the other orphans, especially the younger ones without his survival instincts. It was a sad thought and I mourned for children everywhere who were hungry and had no-one to protect them.

Some of my Vietnamese staff at The Waltzing Matilda

My Saigon apartment near Tan Son Nhut

The Waltzing Matilda and My Linh

The private courtyard and my living quarters behind the Waltzing Matilda

CHAPTER 21

AUSTRALIA

Peter and I were broke and it was my fault!

I discovered soon after earning my first salary from Tamworth's leading department store, P.G. Smith's, that I was hopeless at budgeting. Nothing had changed. The clientele of P.G. Smith's dress department were wealthy land-owners wives. While catering to their high-end fashion tastes, I became enslaved to fashion myself. Talk about champagne taste on a beer budget!

Pre-occupation with clothes must have been an inherited trait. Nan dressed like the Queen mother and owned as many hats as Imelda Marcus owned shoes. Even my overworked, underpaid mother stressed the importance of dressing well.

As a station hand, Peter's salary was modest. That hadn't stopped me from buying a designer ball gown, costing Peter a month's salary. Of course, I charged it. Not by credit card which was unheard of then, but country stores did run accounts for approved farm families.

"You paid how much?" Mrs. Skewes spluttered. To wear only one night? Your pregnancy is already beginning to show."

In an attempt to appease everyone, I decided to pay for the gown myself by trapping rabbits and selling the skins. Unfortunately, my city upbringing failed me once more. Unwittingly, I set the traps on sheep trails, catching few rabbits. The broken legs of so many sheep aroused my father-in-law's ire.

"How could you put us into debt this way?" Peter hollered after his father reprimanded me and rode away.

"Now I'm going to have to work on my days off to pay for it." He was pacing the floor in our kitchen.

"Will your Dad give you extra work?"

"No way! And we need more money than what he pays." He opened the door of the kerosene operated refrigerator, and removed a can of beer. He never drank mid-week but this was an exception.

"There's only one thing for it. I will have to go timber cutting and sell the logs to the timber mill. I'll borrow the truck and tractor from Frank."

Frank, Peter's eldest brother, was currently living on Athlone, a three thousand acre property adjoining the boundary of Glen Barra. Mr. Skewes, a veteran of world war one, had received Athlone under the Australian Government's Soldiers Settlement Act. The Act was initiated to get returned soldiers onto the land and earning a living, albeit a hard one.

The three sons took turns living on Athlone, taking care of the place and helping out at Glen Barra when needed for mustering or other big jobs. Likewise, the family helped out at Athlone when necessary. It was a good arrangement for handling both properties.

"Will Frank lend you the equipment?"

"Yeah. Only last week he was saying that the north end paddock needed clearing." He displayed his displeasure with me by belching.

"Anyway, you will need to help. You got us into this mess."

"How can I help?"

"After I cut the logs, and chain them to the horse, we drag them to the road. The tractor pulls them onto the back of the truck. You will drive the tractor."

Riddled with guilt, I eagerly agreed even though I couldn't drive a tractor.

The following week we started logging on his day off.

"Heavens girl," Mrs. Skewes cried appalled when she drove up and saw us. "If you make a mistake those huge logs could roll back and crush Peter."

I was proud of handling the tractor but obviously she wasn't impressed.

Reaching my fifth month of pregnancy, I was excited as the big day drew closer. All pre-marriage dreams were obliterated by my love of Peter and our plans for a large family. Days were no longer lonely as I rubbed my growing tummy and sang softly to our baby inside. I shared with her my dreams for her future as I perused the baby catalogs which the mailman delivered. Baby clothes all looked pretty much the same in those days and color selection was a dilemma. Blue for boys, pink for girls or white for uncertainty! No-one dreamed that in the future, a baby's sex would be known before birth.

It was about 2 a.m on a wintry night when my bladder screamed for attention. Ignoring it I snuggled further down under the thick, warm eiderdown and tried to go back to sleep. My husband lay curled around me, breathing deeply. My bladder won. Disentangling myself from Peter I stretched my legs towards the bare linoleum floor, slipped into slippers and padded to the outside toilet. Returning through the kitchen, I felt a sudden urge to urinate again. Simultaneously, blood gushed from my nose. Confused and scared I called Peter. Moments later he entered the kitchen and found me doubled over in pain.

"Oh my God," he cried, "Get your dressing gown on. We're going to the nearest hospital. We'd better get Mum."

I stumbled into my dressing gown and then my water broke.

Peter leaped into his trousers and yanked on his boots. Wearing his flannel pajama top, he hoisted me into his arms and ran to his ute.

Taking off in a spurt of gravel, he kept his hand on the horn as we sped up the hill. The lights of the homestead came on when we screeched to a stop and his mother, Stella, ran out, tying her dressing gown.

"What's up?"

"Jump in Mum. We have to get June to hospital."

We bumped over the dirt road at break-neck pace. The intense pain made my heart sink as I realized we had so far to go. In hindsight, I suppose we should have telephoned the ambulance from Glen Barra but Peter thought it was faster to drive me himself. Our nearest small town, Manilla was normally an hour's drive from the property. Every bump made me scream. Squashed on the seat between mother and son, I rocked back and forth, moaning and begging Peter to stop. It seemed a pulsating beast sat with us in that dark, confined cab, soaking us all in pain. I longed to lie down on the road and began beating Peter with my clenched fists but he only drove faster.

Half way there, we reached the cabin of an old hermit. Knowing the man had a phone; Peter jammed on the brakes and ran in to call an ambulance to meet us.

The moment he left, I crawled out the open door and fell, semi-conscious onto the road. Immediately I felt my baby coming. It was too soon. I knew our baby would not live.

Courage must be an acquired thing for at that time, I did not seem to possess any. Dimly I saw Stella and Peter standing beside the hermit who held a flickering yellow lantern. Stella was whispering 'Hail Mary'.

My clothing was up above my knees. I was so modest in those days that I always switched off the light before undressing in front of my husband but I was past caring.

I recall small, unimportant things, like the grit from the road sticking to the blood between the rows of tufts of my chenille dressing gown. My mother-in-law covered me and she was crying. I remember hearing Peter's agitated voice. "I can see the ambulance lights in the distance… Oh no! Those idiots have taken the wrong turn off. I'll have to chase them." I wondered why he was so upset. Nothing mattered now.

I woke up with an unpleasant smell in my nostrils. My stained nightgown was the source of the smell! Gradually, I realized the ambulance must have brought me to the Manilla hospital. My breasts oozed sticky, yellowish milk. An odd thought escaped my dazed mind. Mum's cows' moo-ed for days whenever their calves were taken away. The sound always broke my heart. Now I had joined their ranks – except, I felt too dead to cry.

A nurse entered and said "We've got to get you cleaned up young lady, before your husband comes back.

A second nurse carried in a stack of towels and linens. They wrapped a wide width of heavy fabric tightly around my chest then pinned it down the front. I could hardly breathe.

"That binder should slow the flow of milk." One nurse said "I'm so sorry about your little girl. Is there anything we can get you?"

I jerked my head "A little girl?" I croaked "My baby was a little girl?" That arrow of information pierced every nerve in my body but still I couldn't cry.

Sometime later, I eased myself from the bed and wandered listlessly down the corridor towards the toilet. Coming towards me was a woman whom I vaguely recognized. She carried a bunch of flowers, apparently visiting someone. Seeing me she stopped.

"Oh I see you've had your baby. Was it, a boy or a girl?" I turned, and fled, that inner deadness drowned as the dam burst.

CHAPTER 22

NHA TRANG

A friend of mine, Geri Vay, was visiting Vietnam. We had known each other over the years as we both performed throughout Asia. She was a black American stripper; one of the greatest I had seen.

She had worked in the finest clubs of Paris and I was thrilled when she agreed to do a show in the Waltzing Matilda. Hers, the only show I ever provided, was to be a special treat for my members.

Since I opened The Waltzing Matilda, the 'head honchos' in Saigon had finally started organizing the commercial entertainers who were now pouring into the country. Strippers of course, were banned, but as my club was not on any army base, that was irrelevant.

I quickly spread the word and took reservations.

Few women realize just how beautiful a strip act can be. Unfortunately, most people have a mental picture of today's table-writhers who allow customers to touch them while tucking money into their G strings. The genuine art is all but lost, replaced by simulated sex acts with no tease. In a fast world there's apparently no time for finesse.

The night of my greatly heralded show arrived. The club was tightly packed, the ceiling fans doing little to dispel the heat. I hurried back to my living quarters to check on Geri. "It's awfully hot in there. They are jammed in like sardines. Will you be OK?"

"Sure, maybe I won't need the oil." Geri was sitting on my bed, bending to daub fluorescent paint around her ankles "Just leave a jug of ice water here for when I finish." She never drank alcohol.

Before I could reply, we were plunged into darkness. Nha Trang was having another power outage.

"Shit!" I said, my vocabulary having deteriorated since my arrival in Vietnam. "What now? Can you dance in a circle of candle light?"

"Yes. But I can't dance without music."

"You sit tight. I'll try to rustle up some help." I frowned "We can't disappoint all these men."

They say that if you want anything done, 'Ask a Sergeant' and that is what I did.

Back at the bar Carlos, my Vietnamese bartender had already lit candles. No one seemed perturbed by the heat and darkness. Elbowing my way through the dimly lit room, I found a Special Forces master sergeant. Pulling him aside I said, "We have a crisis here. Geri can't dance without her music and I don't know if or when the power will come back on again. What can I do?"

"Leave it to me," he said "My jeep's downstairs. We'll run out to the base."

I grabbed a flashlight, told Carlos to give everyone a drink on the house and ran after the sergeant.

The gate guards waved us into the camp and I saw a group of soldiers sitting outdoors, watching a John Wayne movie. The sergeant drove past them to a trailer holding a huge generator. He jumped out and hitched the trailer to the jeep.

"What are you doing?" I cried in dismay "What about the mens' movie?

"There's always tomorrow," he chortled, pulling away while John Wayne faded to black. An outraged cry followed as we rumbled off and I was mean-spirited enough to laugh.

Back at the club, we could barely squeeze the noisy monster into my ground floor garage, even with the help of several customers. It started up with an ear-splitting roar, shaking the entire building.

I raced upstairs and announced the show. Geri slithered into view, black and shiny! There was a chorus of low whistles. She undulated to a slow drumbeat which gradually increased in volume and tempo. Light flickered across her lithe body while her small, pert breasts peeped from beneath a cluster of soft feathers. A feathery G string and a few daubs of fluorescent paint completed the costume. The crowd was still as she writhed like a snake, her oiled buttocks gyrating to the hypnotic rhythm pulsating through the room. The pace quickened further and I remembered someone's words from long ago. "Have you ever made love to the music of Caravan. It leads to a terrific climax." Funny, the things that pop into your mind at unexpected moments.

Geri twirled faster, squirming sensuously to the wild rhythm and one by one the small feathers began dropping to the floor. Closing her eyes, she rose to a new dimension as sweat beaded her glistening body. More feathers fell to the floor and we were forgotten. She danced for the sheer joy of it; lost in the heavy drumbeat, lost in her primitive ancestry, ecstatic in her naked freedom until a crash of symbols heralded the finale and she slid away, drained. For several moments the audience remained silent. Finally there was a collective exhalation of breath and they spluttered to life. Some whistled while others applauded. A few laughed self consciously. One bent and scooped up a handful of feathers.

"Drinks for everyone" I called to Carlos, easing the tension.

Geri did not reappear to join the customers. It would spoil her stage illusion if they realized she was from Detroit.

When curfew approached I emptied the club and joined her in my quarters. We sat up late, laughing over old times and mutual friends and I told her about Monique's wedding.

The GI's had a saying that went 'War is swell but combat's hell.'

Life in Vietnam certainly had its extremes for everyone. I often went from exhilarating highs to devastating lows. Running the club had been a year predominately of highs but like they say, "All good things must come to an end." The end for The Waltzing Matilda came all too soon and due to politics.

Premier Nguyen Cao Ky had never found the top role easy. He and the American, Ambassador Taylor, had frequently clashed and some of the hierarchy thought Ky was too military and not political enough. His brash, flyboy image rubbed many the wrong way and some had labeled him "incautious" and "cocky". Ky advocated that the Americans should appear to be more in the background like the Chinese and the Russians did with North Vietnam. The Americans disagreed. One newspaper disparagingly described him as looking like a tango instructor; others were equally unkind.

I was sorry when Nguyen Van Thieu replaced him. My understanding, which was strengthened as time passed, was that Cao Ky was an honest, true-blue patriot. The scuttle butt was that Thieu did not have the same ethics as Ky and eventually it was clear to all that he and his government were corrupt. It was so easy to line your pockets when the USA were pouring one billion dollars a month into South Vietnam. Just stop and think of those figures for a moment. And when Siagon fell, Ky left with nothing but Thieu took his fortune in gold bars.

The escalating street riots back in the USA indicated that most Americans thought Vietnam was a mistake. Maybe the U.S. leaders thought that dropping troops into the jungle by helicopter would win the war the French had lost. It definitely saved lives by evacuating the wounded quickly but the outcome was still unknown. Slogans everywhere reminded us to win the hearts and minds of the people. USAID crates and heavy machinery were plastered with slogans of, clasped hands - one American,- one Vietnamese. Tons of paper leaflets were dropped from planes all over the country.

But it was hard to win hearts and minds when some corrupt Vietnamese officers were stealing the troops' supplies for personal profit and hungry soldiers then looted the hamlets of rice and chickens. Of course, the VC commandeered much more from the peasants but they controlled them by terror, while we continued ineffectually appealing to their hearts and minds.

It was hard to win the farmers' hearts and minds while desecrating their land with bomb craters and defoliating their trees with Agent Orange. Certainly I met Vietnamese who opposed communism but I also met many whose hearts were clearly not in the conflict. The one positive view I consoled myself with in later years was, that in light of the atrocities committed by the VC against their own people, at least America's intervention prevented South Vietnam from ending up like Pol Pot's Cambodia.

Eventually, the death of so many young men and the futility of the war, forced my big mouth open at the most inappropriate gatherings. Whilst dining as a guest at a Commanding General's dinner table, I vehemently proclaimed to all present that the North would conquer the South the moment America left. This did not endear me to some senior officers and I was told later, that they investigated me as a possible spy. No doubt those suspicions were heightened by my constant travels and considerable knowledge of both the camps and the countryside. On one occasion I hitched a ride North on a VIP Beechcraft with a visiting congressman and his MACV major escort. As we flew over each settlement, the congressman asked the major to identify it. The major could not. Excluded from their conversation but braggart that I was, I could not resist supplying the information. By the end of the trip, they were looking at me suspiciously

My conclusions about South Vietnam were further cemented when Ho Chi Minh died. Astounded, I watched as all of Vietnam went into mourning with most businesses in Saigon shut down. In what other war have the people grieved the death of their enemy's leader? Even those opposed to communism revered Ho Chi Minh as an honest man, unlike the reputation of President Thieu and his openly corrupt government..

I had read in Bernard Fall's book, 'Street Without Joy,' that at the end of WW11, Ho Chi Minh had arrived in Saigon with a small band of troops, expecting the Americans to keep their promise of giving the Vietnamese their independence from the French. When that promise was broken, he returned north, the ranks of his troops quickly swelling, and turned to Russia for help.

But whether we were in Vietnam, right or wrong, I was no Jane Fonda. Most young troops had not asked to be sent there. They needed all the support they could get, and that was what I gave. The protests back in the States demoralized them. They had not burned their draft cards or fled to Canada. They were patriots, obedient to their government.

I had befriended. George Simms, a slightly built, twenty year old medic with the 25th infantry Division. George had received a Silver Star for his bravery while attending the wounded under fire. As a reward, he was pulled out of the field and assigned to Medcap duty - a program which sent a handful of medics into the surrounding villages to treat the medical needs of the peasants. George and I became friends after I was privileged to go with the medics on one occasion. His upcoming trip home for R&R was a further reward for his heroism. Whilst R&R breaks were routine after serving a set period of time, there were only so many openings for the States. Many GI's had to settle for Asian destinations. George was in love and excited about re-uniting with his girlfriend.

I met him soon after his return.

"How was it George?" I asked, failing to notice his dark expression.

"It was horseshit." He glowered "I'm over here putting my ass on the line for mother fuckers like those. The day I arrived in my uniform, I was spat upon and abused. If the police hadn't arrived, I might have killed someone."

Unfortunately, he was not the only one I met with similar tales to tell. George never turned to drugs but it's no wonder so many did.

One week after President Nguyen Van Thieu ousted Premier Nguyen Cao Ky, there was a knock on my door. Standing on the threshold was Colonel Uoc and the NhaTrang Chief of Police.

"Come in." I invited "Can I get you a cup of tea?"

"Not this morning," the colonel spoke solemnly, "I'm afraid we're here with bad news. June you are going to have to close the club."

"What? Why? I've done nothing wrong?" my voice rose with panic "There's been no trouble here."

"We know. But Thieu hates Ky and he's kicking out all of Ky's appointee's and putting in his own unqualified cronies." Uoc lowered his head as if embarrassed "Our Chief here has just been replaced and

I could be next. They claim the Chief was taking kickbacks from you."

"What rubbish!" I exploded.

"Yes. But if you don't go before his replacement takes over, you could be arrested."

"Well, this is a shock! What will you all do?"

"There's nothing I can do. It's a bad turn of events for our country." He shook his head. "But how about you June, will you go back to dancing?"

"No. I'm past that now, but I'll be okay. Let me pour you both a stiff whisky. We could use one after this news."

They followed me up the stairs to the empty lounge. I looked around the room sorrowfully. I would hate to leave.

"To the future," I said, clinking glasses.

"Where will you go June?" Ouc persisted, "Back to Australia?"

"No. There's more for me to do here." My mind had already switched into top gear. "During the year I've been running The Waltzing Matilda, more American troops have arrived in country. At last MACV has recognized the entertainment needs and they have set up an office to authorize and control shows."

Uoc absently drummed his fingers on the bar "I thought those USO shows took care of entertainment?"

"No! Bob Hope and Ann-Margaret just left. Those shows are great and cost nothing. But they are few and far between. They appear only at the largest camps and few GI's get to see them. Commercial groups stay longer and travel further. They are paid from club profits." I gulped my drink then choked a little before continuing "I'm told a Clubs and Messes system has been set up. The MACV office in Saigon is interviewing prospective Booking Agents and issuing permits to a lucky few. I'll try my luck."

"Our American allies don't always make wise decisions. You may be turned down."

"True," I grinned "but it's not what you know but who you know. I've covered all bases."

"Will you employ Vietnamese entertainers?"

"I'm sorry Uoc, but when it comes to western music, they haven't caught up with the twentieth century."

The colonel sat his empty glass on the counter "Well we probably won't meet again…. Good luck!"

"And you. Colonel Uoc. Thanks for your friendship." I turned and gestured towards the room. "It's impossible to move things to Saigon. Dispose of my stuff any way you wish."

I screwed the top back onto the whisky bottle, "Here, take this." I handed it to the Chief. "It's not much of a bribe is it?"

CHAPTER 23

AUSTRALIA

The doctors' did not know why I had miscarried. Listlessly, I dragged myself through each day, riddled with guilt. It was my fault I had to drive that bumpy old tractor which probably did the damage. I shouldn't have bought that dress.

Weeks after leaving the Manilla hospital I traveled to Tamworth for a check up. Doctor Stanley advised I give my body a rest before considering pregnancy again. I certainly wasn't ready to try again but these were the days before the pill or the morning after pill. Peter and I tried using a messy contraceptive called ortho-gynol. The application worked by killing all desire, yet only months later I was stunned to find myself pregnant again. There was no pleasurable anticipation this time, only anxiety. Taking Doctor Stanley's advice, I rested frequently.

Spring arrived and with it, lambing season. Peter arrived home one evening with two new born lambs slung across his saddle.

"What have you got?" I called.

"Orphans" he replied "Can you bottle feed them?"

He dismounted and carried them in, one under each arm, then stood them on their shaky legs.

"I'll light a fire in the living room and make up some beds in a box. They must stay warm."

I stroked the soft, curly face of one, sad that they had lost their mother.

For three days I lovingly bottle fed them and they followed me everywhere. Throughout the cold nights Peter got up to replenish the fire.

"The silly things keep climbing out of their boxes." He complained.

On the fourth morning Peter awoke to a dead fire. My 'babies' too were dead. He took them away before I awoke. Heart broken, I saw it as a bad omen.

Nervously approaching the fifth month, I continually exhorted the baby inside me to be strong. Not wanting to jinx myself, I no longer looked at baby catalogs or bought more baby clothes.

Sliding into the sixth month, I allowed a glimmer of optimism and started to dream again. I shared those dreams with little Heather, wondering if my voice soothed her. Peter said I could choose the name if it was a girl. I had not yet shared the name Heather with him, thinking he might scorn my certainty.

Most afternoons I lay on the bed with my feet propped up on pillows, singing lullabies to her. The month passed and anxiety turned to excitement.

Then, on a bright, sunny morning my world crashed down again. Peter broke speed records, driving me and his Mum to the Tamworth Base Hospital. This time we made it and Tamworth hospital was larger and better equipped than the one in Manilla.

While the staff fluttered around me, Stella tried unsuccessfully to phone my mother. Mum must have been working in the dairy as usual. Doctor Stanley gave me the joyful news that my baby's heart was beating. I clung to hope and prayed like I never had before. Once again the pain was unbearable and, not having yet developed my mother's courage, I handled it badly. The doctor said I was having a breach birth.

Drenched in sweat, I stopped screaming long enough to yell "For God's sake, give me something to ease this pain!"

"That's impossible." The doctor snapped. "Pain killers will only weaken the baby....... And now Mr. Skewes, if you don't mind, you and your mother will have to wait outside." It was a different time, different rules.

Peter's face twisted with stress as he kissed my damp forehead. My tumultuous brain was singing through the pain 'She's alive. She's alive. Please God, save her.'

I don't know when I left my body but I found myself floating up near the ceiling. All pain was gone and I felt indescribably mellow despite hearing distant screams. I wanted the sound to stop disturbing my bliss. In curious slow motion, I became aware the screams were coming from a young woman lying on a bed below me. Gradually I realized I was looking at myself yet we were disconnected. I could see right through the wall to Peter and his mother and hear their anxious conversation. Stella was softly crying and I felt an urge to comfort her but could not.

I never rushed through any tunnel or saw any light like people say and I don't know how or when I came down off the ceiling. I awoke back inside my body with the doctor standing above me.

I grabbed his white jacket, wondering if I was in heaven.

"Are you an angel?"

"No" he replied "and you have a baby daughter. She's weak but she has a fighting chance." I crashed to earth, breathless beneath a wave of incredulous joy. I wanted to cry-I wanted to laugh- I wanted to pray. I did all those things! I wanted to see her. I wanted to hold her. They allowed me neither.

Time held no concept as the doctor and nurses tended to little Heather at the foot of the bed. I floundered like a jelly on a plate, struggling to find enough strength to sit up and see her. "For God's sake. Somebody help me up. I want to see her." My hysterical pleas must have hindered the staff who was doing their best to save my child's life. Sick of me, they clamped chloroform over my face and I fought all the way into blackness.

When I regained consciousness, Peter and Stella were hovering over me.

"Where is she?" I gasped, staring around.

"They've put her in a humicrib. She is very weak." Peter stroked my hair.

"You've seen her? What is she like?" Questions tumbled over each other in my head.

"Like you." He lied. "She is a perfect little dark haired girl."

"She has hair? Why can't I see her?" My voice was sharp, full of panic.

"The doctor said you can see her in the morning.....if she makes it through the night." Apparently, that was the rule back then if a baby's survival was uncertain. Peter hesitated and glanced at his mother, "While you were sleeping...... we called a priest in to Christian her."

"What? She's been christened?" I was becoming hysterical again. "And where's my mother?"

"I'm sorry dear" Stella sounded apologetic "I didn't know what you planned to name her so we christened her Mary after my mother."

"It's alright Mum." I choked out "What does her name matter as long as she lives?"

She did not! After five hours my little girl slipped away. I put violets on her grave.

CHAPTER 24

SAIGON.

The moment I arrived back in Saigon I was again hit by the atmosphere. The air throbbed with life – with anticipation of imminent action; a jarring place of swirling dust, and strident noise – of horns, of helicopters, of planes, of blaring '60's music and occasional gunfire. It was completely different from the more laid back atmosphere of NhaTrang.

I left the Tan Son Nhut airfield and walked along Plantation road in the blazing sun, waving off the hopeful GI's who stopped their jeeps to offer me a ride.

It was a short distance to the gate of the apartment building where I had stayed during my dancing days. The landlord answered my knock and smiled, "Ah, Miss June. You're back?" He was another good Vietnamese; a transplanted college professor from Hanoi who spoke English and hated communism.

We had in the past enjoyed several chats about Vietnam and communism.

"Yes. I don't suppose you have a vacant apartment? This location is so handy." He smiled and disappeared to get a key. Not many people wanted to live near the airport, a prime target.

After handing over the rent money I left. I needed to retrieve my luggage, buy a few sticks of furniture and some groceries. But first priority was to visit MACV and apply for that agents permit.

A Sergeant led me to the office of the Major in charge of entertainment.

"Miss Collins. Take a seat." The square jawed officer rose from behind his meticulously tidy desk.

"Thank you major. As you may have guessed, I am here to apply for a permit to book Filipino entertainers into the camps."

"Why not Australians?"

"I haven't lived there for many years and I am out of touch. Besides, I am familiar with the Philippines and they have great talent."

"And what about you Miss Collins? Will you be part of the act?" he spoke coldly.

"I quit performing a year ago. I plan to produce shows with good music, plenty of singing and just a go-go dancer or two."

The major raised his eyebrow skeptically.

"Is that the truth? I've had a complaint from a liquor salesman named O'Halloran. He claims he arrived in a camp the day after you had done a strip act there."

I blushed "There's no love lost between him and me but I've stopped performing. Anyway, they were big boys."

"Ma am, we don't allow strippers in the camps."

I thought of the two hundred 'masseuses' on the Long Binh post but bit my tongue. O'Halloran must have reported a show I had done for a small band of Signal Corps officers. I rarely stripped in Vietnam but a Captain had become excited when he saw me.

"I recognize you," he exclaimed, "I can't believe it's you. I saw you in '65 at The Crown Nightclub on the Ginza in Tokyo. I was on R&R from my first tour. You were terrific."

The Crown nightclub was the best in Japan. I recalled the glamour of working there. The unique stage was cranked up from the basement into the cavernous, two story club by hydraulics. Shaped like an open clam shell, this stage was made entirely of mirrors. My sparkling, small stage appeared hung in space between the circular mezzanine upstairs and the dance floor and diners below.

Draped in rhinestones, I had posed madly as that sparkling shell cranked into view with fountains of pink tinged bubbles spraying into the air all around me. The mirrors created an optical illusion as if there were six of me.

Unfortunately, this spectacular entrance had logistical drawbacks.

The shell was small and the bursting bubbles made the glass floor slippery. For strippers who didn't move about much, it was okay. Even though I removed, my bra at the finale I was a dancer with expansive movements requiring considerably more space — and definitely a dry floor. One part of my routine had me sliding across the floor in the splits. Every night at the Crown, I feared I would slide right over the edge and out into space. Despite the Japanese patrons' penchant for white breasts, I doubted they would appreciate me dropping into their bowls of fish head soup. But who knows? They could be quirky!

"Won't you do that show for us?" the excited Captain begged.

"You're joking?...... Here?" I looked around.

"Forget the props." He grinned "Just give us the same performance."

"Yeah," others urged.

"Say what you mean! My strip act."

"Well .... the dancing is good too"

"And you only buy Playboy for the articles!" I said "Military clubs don't have the separation of a night club stage. Someone could touch me."

"Aw, we are only a small group. Haven't you heard, we are officers and gentlemen." They laughed. I capitulated. Of course the word traveled. And then there were other times, other places. It boosted my bank account.

I never considered either Geri Vay or myself as strippers. We were dancers who dispensed with modesty.

It was an era when vaudeville put strippers in hot demand and many were terrific.

My dancing/stripping performances were probably 60/40, depending on which country I was in and their requirements. Throughout life I have prided myself on disarming honesty, yet when it came to stripping I was a hypocrite. Abhorring the 'stripper' label, I preferred the title 'exotic dancer' and I lay this annoying hang-up at the door of my middle class upbringing. Surely the glamour girls of the Moulin Rouge harbored no such hang-ups.

The MACV major's voice brought me back to the present "This is not the wild west you know. We're throwing strippers out of country." He stared at me disdainfully "Things are going to be differ........" a knock on the door interrupted his sentence. My optimism was fading.

"Enter!" he growled. Seconds later he scrambled to his feet and saluted. A bird colonel returned the salute.

"As you were Major" the older officer said, and then realizing they were not alone added "You're busy? Come see me in my office when you finish here." He turned to leave then stopped abruptly and faced me, looking surprised. "June.......Miss Collins" he corrected himself "What are you doing here? How are things in Nha Trang?"

"Not too good colonel. That's why I'm here. I need to change direction and I want to become a booking agent."

"Well I'm sure that's no problem. Right major?"

The major spluttered something unfathomable, finishing his sentence with 'Yes sir.' I almost felt sorry for him. Avoiding my eyes he got up and went to the door, calling his sergeant in.

"Sergeant, I would like you to get the paperwork for Miss Collins and see what assistance she needs with her application. I have to leave now." He turned back to me "Well, congratulations Miss Collins. It looks like you're in. But just remember, one foot wrong and your permit will be revoked. This is a man's job and I am not without reservations."

I left later, thanking my lucky stars – or whatever you want to call it.

Ching Imperial, a tall, dignified mix of Filipino and Chinese blood, was a well respected booking agent in South East Asia. I had met him in Manila a few years earlier. He was expecting me and had lined up a selection of musicians, dancers and singers. There was an abundance of talent in the Philippines and never enough work. We auditioned all day until I made my selection. The four-piece band had a couple of hot guitarists. A singing group of four men sounded exactly like the Platters. Mary Jane, a pretty diminutive girl had a surprisingly powerful voice. Last was the sassy little teenager Rose Marie. She had a blinding smile and could really shake her way through the popular go-go numbers.

For a few days we rehearsed the format of the show and in between rehearsals I arranged their passports, work visas and plane tickets. The girls' mothers met with me and I assured them that I would protect their daughters with my life if necessary. Rose Marie was only eighteen year old. Of course her mother was worried but I'm sure the money her daughter would be sending home was a big incentive.

I flew back to Saigon, leaving them to await their visas and follow a few days later. That gave me time to rent a Saigon villa large enough to house them. I needed to rent a van and driver for getting them to and from the airfield and to the camps close enough to Saigon for road travel. Logistically there was a lot to do. Permits had to be arranged to get the vehicle onto the base. I needed I.D. cards and travel permits, enabling them to board military aircraft. Gone were those early days when anyone could just hitch a ride with the pilots.

Armed with glossy, ten by eight photos, I began traveling the military bases, setting up show dates.

Glamour Queen at the Ginza Tokyo

CHAPTER 25

AUSTRALIA

Had Heather been conceived when technology was more advanced, she would have lived. Years later, a problem with my uterus was discovered which could have been rectified. I would have had my large family and may still have been driving a tractor in the Australian bush.

Between grief and money worries Peter and I were drifting apart. Peter began drinking heavily. Conversely, tragedy had altered my relationship with his mother, Stella, from skeptical in-laws to one of dear friends.

We were standing before the big enamel stove in her kitchen one day when she pushed a strand of snow white hair back, saying "June, I've had several children but I swear these white hairs have come from the heartache of watching you lose your babies."

A few months after Heather died there was a shearers strike in Queensland. The shearers hated the strike breakers, calling them scabs and attacking them. Most of the so-called 'scabs' were graziers' sons like Peter who saw the problem from the other side. Violence escalated and police had to be called to the shearing sheds.

"I'm going shearing." Peter informed me one night.

"Don't," I said "You might get hurt."

"It's a way out. We're up to our ears in debt. I'll never get out from under on what Dad pays me and a good shearer earns big money."

"Then I'm coming with you."

"Sorry. Families are not allowed. Besides, there's nowhere for you to stay."

"Well I'm not staying here alone for months. I'll rent a place in the nearest town and you can visit me on weekends."

With no concept of how remote the locations were, I was unaware there were no nearby towns.

We headed to Queensland where Peter would join a team in Charleville. It was my first trip to our northern, sub-tropical state. We stopped at a town called Toowoomba and Peter helped me settle into a cheerful, yellow, two roomed flat with lawns and gardens back and front.

Soon after Peter left I became bored and lonely, filling my days by reading. Television and mobile phones were still in the future. Letters went unanswered or were returned as he moved from place to place before the mail could reach him. Then, after six weeks, I was excited to receive a telegram saying he was coming to visit .

Early one Saturday morning he arrived accompanied by another shearer. They were dusty and unshaven. That night they stayed out late, returning when the pubs closed. After eating the dinner I had prepared earlier, they sat up even later, playing cards. I was furious.

"You don't understand," Peter protested. "It's too far to travel for a weekend. The only way I could come was if I had someone to help me drive. We drove all night. We'll have to travel all night tomorrow then go straight to work. Please don't embarrass me in front of my friend."

I tried to be understanding even though I was left to go to bed alone. When Peter did come to bed, overtired and the worse for drink, he promptly fell asleep and snored. I went to the toilet and saw his friend passed out on the verandah floor.

A few hours later Peter awoke with an erection. I was not much of a morning person, but being a dutiful wife; I ignored his stale beer breath and complied, minus any reciprocal passion.

Three months later I was flabbergasted to discover, that one perfunctory performance had made me pregnant again. Now, with my life in disarray and my recent history, I knew this baby had no chance. Had abortions been legal, I would have had one.

Weeks passed and I didn't know if Peter had received my letter telling him the news. Alone and cut off from my world I was overcome by depression and even thought fleetingly of suicide.

Then my money ran out. Sitting in the yellow kitchen one afternoon, I tried to ignore my rumbling tummy. I opened the kitchen cupboard, hoping to find some food. Maybe an overlooked can of tuna? Nothing! The previous day I had eaten the last of the bread.

The temptation to phone our parents and throw myself on their mercy was great, but how could I tell them our marriage was crumbling? They had warned us we were too young. Looking around the little kitchen, my eyes fell on three empty soft drink bottles. I had been meaning to return those bottles for a refund. If I could increase their numbers, I might have enough money to buy a little food. I remembered seeing some empties lying on the side of the road the previous day.

Telling myself that today's walk would be just like any other; except, I would be doing my civic duty, I picked up a sugar bag from the laundry and left.

After walking a couple of blocks I spotted the first 'empties' lying beside the road. I was hurrying towards them when I saw a lady pushing a pram in my direction. Striding past the bottles, I waited until she turned the corner then I ran back, checked that no-one was looking, grabbed them fast and stuffed them into the bag.

`Eventually the half filled bag was becoming heavy. I lugged it back to the small shop near the flat. The bell rang as I pushed open the wire screen door and I traded the bottles for enough coins to buy a few potatoes.

Back in my kitchen I watched the potato's boil. There was no butter to mash them. This was rock bottom. I should have stopped relying on Peter sooner. It was time to look for work!

Following in my mother's footsteps, I found a job as a barmaid at The Portadown Hotel, which was within walking distance.

I learned the ropes quickly and just to be around other people was a great improvement. The morning sickness was awkward but my trips to the 'Ladies Room' seemed to go unnoticed until one day when the proprietor's wife called me aside.

"I don't want to let you go June, but I can tell you're in the family way. I'm afraid you will have to finish up at the end of the week."

Pregnant women were supposed to stay out of sight, respecting societies' sensibilities by denying any evidence of sex.

My dismissal was devastating. Who would hire me now?

During my few remaining days at the pub I mentioned my predicament to one of my regular customers. He worked as a warden at the Willowburn Mental Asylum on the outskirts of Toowoomba.

"Maybe I can help." He offered "We are always understaffed out there. They're happy to take on anyone. The work can be dangerous but the money is good."

"Well I'll try anything."

They hired me as an assistant in the women's ward. My duties entailed little more than patrolling the grounds during daylight hours and keeping an eye on the inmates, intervening in problems where I could and calling for help where I couldn't. The warden had not exaggerated the unpleasantness and I was unprepared for the experience.

Inmates wandered about 'in the yard' under the boiling sun during summer and I assumed, in the wind and cold in the winter. Consequently, their skin was burned and cracked. Most of them had missing or no teeth and their hair was rarely brushed. Each morning a basket filled with shapeless blue-grey cotton dresses was brought into the wards. The inmates grabbed whatever dress was closest, regardless of fit or stains from the previous wearer. Some walked about barefoot, others slopped around in oversized men's shoes without laces.

Many of them talked to themselves and followed me around, sprouting gibberish or using obscenities the likes of which I had never heard.

Several were fascinated by the toilets and continually disappeared there as an inner urge compelled them to dip their head into the bowl. They played in their own faeces and hurled it at the staff. The smell was nauseating. I carried a whistle in the pocket of my starched, blue uniform, in case of attack. The first time I tried to use the whistle; the crazed creature grabbed my hair and shoved the whistle down my throat. My eyes streamed and my heart pounded as I choked, unable to blow. Instead of being my means of help, it almost became the weapon of my demise. Luckily, I was rescued, none too soon.

Many of the patients spent hours each day just twirling strands of hair around their fingers until it tore away from their scalp, leaving large bald patches.

I dreaded going to work. Never hearing from Peter, I wondered if he had left me without saying so, just as my father had done to my mother. I could not continue living this way.

Desperately lonely, one night I slept with the married warden who steered me into the job. He held no attraction for me. Maybe I felt I 'owed him'. Maybe I just needed human touch. That depressed me further. All my dreams were shattered! My marriage was over! I blamed it on a combination of my spendthrift ways, Peter's immaturity and the loss of my children.

I never knew my neighbor in the duplex. She was older than I, and some evenings I saw her carrying home a bottle of whisky. We smiled and exchanged greetings. She had a dry sense of humor and dressed oddly. I tagged her as a likeable eccentric.

One night I stopped at the bottle department of the pub where I had previously worked and bought a bottle of gin. I had been involved in breaking up several fights between the patients that day. One of them had spat in my face. Although they were the days before anyone knew about Aids, I was revolted.

Turning on the small Bakelite radio in the kitchen, I removed my soiled uniform and mixed a stiff drink. Sitting at the table in my underwear, I gazed at a single red rose in a jar of water. A loose petal fell to the table and suddenly I burst out crying.

Controlling myself, I poured another drink and made a ham and pickle sandwich. I ate, not tasting the food, occasionally refilling my glass. I switched radio stations back and forth, avoiding anything sentimental.

Around ten o'clock I stood to wash my uniform. The room swayed and I realized the gin bottle was half-empty. Suddenly I wanted to throw-up. Dropping the uniform, I bolted for the bathroom and vomited. Immediately the pains started. The room spun, I began sweating and I thought I might collapse. My neighbor must have heard me through the thin walls. She banged on the separating partition and called out "Are you alright? Do you need any help?"

"No. I'm fine." I lied before my water broke. Oh no! Not now… I was still retching and dizzy. Bent in a haze of pain, I flushed the toilet then turned and sat. The miscarriage which would have been my third child occurred over the toilet bowl. Technically I suppose it was an embryo, not yet a child but emotionally it was my doomed child. I was further traumatized when it seemed to stop half way, as if wanting to retreat to the familiar warmth. Tears streamed down my face as I gently eased it into the world, all the while begging for the nightmare to end. Unable to look as I held it, I opened the medicine cabinet and withdrew a roll of cotton wool. Unraveling the blue paper with one hand I finally forced myself to look and almost collapsed. This little miniature figure would have been the son Peter wanted.

This pregnancy was of the same duration as my first one. Back then I had a family, an ambulance and a hospital on hand and I was relieved of all details. Now I was alone, distraught and not knowing what to do next. Gasping for air and choking, I barely looked as I awkwardly wrapped my embryonic son in the cotton wool then stumbled to the kitchen and collapsed onto a chair with the little bundle in my lap

I never thought of reporting the miscarriage or going to a hospital. It was not a live birth and I no longer cared what happened to me. Eventually I rose and lurched into the back yard. It was a moonlit night with tree shadows falling across the lawn. Kneeling between two azalea bushes I tore a deep hole in the soft earth with my bare hands and lay the end of my dreams to rest. I covered him with night soil, picked some white azalea blossoms and sprinkled them over him. How could I go inside and leave him all alone? Curling up on the grass, in the eerie shadows, I cried as I prayed for forgiveness. A deathly, black sleep engulfed me and when I awoke, shivering in my underwear, the wind had risen. I watched hollowly as one by one, the little blossoms blew away.

CHAPTER 26

Several of my military friends had queried me about selecting such a dangerous location to rent an apartment.

"The first place the enemy aims for is the airfield." One of them said. "And you are right outside the gate."

"Well so far, so good." I replied. "It is handy to be able to walk in to catch a flight."

My Saigon apartment was no luxury abode; however, I rarely brought anyone home and seldom ate there. The building was the usual, box-shaped, two-story cement structure with small balconies that one sees throughout Asia. I seldom saw anyone going in or out, and certainly no Westerners.

Most nights, I was out of town, but on the night of 30 January 1968 I was home and went to bed by curfew. It was the Lunar New Year, a time of year I had grown to hate. In previous years I had found myself trapped amid the celebrating, Chinese crowds in Hong Kong who were doing their best to frighten away the devils. The streets of Kowloon were filled with smoke, noise and torn scraps of red paper from exploding strings of Tom Thumbs. It may well have been my imagination but I felt certain they targeted Caucasians when throwing down the fire crackers.

The previous year in Nha Trang, the Lunar New Year celebrations had been no better. Bullets replaced Tom Thumbs as the ARVN's went berserk; shooting their rifles frenziedly into the air. The celebratory firestorm was not without casualties.

About four or five a.m., the noise first penetrated my sleep. I rolled onto my side and pulled the pillow over my head, trying unsuccessfully to muffle the sound.

"Shit." I said, throwing the pillow to the floor, "These bloody assholes are worse than the Chinese."

Staggering to the kitchen, I made a cup of tea and was taking the first sip when my phone rang. This unauthorized, therefore illegal, military Tiger line had been installed by my friends in the Signal Corp., civilian phone connections being impossible to get.

"Damn it!" I grumbled, snatching up the large, khaki colored handset.

"What idiot is calling this early?" It took me a few seconds to recognize the voice of My Linh, my assistant manager from The Waltzing Matilda.

"June..." She was breathless. "June, all hell has broken loose up here. We're under attack. And the old Waltzing Matilda has been shelled."

"Hell. It's never been that bad before. This is a..." mid sentence, the phone went dead.

I absently picked up my cup. The tea was half cold. As I walked towards the gas ring, the lights went out.

"Shit. What next?" Glancing out the window I noticed it was daylight. Going back to bed was pointless. I decided on a quick walk before the day turned too hot. Locking the door, I headed down the gravel drive way. The Large black metal entry gates were open as usual. Stepping onto Plantation Road, I noticed the military traffic was heavier than usual at this hour. And the noise was louder. I stopped abruptly and saw a flash of light from the direction of the airfield, then another - and another. My brain was turning on at last when an American jeep shot by and a G.I. leaned out and yelled, "Get off the goddamn street! We're under attack."

I remembered O'Halloran's words "If they ever get as far as Long Binh, were finished."

Stunned, I raced back to the apartment. I never expected my predictions about the North would happen this soon and while the American's were still in country.

Taking the stairs two at a time, I unlocked my door and rushed out onto the balcony for a better look. Dark plumes of smoke poured into the sky amid mortar flashes. Sirens wailed. Helicopters buzzed like angry hornets and tracers streamed in all directions. One helicopter was sending streams of bullets towards a building only two removed from mine. "That's a bit too close for comfort" I thought as gun-fire was returned and I decided to take cover. Before I could leave the balcony, the sound of breaking glass stunned me. It was my bedroom window. Slamming the door behind me, I gaped at the shards of glass lying on the cement floor. The veneered closet door hung carelessly open just as I had left it, except it now had two bullet holes angled down through the lower part of the door. Crouching on my hands and knees, I found a bent-nosed AK 47 bullet on the floor and the other inside the closet. For some stupid reason, I was surprised.

Nervous at last, I removed my small Browning 25 revolver from my bag and slipped it into my pants pocket. Against an AK47 it was useless but it was all I had.

Anxious for news, I switched on my battery operated radio and discovered the batteries were dead! Frustrated, I threw it down and paced the floor. The day dragged on, punctuated by booming noise and occasional furtive trips to the balcony. Nerves kept hunger at bay but I drank gallons of tea, grateful for the gas stove. On my last trip to the balcony, I saw a couple of Charley's running down Plantation road. Slamming the door, I locked it, my curiosity sated. In the dark, with no information about what was happening outside, it was a long, sleepless night.

I never kept much food in the apartment. By day two I had eaten all the cereal. The ice cream had melted after the power quit. All my outdated magazines had been read and re read... in poor light. Boredom set in!

By day three the last of the candy was gone and my belly was rumbling. Things outside seemed to have quieted down. From my balcony, I saw that Plantation Road now looked completely deserted. I needed to eat but I knew we must be on twenty four hour curfew. No phone – no radio – no-one to talk too – no food- it was all too much.

Then I remembered a handful of assault helicopter pilots who lived in a small, BOQ villa less than a mile away. Uncle Sam rented many Saigon villas to accommodate the overflow of officers from the bases. Certainly my friends would be out engaging the enemy but they had a generator and a big refrigerator which might still have food in it.

Almost numb from inaction and boredom, I quietly closed my apartment door and crept down the stairs. Reaching the open, entry gates, I saw a black clad figure sprawled out in the middle of our driveway, obviously dead. I wondered was it he who had fired at me. All was eerily quiet. This normally hectic thoroughfare had no vehicles, no people, no animals, and no birds. Had I entered the twilight zone? Slouching along the silent streets, my heart was going faster than my feet. Was I really that hungry or was I just insane? Even an American jeep would be a problem, its occupants ordering me off the street. But I saw ne'er a cat. I felt like I was the last living person on the planet.

Reaching the villa, I found the door was unlocked – as always. The Vietnamese civilian 'guard' who usually slept out front had disappeared. I headed straight for the kitchen and the refrigerator. There wasn't much but I found some stale bread, margarine and peanut butter. I was tying it into a kitchen towel when a noise spun me around, warning bells clanging in my brain. I grabbed my Browning and raised it. Someone was in the hallway. My finger shook on the trigger. A shadowy figure came into view.......... Wham. It was one of the Warrant Officers.

"You fucking idiot. You almost gave me a heart attack." I gasped, trembling.

"Put that thing away. You could have shot me. What in God's name are you doing here?"

"I'm looking for food. Why else why would I be here? And why aren't you out chasing the bad guys?" I accused.

"Shit! I should be! What a great fucking time to come down with food poisoning." He strode to the door and looked outside. "There's a Goddamn curfew. How the hell did you get here?"

"I walked."

"Oh bullshit!

"No bullshit, and now I've got to walk back so I had better hurry before it gets dark. I don't want a nervous MP shooting me."

"Don't chance it. You had better stay here the night."

"Thanks but no thanks. If any choppers spot me, I'm definitely not dressed like Charlie."

"You are crazy! Everyone's trigger happy right now."

"Don't you talk! Your door was unlocked.

"Son of a bitch!"

"Anyhow, the fighting must have moved further away. I'm guessing down towards the Chinese area of Cholon."

"Well if you won't stay, be careful. You wouldn't have died from hunger."

He shook his head as I left with my little bundle.

The adrenalin which made the outward journey exciting had now dissipated. I couldn't wait to get home.

Dead Charlie was still lying where I had left him, a swarm of flies keeping him company. His small, leather wallet lay open in the dirt beside him, stained with blood. I wondered had one of our soldiers taken it out of his pocket and thrown it down or had he managed to pull it out for a dying last look at photos of his loved ones? For a moment I thought of picking it up and looking through it but I didn't want to see his photos. That would make him too human to me. I skirted him and hurried down the driveway, wondering would anyone move him before he began to stink. I said a silent prayer for his soul, but better him than one of ours, I reminded myself.

CHAPTER 27

AUSTRALIA

I left Toowoomba, hung-over and empty, convinced love was a farce. How could Peter dump me in a strange town and not even bother sending money to support me? As I didn't know where he was, he was unaware I had miscarried our son. I left with no goodbyes.

Stepping to the gutter I threw up, wiped my mouth then stumbled on towards the Greyhound bus stop.

"When is the next bus due in?" I asked the ticket agent.

"Not for three more hours' lady."

"Where's it going?"

"Brisbane."

"Give me a one way ticket please." I really did not care where it was going. I just wanted to get as far away from my life as possible.

Sitting on the bus I analyzed my situation. I would never go back to Peter and I would never marry again. I saw no point to marriage if I couldn't have children. Since leaving Glen Barra, I had seldom written home, not wanting them to know my problems. They would disapprove of me leaving Peter. In the fifties, 'decent' people didn't divorce. I was now a third generation marriage failure.

Falling in love had been my downfall! I abandoned all my dreams to be with Peter. But maybe that's all they were – impossible dreams. Did I run to him to escape? Or did I run from the fear of not being able to make it alone? Or maybe fear that Dennis had blackened my name? I had to stop allowing a faint heart to impede me. Love would never again make me falter.

Houses appeared among the trees as the bus approached Brisbane. I took a deep breath. It was time to take a new name for the new me.

Peter's name of Skewes had to go. My father had deserted us so his name was out. The only man who never hurt me was my step dad, Bake. I would adopt his name, Collins. I whispered softly to myself "Goodbye, June Skewes. Hello June Collins."

Fate was never far away. Days after I arrived in Brisbane I saw an advertisement in the Courier Mail for dance instructor trainees at Arthur Murray's Dance Studios. My mother had sacrificed for years to have Clarice and I taught dancing when we lived in Sydney. I could put all those early dance lessons to good use.

The studio manager hired me immediately. Every day I trained for long hours until I was sufficiently skilled to commence teaching.

People from the southern states, especially the city dwellers of Sydney and Melbourne, used to scorn Queenslanders, calling them 'banana benders'. This reference was directed at the state's many banana and sugar cane growers. Queensland had minimal industry and tourism was yet to become big. Few Australians had money for holidays. They ridiculed Brisbane as a big country town and further south, The Gold Coast was little more than a coastal village. The 'Queenslander' houses were elevated on 'sticks', allowing the air to circulate below, supposedly to cool them. I loved the houses, loved the warmer climate, and didn't mind being called a hick.

Arthur Murray's dance studio was located in Fortitude Valley, the seamy side of town. After being buried in the bush, I found it exciting. The studio opened at 10 am and closed at 10 p.m. Teachers were paid according to the number of hours they taught plus bonuses for dance courses sold.

Most of the male teachers were gay, and it was my first awareness of homosexuality, middle class society being sheltered from such worldly knowledge. That is hard to believe today when primary school children know all about sex and many have openly gay parents.

The Arthur Murray's staff was fun and seemed very sophisticated to me. I longed to be accepted as 'one of them'.

When the studio closed each night a group of us danced the night away in Brisbane's night clubs. I soon became as extravert as the others, showing off before the lesser skilled patrons. The past began fading.

Shortly after commencing at Arthur Murray's Studio I found a spectacular, spacious apartment just perfect for parties. The rent was prohibitive but old habits die hard. By then, I was morphing into a party girl. Life had never been so exciting nor alcohol tasted so good.

The apartment, a huge place atop a men's wear store, was located around the corner from the Wickham Street studio. Set amongst the shops, there were no nearby residences. Originally it was intended for the manager of the men's wear store but his wife turned it down. There was nowhere for her children to play and it was in that bad part of town.

The bathroom, my favorite room, was a huge expanse of crème tile beneath a sky-light ceiling. In true Hollywood style, the oversized bath tub was adorned by a roaring lion's head. Water shot from its gaping mouth with the power of an artesian bore, hitting the opposite end while filling the tub within minutes. I habitually soaked in supreme hedonism amid the scented bubbles, a glass of wine in hand and stars blinking at me from above. Soft background music and perfumed candles completed the ambience.

It was not unusual to awaken after a party and find a guest passed out in the tub.

My ballroom – I mean, living room, had a soaring ceiling and ornate moldings. Party noise went unheard with no-one around after the stores closed (at 5.20 in those days).

The only drawback was my entrance which was accessed by a narrow staircase between the men's wear shop and the store beside it. I shared the stairs and landing with the shop employee's lunch room. Careless employees sometimes forgot to lock the door onto the street. Those stairs would then become a retreat for every vagabond in The Valley. My co-workers seemed to find this obstacle course amusing as they squeezed past unconscious bodies and pools of pee and vomit.

Naturally, my place was voted as our unofficial party pad. My routine became long hours of work and partying punctuated by short periods of sleep.

The Australian television personality, Barry Crocker was not well known in those days. His duo act included a young Englishman named David, surname forgotten. David played sax and drums, sang and danced. He was soooo handsome. We began dating and I hung out at the clubs where he and Barry performed.

His landlady, sick of the noise when he practiced the drums, threw him out. Homeless, he asked could he move into my place. With clear thought impaired by his good looks, I agreed and he arrived with his drum set and sax. The noise was too much even for me and I was thrilled when he and Barry left for an engagement in Melbourne. Shortly thereafter, they separated but it was David who inspired me to seek a show biz career.

I realized, that as an entertainer I could travel far and get paid to do so.

CHAPTER 28

VIETNAM

My Filipinos surpassed my hopes! They were professional and cheerful, never complaining about the rough conditions. After six months we were riding high, travelling from camp to camp. However, to my knowledge, no-one worked in camps as small and remote as some in which I had performed. Transporting a band with all its equipment required two empty helicopters. As a solo dancer, I had traveled with only my tape recorder, making it logistically easy for me to hitch a ride anywhere.

Pre-booking shows, I traveled on ahead of the group, and tried to spend at least one night checking on them in each camp. We were seldom in Saigon, and when we were, there was laundry and friends to catch up with.

The band performed all the current hits. That fabulous 60's music with its demanding beat- its surge of life; they played it to perfection, bringing the GI's to their feet, capturing the moment as they belted it out.

Songs like;

Chain, Chain, Chain, Chain of Fools.

Mustang Sally – All you wanta do is ride around Sally,………....

Born To Be Wild

Just Give Me Money – that's what I want.

Here We Come Now, Say Mony Mony.

I Can't Get No Satisfaction… But I tried, and I tried, and I tried.

My Baby Just Wrote Me a Letter…. I don't care how much money…

I'm Leaving on a Jet Plane

Running Through The Jungle

R.E.S.P.E.C.T. Wow, Aretha Franklin was HOT. And how about Wilson Pickett doing his 'Mashed Potato."

Every show finished with the same song; "WE GOTTA GET OUTTA THIS PLACE – If it's the last thing we ever do." This song became the GI's national anthem. By the time that number was played, there was never a soul sitting. Every man in the room stood tall, punching the air and screaming the words. "WE GOTTA GET OUTTA THIS PLACE" They stood on tables, stood on chairs, hung from the rafters –the noise swelling like a huge wave, swamping one and all in a fervent crescendo "WE GOTTA GET OUTTA THIS PLACE."... 50,000 of them never did.

To this day, whenever I hear the overhead whomp, whomp of helicopter rotor blades, it brings it all back to me. I still picture the beads of sweat on the sun-bronzed flesh of the young G.I's as they squatted on sand bags in front of their hooch's. I see them re-reading letters, powdering their feet, polishing their boots and cleaning their M16 rifles. The music was always blaring in the background, the helicopters passing noisily overhead. A few years later, Charlie Daniels recorded a song "Still in Saigon." That song grabbed me. I still relate!

Each division comprised numerous battalions and eventually all battalions had their own clubs; a small one for the officers, a larger one for the NCO's and the largest of all for the E.M's (enlisted men). Naturally, the NCO's and EM's generated the most money and therefore bought the most shows. These were paid for out of club profits. Each club had its own club manager, but the sergeants who managed the NCO and EM clubs usually had a custodian, a head man in charge of all the NCO and EM clubs within the entire division. This was a huge responsibility as they controlled enormous sums of money. The officers' clubs, being smaller, were not part of this system and did not require much management. That job usually fell to one of the more junior officers. Smaller clubs meant fewer profits which meant fewer shows.

For the first six months my bookings ran smoothly and we kept getting return engagements. Then gradually I noticed an unpleasant change among the club managers. Many of the old familiar faces had rotated back to the USA and the newcomers were rude and began demanding money.

Furthermore, I noticed that the new club managers, from division to division, seemed to be mates. It was not unusual to find them, sitting around drinking, chatting, and playing cards awhile listening to Country and Western music in each others offices. It was a regular 'Good Ole Boys Club'. Far from the fighting, these clone-like older men with southern accents, all favored diamond rings and gold Rolex watches, a seemingly inappropriate accessory for a 'war zone'. Budweiser Beer or Bourbon were the drinks of choice and Cuban cigars the preferred smoke. So many common denominators were perplexing.

Sergeant Bill Higdon was the newly arrived custodian for Long Binh and therefore, the most powerful of the aforementioned group. My band had just finished a ten day stint on the base which the previous custodian had booked before departing. I arrived at Higdon's office to introduce myself and collect the ten days' payment. At three hundred dollars per night I anticipated receiving three thousand dollars.

Higdon, big and gruff, was alone when I entered

"My managers' tell me the men liked your group. We'll book them back again."

I was pleased. Repeat bookings made my job easier. Higdon sat at the desk to write a check. I gazed in amazement at the sizable diamond glinting on his big square hand. Then I recalled the roaring trade the diamond vendor was rumored to be doing in Long Binh's PX.

"Here, sign for the $3,000." He shoved the receipt book towards me.

"Thank you, sergeant." I scribbled my name then reached for the check.

"Not so fast..... " He pulled the check back. "You've forgotten something, haven't you?"

I frowned

"What?"

"My cut woman - where is it?"

"Money?" I was confused.

"Jesus Christ. Does a bear shit in the woods? What else would I mean?"

"I never paid Sergeant Brookes. How much are you talking about?"

He looked exasperated "Fifty a show. Ten shows means five hundred."

I thought I had heard wrong "After I pay my kids and cover the overhead, that doesn't leave much profit."

"Take it or leave it. If you leave it you can say goodbye to working here again and, I run the bulk of the shows around here."

"I guess I'll take it then." Reluctantly I opened my purse and counted out five hundred MPC.

"What the fuck is this?"

"What do you think it is? Haven't you seen your own military script before?"

"You stupid broad. I need dollars. Green backs. Uncle Sam. Got it?"

"I only have piaster or MPC and please don't call me a stupid broad. Anyway I can write you a check on an American bank."

"God, save me from idiots." He spluttered and I watched him put my check back into the safe.

"Come back when you've got the goods and then I'll pay you." He was already turning away.

"The only way I can get U.S. dollars is through the Indians on Tu-Do's black market and the CID is always raiding those places."

"That's your problem lady. The sooner you bring my cut the sooner you'll get yours. And one little bit of advice; wise up quick if you want to stay in business around here."

My mind racing, I left. Could I work here again? It was the closest and most lucrative base in Vietnam with dozens of clubs in one location. It meant no hanging around the hot, dusty airfields. We could drive the short distance back to Saigon each night and sleep in our own beds. But doing business this way sickened me.

From Higdon's implication, it would appear the other agents were not complaining about this kickback. However, my immediate concern was to get my money and one thing was certain – I despised this new custodian.

At first I thought Sergeant Higdon just one bad apple in the barrel. But days passed and I began encountering the same problem everywhere.

"What the hell is happening?" I wondered. "Are all Americans crooks?" I decided to speak to some of the other booking agents.

The International House, commonly referred to as 'The "I" House' was the hang-out for booking agents when not out on the road. It was an immense, private membership club on Tu Do with the stupendous advantage of being air-conditioned. Membership was supposedly limited to American Embassy staff, USAID, and various other privileged American nationals. However, the old rule of 'who you knew' worked here.

Entering the brightly lit lounge I saw a group of acquaintances sitting drinking in jovial mood. Randy Crane, a prominent American booking agent was among them and I made a beeline in his direction. Pulling up a chair, I squeezed in beside him and ordered a gin and tonic. Randy had American and Australian bands working in country.

With his dark, curly hair and good bone structure, he was almost handsome.

"I hear you rode a Honda down an unsecured road last week. Is that true?"

"I don't deny it." I lifted my gin and tonic from the waiter's tray. "There were no choppers heading my way and I had promised to book a show into a small camp."

"You must be damned mad, traveling an unsecured road for a small camp…. meaning only one show."

“I couldn’t let them down! I bought the Honda when my driver refused to drive me……. You don’t want to buy it do you? I didn’t scratch it when I fell off.”

“Seriously June, you should cool it or you won’t be around much longer.”

“I can’t worry about what MIGHT happen. Anyway, it was worth it just to see the expression on their faces when I walked in. The major said ‘I didn’t hear a chopper land.’ Until he saw the bike, he didn’t believe me.”

Randy shook his head “Well, the regulars here are placing weekly bets on whether you will survive each week. Stunts like that are stupid.”

“Gotta keep life interesting!” I replied, knowing I was pushing the envelope. I seemed to have become a slave to my ego and the reputation I had built. What insane urge impelled me to perpetuate that reputation by placing myself in harm’s way? Was I a phony? For in truth, I was often scared, yet with that fear came an irresistible excitement.

“Changing the subject, Randy, how do you like this new Higdon bloke?”

“He’s a bit rough about the edges but he knows the club business.”

“Well, he’s taking a cut from my money. Is that the same with everyone?”

“So? We all pay now. With the troop build up, there’s plenty for everyone. Gotta be a team player.”

“Don’t make me laugh for God’s sake. Everyone here would stab one another in the back to get an edge. Anyway, I’ve never been short of work and I never had to pay. I don’t like Higdon.”

“Loose lips sink ships.” Randy shot me a tight look. “Watch your mouth.”

Shown here with some of my wonderful Philippine entertainers; Ding, Rose-Marie, Joe, Mary-Jane. Soc-Trang January '69

CHAPTER 29

AUSTRALIA

Despite the partying lifestyle, I had not become particularly promiscuous; probably because most of my friends were gay. David's departure made little difference for his sax, not sex seemed to meet his needs.

Therefore I was shocked one morning to wake up naked in bed, and find another dance instructors boyfriend snoring beside me. Sid was a prim and proper Englishman when dressed, which he wasn't at that moment. What the hell had happened? I knew I had changed, but THIS much? Loyalty had always been one of my inviolable traits. Trying to reconstruct the previous night's events gave me a headache. I staggered to the kitchen in search of aspirin and a pint or two of orange juice.

Passing through the laundry area, heading for the toilet, I spotted a body curled up in my cement laundry tub. 'What idiot would sleep there" I wondered "when there was a perfectly good bath tub inside?' On closer observation I saw it was Patti, Sid's girl friend. She too was English; petite, attractive, blonde and totally scatter brained. She had passed out in eighteen inches of water. I checked to see that she was still breathing. It was best to leave her there until her boyfriend was out of my bed.

Returning to the dimness of my bedroom, I tried to shake Sid awake. He snored louder and mumbled. This required drastic action such as dousing him with water.

I was running the kitchen tap when Patti awoke and staggered in, trailing water.

"Have you got any orange juice?" she moaned, opening the refrigerator "I think I'm dying."

"I don't wonder" I was flustered that she had revived already. "Check the second shelf. I'll make some tea in a jiffy."

She found juice and gulped it straight from the bottle. I was planning how to get rid of her when she began stumbling towards my bedroom.

"Where are you going?"

"Gonna borrow a dressing gown. I'm bloody cold. And wet. Hadn't you noticed?"

"I haven't got one" I panicked. "Take your clothes off while I get a couple of dry towels."

She continued on towards my bedroom.

"Pat" I took a deep breath "I have something to tell you."

"Can't it wait? I'm dripping wet."

"Er. Er. It's about Sid...... Look,......I don't know how to tell you this but he's asleep in my bed."

Her eyes widened, her face twitched.

"You bitch!"

"Truly, I don't know what happened. I can't remember a thing. Honest...."

"A great friend you....." she spluttered with anger, unable to finish.

"Errrr......I don't think anything happened."

What could I say? I didn't even fancy Sid. Suddenly she stunned me by roaring with laughter.

"What a sucker you are." she gasped.

"What's so damned funny? I'm too hungover for games."

"You silly bitch! You both passed out. We undressed you and put you into bed......... together."

"What a dumb joke. You wouldn't be laughing if the joke backfired!"

"Lighten up girl. Make me that cuppa and I'll forgive you."

I shook my head, disgusted.

Sometimes I swear that English television show "Absolutely Fabulous" was based on those years.

Eventually I discovered I was not the only person living in that non-residential area of The Valley. A struggling young artist by the name of Andrew Sibley was living in a cavernous rat-hole of an uninhabitable basement beneath the shops. The back was open to the elements and one had to walk far into the building's bowels before discovering Andrew painting away in a blaze of artificial light. It is doubtful the landlord knew there was a mad artist living beneath the building and I don't know from what source Andrew obtained his electricity.

He painted to a background of loud, classical music. After giving me permission to visit, he warned that if he was painting I must not speak until he put his paint brush down. After I knew him better I gave him a key to my apartment so he could come up and shower occasionally. That key became an important factor a few months later.

Andrew was a sensitive and proud man. He was straight, somewhat eccentric and vastly different from my other friends. His characteristics were rare in Australia where most blokes were obsessed with sports, beer and mates.

The typical starving artist, he was thin and rarely accepted my offer to join me in a meal unless it was one of those rare days when he had money in his pocket. Misguided pride!

I knew little about contemporary art but I listened and watched, trying to learn.

He came to my apartment for a shower one Sunday and after much persuasion, stayed on to share a corned beef and mustard sandwich.

"I live to paint" he said as we sat on the sofa eating "I can go without food for days and my part time job as an art teacher at the university usually pays for my paints and brushes and an occasional bottle of cheap red." He lifted the wine I handed him and drained it before continuing.

"Sometimes it's not enough and unfortunately, the last couple of weeks I have been forced to take outside work. Then last night I had a humbling experience."

He wiped a speck of mustard from his mouth before continuing.

"I took a night job selling pies at one of those late night pie kiosks on the side of the road in Brisbane."

I waited.

"Usually my only customers are drunks staggering home and last night it was particularly wet and blustery. Newspapers were blowing about in the empty streets and I decided to close up early. But before I could lower the shutters I saw a group of my rich, young Uni students heading towards me." He looked for my re-action.

"I panicked. What would these privileged kids think about their Uni professor selling pies out on the street in the middle of the night?"

I understood his dilemma. Andrew was just becoming recognized as one of Australia's emerging young painters.

"I was so embarrassed that I turned and prayed they would pass by but as I stood with my back to them, I recognized how hypocritical my humiliation was. I turned back and spoke to them."

"Did they buy a pie?"

"Several. I underestimated them. They thought it was a lark."

"You know Andrew;" I said thoughtfully, "you haven't been able to teach me much about modern art, but you've constantly taught me much about life."

By the time I befriended Andrew I was seriously trying to live without sleep, sustained by pills and alcohol. Those little 'greenies' (Dexedrine) had become my best friend followed closely by 'Ludes' (Quaaludes) and without 'downers' I couldn't sleep.

It was a fateful day when I gave Andrew that key. Late one afternoon I opened my eyes to see the sun weakly peering through the tall living room windows as it sank below the roof tops. What time was it? When did I fall asleep on the sofa? My stomach hurt, my throat was raw, and I smelled of vomit. The room swam when I tried to sit up, and I fell back onto the cushion. I heard footsteps and Andrew entered from the kitchen. He was accompanied by a stranger dressed in a suit.

"What are you doing here Andrew? What time is it?"

"Just be grateful he is here" the stranger said "I've had to pump your stomach. If it hadn't been for your friend here I may have been too late to save you."

His words shocked me awake. I tried desperately to recall the previous night's events but it was a complete black-out. I had a vague vision of lying on the roof, staring up at the stars, crying. Why on earth had I cried? I loved my work, I had plenty of friends. I was independent. I never thought of the past. I had no reason to take my life! It must have been a drunken accident!

For months I cut back on my drinking but I still needed pills to cope with the long hours. I curbed my spending habits and started saving. When I had enough money, I flew to Sydney to meet Keith Bane, one of Sydney's top choreographers.

During my time in Sydney I stayed with my grandparents. Pop claimed I was wasting money on an unstable lifestyle. He disapproved of me leaving Peter. With the exception of ballerinas, dancers were considered lower than barmaids.

"Why don't you settle down like other girls and get a good steady job in the Post Office?" He was prone to ask.

Returning to Brisbane, I resumed teaching while auditioning for additional work in the nightclubs. Soon I was hired to perform in a lively spot named Tommy's. Owned by a Chinese gentleman of the same name, it was located not far from the studio.

I became busier than ever, working at the studio from 10 am until 10pm then racing down to Tommy's to do the late floorshow. Of course I seldom fell into bed before daylight.

I planned to end my dependence on pills by working less and sleeping more. If I earned enough money as an entertainer, I could give up teaching and sleep during the day.

CHAPTER 30

VIETNAM

I had begun paying the kick backs like everyone else. Apparently no-one could work any longer in many army bases unless they did. Kickbacks were paid by the liquor and snack salesmen, the furniture salesmen and of course, the entertainment booking agents. It galled me. Consequently I began avoiding the kickbacks by booking my people further away in camps not yet swallowed up by the Army Clubs and Messes scheme.

We began working regularly with the 25th Infantry Division. It was located only twenty three miles west of Saigon in an area called Cu Chi. It could be reached by road but as the road was not secure at night, we never drove back to Saigon between shows.

The Division Headquarters camp was large, barren and dusty. Trucks oiled the dirt roads down daily in an effort to combat the swirling red dust. Fires constantly burned in blackened forty four gallon drums as GI work details emptied the latrines.

The camp held Brigades one and two, the division's third brigade was separated some miles away in an area named Dau Tieng.

These 25th Infantry Division troops were constantly away in the field. Whenever they returned to camp, tired and dirty, they were welcomed by the Divisions Donut Dollies (Red Cross girls.) I was never an admirer of this program, although it was not a reflection on the girls who were young and mostly pretty. However, few of the returning warriors accepted their invitation to join them for coffee and donuts followed by childish games. What man wants to come in from killing fields to turn around and play guessing games while drinking coffee? Most preferred a stiff drink and besides, the girls were tagged as 'officer material'.

When performing in Cu Chi we usually slept in the clubhouse of the 1/27 Wolfhound Battalion. It was more convenient to establish one temporary 'home base'. And as time passed, we naturally made many friends among these 'Wolfhounds'.

It was another hot day and the men of the 1/27th Wolfhound battalion had just returned to Cu Chi after a deadlier than usual field operation. This time, too many Wolfhounds were going home in body bags.

The lucky ones lined up in somber formation. Beneath the blazing sun, they grimly waited for their battalion commander, Lt. Colonel Ernie Condina, to address them. I stood unobtrusively back with a handful of my band members.

The Commanding General spoke into the microphone praising the battalion for their courage during the recent operation. I silently, changed my weight from leg to leg. The finale was a roll call for those who weren't present.

As Lt. Col. Condina called each name, a 'Wolfhound' stepped forward and plunged the deceased soldier's bayoneted rifle into the hard ground. The empty helmet was then placed over the rifle butt. Last of all, the KIA's no longer needed boots were set on the ground in front of the bayonet.

The roll call seemed interminable; a poignant space in time as the row of rifles grew longer. Men stared straight ahead, avoiding other eyes. In the silence between names, the flapping headquarters building's flags sounded extraordinarily loud. Occasionally a nervous tic pulsated in a soldier's cheek. The swelling lump in my throat almost choked me but I'd die before I broke down. This was no place for weakness.

After the last pair of boots was placed, the bugler's trumpet sounded taps. There is no more final sound than that recognition of a soldier's death. The hairs stood up on my arms. It didn't take a clairvoyant to read every man's mind.

People disbanded quietly. Many headed for the club, me along with them. Some would be drunk by nightfall. Fear and anger would find release in obscene language. Eventually alcohol would loosen the tension and they could laugh; loudly – hollowly. I drank with the best of them and hid my tears as well. By 1968 my language was no better than theirs. In a way, I had become one with them.

Such incidents intensified my disgust at the club sergeants. They never left their comfortable quarters to go near any battle. While the young fighting men counted the days, hours and minutes until they could climb into that 'freedom bird' and 'deros' home, the custodians extended their tours, year after year, sometimes up to four years. So confident were they, that they openly bragged about building their Swiss bank accounts. Such lack of discretion puzzled me.

Some weeks after that emotional ceremony, I was back in Sergeant Higdon's custodial office at Long Binh. Kickbacks or not, I had to keep working. The air was clouded with cigar smoke and a handful of club managers sat around listening to Johnny Cash. A thin Vietnamese hooch maid entered carrying a tray filled with cans of Budweiser beer.

"How about joining us for a beer?" Higdon asked.

For the sake of business I hid my reluctance and accepted a can, adding little to their man talk until there was a lull in the conversation.

"Did anyone hear the news? The Paris Peace talks have stalled. The North is being pig-headed again." I remarked.

"I'll drink to that." One of them said, draining his can and burping.

"They'll never get an agreement signed." Higdon smirked "And a good thing too. I hope this Goddamn war lasts another ten years. Every year here is worth another half a million in my bank account."

"Right on." Someone agreed.

A wave of revulsion made me blurt "What a pile of shit. Don't any of you give a damn that your young men are dying?"

The silence was ominous. One of them broke it.

"What's your gripe lady? You're a carpetbagger. No better than the rest of us."

I had made a mistake.

"You need a change of attitude, ma'am. Those asshole officers you hang out with have you brainwashed." Higdon stared stonily at me. "They won't get you anywhere."

"You're right" I tried to undo the damage "but it's those body bags being loaded onto the planes that bother me."

"We've all done our time in the field. We've seen our share. Nineteen goddamned long years in this man's army. Get over it lady. This is war and people die."

When would I learn to shut my big mouth?

There is always an explosion of business going on with any war. On a larger scale back on the home front there is the purchase of weaponry, machinery, vehicles, air craft, uniforms etc. What enormous amounts of 'under the table' money must pass hands there? The defense budget runs into billions.

On a smaller scale involving millions is the underhand business going on in the war zone itself. It starts with the locals the Americans employ for menial chores around the base. The guards check them as they go through the camp gates but still many get away with the plunder. I saw the guards stop a woman one time who had six huge T-bone steaks taped beneath her clothes.

Some soldiers share responsibility for the black markets which flourish in the back streets. The Military Police seem disinclined or unable to stamp it out. Just about anything available in the PX or commissary can be illegally bought from those underhand vendors. I heard one American airman lament. "Uncle Sam is supposed to supply us with fire proof flight jackets. There are never enough to go around so I've missed out. But I go down to Black Market Alley and the old Vietnamese hag is trying to sell me one for a stiff price. How did she get it, huh? This war stinks!"

Fortunes were being made with the illegal money exchange on the local economy. In Vietnam we had the MPC (Military Payment Certificates) paid to the troops, green backs and the local money, piaster. Not even the Vietnamese wanted their own worthless currency. It was impossible to keep up with the illegal money trading. In a futile effort to bring things under control the military occasionally, without warning, would change the printing of MPC script so that those holding a quantity of it suddenly found it as worthless as toilet paper. The Indian shop-keepers on Tu Do Street openly exchanged all kinds of money, not too inhibited by the occasional police raid.

Corruption was everywhere. My experiences were with the club custodians who took their cut on every show they hired, on every drink they sold, on every bar snack and every table or chair the men used. The millions they bragged about making were peanuts however, when compared to what the big companies were doing.

At the top of these immoral business dealings were the big engineering and construction companies who were contracted to build the airfields, roads, camps; the entire reconstruction of Vietnam. They hired tens of thousands of civilians, foreign and local, in Vietnam. There was PAE (Pacific Architects and Engineers), Halliburton and RMK-BRJ. These companies obtained billions of tax payer's money yet any discerning G I could see something wasn't right. I heard GI's scoff bitterly about LBJ their President, and his wife having substantial shares in RMK-BRJ. How could that be good for morale? (This is a subject I'll return to later.)

The longer I remained in Vietnam, the more aware I became of the corruption at every level, the more my bitterness increased. All this money was being stolen by people in relative safety while a PFC received only U.S. $100 a week for risking his life. My own part in enabling some corrupters had me conflicted. I began to wonder what I could do to change things.

Already I had complained to several high ranking officers. They listened attentively but none seemed inclined to become involved. Their focus was on the war and the enemy body count; things which would look good on their records.

Why were club custodians given free reign with no officers supervising them? They handled money in sums as large as some company CEO's yet none were accountants, had college educations or business training.

My obsession to stop the brazen custodians was building.

One night, after the club closed in Bien Hoa, my band and I packed up my old De Soto. We went back to collect the last of our equipment. Inside the empty club the manager and his helpers were calmly filling buckets with coins from the slot machines. They must have removed half the night's takings before carrying the buckets out to the manager's jeep with little thought of secrecy. The Sego machines were regularly serviced and emptied by the representatives of the leasing agent. I wished I had a camera. Without evidence I couldn't report anyone. It was the first time I thought of doing so yet I shuddered at the danger involved.

CHAPTER 31

BRISBANE – SYDNEY

Brisbane was considered a backwaters in the fifties and sixties. When top name American entertainers came to Australia they usually gave it a by-pass. Determined to leave Australia, I decided I must move to Sydney or Melbourne for exposure to the bigger agents. With no work lined up in either city, I gave notice at Arthur Murray's and Tommy's.

On my way to Sydney, I stopped off in Tamworth. All but Jan, the youngest of Mum's children from her second marriage, was now in school. Clarice and Russell had both moved to Sydney; Clarice to take up nursing at Balmain hospital, Russell to do an aeronautical engineering apprenticeship at Bankstown airport. As a teenager, through a clerical error, he became the youngest pilot to ever pass his private, fixed wing license in Australia and he was already working at obtaining his helicopter license.

I arrived in Tamworth dressed to the nines. My hair was dyed red and I thought I looked hot (or was the terminology 'cool'?) Mum disagreed.

"What have you done to your hair?" she greeted me. "Are you morally bereft? Last week Clarice visited us smoking a cigarette. Now you arrive looking like a flaming haired hussy." She moaned. "Where did I go wrong?"

In the ensuing years as I changed my hair from one color to another, she repeated that lament until finally taking it one step further and declaring that she was sure the hospital had given her the wrong baby.

The children from the second marriage were not finding life quite as hard as we had. There was still plenty of work but money was no longer as tight. They could afford music lessons and Mum bought a piano. Whenever I visited we had some pleasant musical nights with Bake singing along and me dancing.

The day before I left for Sydney, I took Lorraine and Della into town to do a bit of shopping and have lunch. I thought I looked pretty good in a red and white gingham, full skirted pinafore over a white silk blouse. The two little girls wore their best Sunday frocks and heads turned as we walked along Peel Street. Suddenly, walking towards me was Peter. Unexpectedly, my hands shook. He looked handsome in his wide-brimmed Akubra, hat. We had not had any contact since I left Toowoomba and I thought he was still away shearing. As he drew nearer, I was pleased that I looked good and I hoped he regretted losing me.

He stopped and I couldn't find words.

"Hullo Peter." My voice trembled.

"You look terrible." He said "You've got too much make-up on."

They were the last words he ever spoke to me.

In Sydney I conserved money by renting a room, not an apartment. It squatted, small and gloomy, at the top of a narrow unlit staircase. The landlady was a busy-body and I missed my spacious Brisbane apartment. But I told myself 'it wouldn't be for long'.

Work was sporadic; a few engagements in various RSL clubs (Returned Soldiers League - Australia's equivalent of an American Veterans club but larger, with many more facilities), and a few shows in the beer-gardens of the pubs.

Exploring the city I discovered the infamous Abe Saffron's strip clubs in the notorious part of town, King's Cross. The clubs were dark and dinghy. Girls in high heels, with pasties covering their nipples, jerked gracelessly to taped music. Shuddering, I told myself I would take Pop's advice and sell stamps in the Post Office before ending up there.

Speaking to my brother Russell on the phone one night I invited him to watch me dance the following week-end in the beer garden of the Belmont Hotel. My upcoming performance was advertised alongside my picture in the Sydney Telegraph.

The day arrived and I dressed in a two piece, red-sequined number with sheer floating back panels. My family had never seen me dance and I was nervous. Russell was always the perfectionist.

The beer garden overflowed with noisy, beer swilling louts. Russell, quiet and neatly dressed, looked around critically. The music trio blasted my intro and when I shot onto the floor, the crowd went wild; but not appreciatively so. They yelled and whistled and some made crude comments. This had never happened in Brisbane and I was humiliated. When I joined Russell after dressing, he was in a foul mood.

"How can you lower yourself to dance half naked before a bunch of boozers like these?"

"I'm not half naked" I replied, hurt "And you can see more on Bondi Beach any day. I'm sorry I'm not smart enough to be a pilot like you."

"Well if Nan and Pop ever saw you dance, they'd have a heart attack."

His words stung. We had always been close. I realized then that while I was trying to break free from my middle class bonds, Russell was still quite comfortable in his.

A few weeks later my luck changed. An agent caught my performance in a Sydney RSL club and offered me a week's engagement in Melbourne. I had never been to Melbourne but I knew The Embers was the finest night-club in that city. The offer left me speechless.

CHAPTER 32

VIETNAM

My life in Vietnam was not without lovers. Only a fool or a lesbian would pass up such an opportunity. I was surrounded by good looking men whose women were on another planet, far away. This suited me perfectly for after leaving Peter I spurned the idea of marriage.

As long as wives were temporarily out of the picture, I preferred married men. They would never require a permanent commitment from me. My definition of a perfect relationship was good sex, genuine affection and mutual respect. Love was avoided! A little bit was great –too much was disastrous. I was not immune to pain.

I have met many women who claim to have found their soul mate, - their one great love. I have had several great loves. In Vietnam, once my lover climbed onto that big 'Freedom Bird" the door was firmly shut. No matter how much I yearned for him, never again would I attempt any contact for he had left my world. I was grateful for the time we had shared but when the end came, I returned him in good condition.

We were in such a world of our own with no certainty of getting out. That was possibly part of the excitement. Like the old saying goes, 'You've never really lived until you've nearly died,' and I was living more intensely than I ever thought possible. This may sound crass, but that intensity overflowed into the sex.

Mail call became the one pin-prick of intrusion from the outside world for many men; a thread to sanity for others. My own correspondence was negligible, consisting of a few, guilt inspired scribbled lines. It was impossible to describe my life in a manner which my family would understand. Certainly not to a mother whom I had once traumatized simply by changing my hair color!

Colonel Larry Mowery was a huge, gruff man with a deep voice, coarse skin and intelligent eyes. He was a combat soldier through and through and his men would follow 'The Old Man' to hell and back. This told me a lot about him for I was well aware that not all officers were held in such esteem. Some were disrespected or hated and there were occasional incidences of fragging an unpopular or incompetent officer. Colonel Mowery was infantry-airborne, the commander of the 3rd Brigade, 101st Airborne. They were commonly known as The Screaming Eagles due to the eagle patch on their uniform sleeve.

Located North, at Hue Phu Bai, his brigade consisted of battle hardened soldiers who were constantly in the field. As they were seldom in camp, their clubs generated insufficient profits to lure the crooked club sergeants.

My group and I had been working there for three days, doing shows for various battalions as they returned from missions. We slept on army cots at night and by day we read, chatted with the men, or rehearsed new numbers.

On our third night, Colonel Mowery entered the officer's club accompanied by a group of staff officers. I was watching my band perform when a major approached, saying "The Colonel would like to meet you ma'am. Please follow me."

When we reached the colonel's table, he half rose from his chair, saying "Take a seat. Entertainment is good for my men's morale and we don't get enough of it. Welcome aboard."

His officers' apparent adulation impressed me .The drinks flowed and conversation was stimulating. We talked and laughed long after my band had finished playing and retired to their cots. As the night progressed, a major challenged his commander to a one-armed push-up contest. Colonel Mowery enthusiastically agreed and stood. He was a giant.

A space was cleared in the centre of the room and immediately the two officers became the centre of attention. The crowd gathered and noisily placed bets. Teams of supporters gathered around the contestants who now lay stretched out on the floor.

"Who are you putting your money on June?" The XO (Executive officer) asked.

"Why, the colonel, of course. He's got to be older by at least ten years. We Aussie's always root for the under dog." The XO raised his eyebrows, possibly misinterpreting my Aussie slang.

I joined the men cheering-on the duo who were becoming flushed as they pumped, one arm held skywards, to a chorus of counting. By the count of forty, both men were breathing hard. By fifty they were dripping sweat. The tempo slowed but they struggled valiantly on. The crowd yelled louder, egging them on. Both officers were obviously fading but neither wanted to concede.

"Go Colonel, go." I urged loudly. Whether that made the difference, I don't know, but Colonel Mowery got a last burst of energy as his younger opponent collapsed. Rising to his feet to a mix of cheers from the winners and grumbles from the losers, he glanced at me with the satisfied expression of a conqueror.

Around midnight, only the colonel, his X.O and two bleary eyed staff officers remained. Feeling the effects of the alcohol, I was loath to leave, but finally I stood and said "Goodnight everyone. I need my beauty sleep."

."Where are you staying June?" Colonel Mowery grabbed my hand.

"With my band in the NCO club! Thanks for a fun night."

"How would you feel about doing a little more for the war effort, June?" He searched my eyes intently. "You would make an old warrior happy."

"I'm not a one night stand." I snapped; my feelings hurt.

"I wouldn't have asked if I thought you were. Circumstances don't allow for the usual niceties. Besides, I have more than one night in mind."

I was undeniably drawn to power and courage and the vibes between us had grown as the night progressed.

"In that case, I don't play games anyway. Lead on!"

That night I spent the first of many in his 20 foot metal, shipping container. This container doubled as his small office /sleeping quarters and I later saw it sling-hooked by Chinook helicopter from location to location as he and his men chased the enemy.

For months I used the colonel's camp as my base. There was an awkward moment one morning when the 101st's Commanding General chopper-ed in, unannounced from Division Headquarters. I was wearing pajamas, reading 'Readers Digest', when Larry's driver, Ron, a wholesome young spec.4 from West Virginia, banged violently on the door of the air conditioned container.

"Quick June, quick! You've gotta get outta here. The General has arrived. The old man will be dead if you're caught here."

I leaped into my nearest clothes and ran to the jeep, stuffing my long hair inside an army cap.

"Where can I hide?"

The treeless camp was exposed, in the middle of nowhere.

"The Colonel said to keep driving around the perimeter until the General's chopper takes off."

Ron had long ago placed his boss on a tall pedestal and he would die before letting his Colonel down.

We spent a long time circling the camp in an open-topped jeep, trails of red dust spiraling behind as we waited impatiently for that general to fly away.

What instinct caused me to unconsciously challenge my mates? If I mastered them I was disappointed and gave them hell until I left or drove them away. I needed a man stronger than myself. Colonel Mowery was definitely that man.

A few months after becoming 'the colonel's woman', I found him in the trailer one evening, obviously stressed. He was sitting at his small desk, writing a letter in the yellow glow from a desk lamp. A nerve visibly bounced in his cheek! Sensing his mood, I sat silently on the bed. He folded the letter into an envelope then laid his forehead on the palm of his hand.

"What's wrong Larry?"

He lifted his head and looked at me with such profound sadness that I had to look away.

"This is the job I hate most." He said "It's been a shit of a week and I've lost some fine, young men. What do you write to their parents? Nothing I can say is ever adequate."

No-one has that answer. Like all good officers, he loved his men and felt responsible, even though a lesser leader would have lost more.

CHAPTER 33

MELBOURNE

I arrived at The Embers Club for rehearsal. The dim room looked the epitome of elegance. The eight band members struck up my opener of Peter Gunn. They were terrific! My nervousness disappeared as the rehearsal progressed.

Coincidentally, Sammy Davis Jr. was in town for two concerts that same week and I was disappointed my schedule would collide with the timing of his shows. His warm-up act was an American dance duo named Audie and Margo. I had only ever seen them on the new media called television. They had appeared as a guest act on the Ed Sullivan Show and I was spellbound by their sensual performance.

Opening night! On my way to the dressing room I stopped at the bar and ordered a gin and tonic to quell my jitters. The crowded club felt warm and intimate. Soft yellow lights flickered atop white table cloths-- pinpoints in the dark. Long legged girls wearing black stockings and short stiff, black skirts weaved among the tables, selling cigarettes from trays hung around their necks. A handsome young, tuxedo clad man was selling red roses to the ladies. Occasionally a light flashed as the photographer found a buying customer.

I thanked the bartender for my drink and was carrying it to the dressing room when I sensed a stir in the crowd. Looking curiously towards the entryway I caught my breath. A large group of tall, black men were entering, surrounding a white couple and a short black man. Stunned, I recognized Sammy and Audie and Margo.

The club manager hurried to greet them and led them to a table, centre front of the stage. Realizing they were to be in the audience of my opening show, I shook like a Brazilian Samba dancer and almost dropped my drink. Opening night was always nerve racking. To open in the best club I'd yet performed in, and before celebrities of such magnitude was terrifying.

In the dressing room I zipped up my long sleeved, red lace leotard in a state of shock. It fit like a second skin. 'Calm down' I told myself "You are not as good as Audie and Margo and never will be. But you have the passion. Get out there and let it flow. Close your eyes and let the music carry you."

And so I did! Every kick stretched higher than my legs had ever reached. Every twirl was pure and sharp; every beat of the music inspired me to new heights. I danced so hard I thought my heart might just fly out of my body and lay quivering at their feet.

It was over and I stood breathless at centre-stage, humbly bowing my head. The applause was thunderous. I couldn't believe my ears. I looked up smiling and saw Sammy, Audie, Margo, the whole entourage, giving me a standing ovation. Following their cue, one by one, the entire audience stood and the room shook with applause such as I had never experienced. Elated, I ran from the stage. 'If only Russell could see me now,' I thought, climbing down the side steps. But even then it wasn't over. Sammy left his table and blocked my exit.

"That was too cool. Woman, you've got heart. Will you join us?" I looked into his smiling face and listened to that familiar voice, wondering if I was dreaming.

"I'm sure the manager won't allow me to sit out front in my costume." I mumbled nervously.

"Don't you worry about the manager." And so saying, he removed his jacket and placed it over my shoulders. "I'll take care of him." He finished.

This was my first encounter with celebrities and I was surprised to discover they were just like 'real people'. In fact Sammy was warmer and more considerate than many people I knew.

Over the next two days, Sammy invited me to join his group each afternoon at the hotel. The front desk cleared me through Sammy's road manager before allowing me up to their floor. There wasn't much happening in the crowded, smoke filled suite yet it was new and exciting to me. The musicians spent most of their time playing cards and ordering room service.

On the second day, I brought a girlfriend with me, an aboriginal singer. Our inter-racial friendship pleased Sammy who was at that time newly wed to the white actress, Britt Eklund.

Screaming newspaper headlines ruined the ambiance of our last get-together. Back in the USA a Ku Klux Klan member had thrown a bomb into a Southern Baptist church, killing many black children. Sammy was almost in tears as he paced angrily back and forth, raving about America's racism. "As soon as I get home, I'm going straight down there to rebuild that church," He vowed.

My first week in Melbourne was coming to an end and it had been such a heady experience that I had no intentions of returning to Sydney. Sammy and his group had already left and I was feeling a bit of a let-down.

It was my last night at The Embers. As I finished changing, the manager came to my dressing room to tell me a man was waiting outside to see me.

"Who is he?"

"I don't know. Here's his card." I looked at the name. Ray Bolwell. I didn't know him.

"What's he like?"

"Don't ask me. Looks like a player. Go see for yourself."

I patted my hair into place and followed him into the club. He pointed to a table. The customer rose from his seat as I approached. He looked late thirties, early forties. An expensive three piece suit covered a well built body. He was smoking. I hated cigarettes but most everyone did it.

"Good evening, Miss Collins. I am Ray Bolwell. Can I buy you a drink?"

"A gin and tonic would be nice" I said, sitting." May I ask why you asked to meet me?"

"I enjoyed your dance performance." He exhaled a stream of cigarette smoke towards the ceiling.

"Thanks."

"I run a club near here in St. Kilda."

He had my interest. I would be out of work tomorrow.

"Have you ever considered stripping?"

I remembered the women I had seen at Abe Saffron's joints in King's Cross and stifled a shudder.

"I have not." I spoke indignantly "And please say no more. I've put too much effort into dance training to consider throwing it away just to bare my body."

"No offence." He smiled briefly "Please hear me out."

My interest had faded.

"I don't run a joint" he continued "It's a dinner theatre catering to couples. The fur stole, suit and tie class. It's a high class vaudeville type show."

Never having seen a vaudeville show; that meant little to me.

"We have a twelve piece orchestra, a fine vocalist, and a comedian"

I pondered this information, thinking it must be pretty good to have a twelve piece band.

"And the highlight is, of course, our six ladies." He stubbed his cigarette in the ash tray.

"Six strippers?"

"I like to refer to them as exotic dancers. Every one of them is a budding Gypsy Rose Lee. We don't hire any of that Abe Saffron sleaze."

"Really Mr. Bolwell, it took me months to feel comfortable wearing my flimsy costumes on stage. I couldn't possibly bring myself to wear less."

"I'm sorry to hear that. I'm always looking to improve my show and keep it balanced. It's never raunchy so our female customers are not embarrassed but it's sexy enough to titillate their men." He smiled at his choice of words and I guessed it was a practiced line. "You have just the right mix of elegance and sensuality."

"Yes, and big boobs." I said sarcastically. "Is that my draw card? Thank you but no thank you. I'm not a stripper."

"Well then. I'm sorry for wasting your time. Where is your next engagement?"

I hated to admit I had none. "Nothing is finalized yet," I stammered.

"In that case, why don't you come around to The Ritz Hotel and catch my show tomorrow night? You can have dinner on me. There's no commitment of any kind."

I looked at his card again. "Where is St. Kilda?"

"Any taxi can bring you there.... If you change your mind, you could continue to do the same act you are doing now."

I brightened. "The same act?"

"Of course, you would have to throw your bra into the wings as a finale."

Hope vanished.

"Well, I couldn't. But I will come tomorrow night."

"Just remember, working for me is a permanent job. You don't need to pay an agent to find work every week. And because of your dancing ability, you would be the star of the show. Keep in mind that we get regular visits from overseas agents looking to find girls."

I took a deep breathe. Now he had my attention!

"Did I tell you how much you would earn?" He mentioned a sum. My mouth fell open.

CHAPTER 34

VIETNAM

I was complaining to Colonel Mowery about the corruption in the club system in many of the camps.

"We don't have it in the 101st" Larry said. "We're too busy fighting the war to sit around the clubs drinking."

"I understand, but corruption is hurting my business. The big support camps that hire most of the shows aren't hiring mine and that's where the money is. Wasn't it you who told me that for every combat soldier out there fighting, there are ten support troops who rarely, if ever, see battle?"

"Something like that."

"Well the crooked sergeants say that I bitch too much and they don't trust me. I tell you Larry, if I knew how to destroy them I would."

"If they didn't destroy you first." He replied grimly.

"The last time we worked Long Binh the damn sergeant put a move on Rose Marie. Thank God I arrived when I did. I promised her mother I'd keep her safe. You know, I hear some of the agents are providing the club sergeants with hookers, putting them in the shows under the guise of go-go dancers. I won't do business that way. There's a limit to the things I will do for money."

We were striding towards the helipad and I frowned, pondering my situation. Larry's chopper was preparing for take-off. He bent low and ran beneath the twirling blades.

"Mind your head," he yelled, clambering aboard. I ran after him and scrambled in. Seconds later, the powerful machine lifted, nose down from the ground. We slowly circled then headed south.

Wind rushed through the open doors whipping my hair across my face. I cursed myself for not braiding it and pulled on a headset. The intercom was silent. I motioned to Larry.

"You know Larry, my troupe sat around without work for four days last week. I have to pay them whether they work or not. Then there's the rent on their villa and wages for the driver. We used to work seven days a week."

I hated to burden him with my problems when his concerns were of much greater import but there was no-one else to share them with.

"Yeah!" He replied "I've thought about that. While I'm taking care of business in Saigon, I've told the pilots to take you up to Dau Tieng. One of my best buddies, we went through OCS (Officer Candidate School) together, commands a brigade there. I radioed him that you're coming. He'll make damn sure that his sergeant gives you some shows. If he says book your show, you bet they'll fuckin book it! Daems is a real renegade." He chuckled.

"I planned to stop by my Tan Son Nhut apartment and grab some clean clothes." I frowned.

"My pilots will wait. Gives them a chance to visit the PX."

"What time will we meet up?"

"I'll be busy all day. The chopper will return for me later and I'll join you at Dau Tieng. Daems puts on a damned good dinner. Considers himself a gourmet." Larry snorted "I daren't leave you alone too long with that old fox."

Later, when I returned to the helipad, the crew was loading several large cardboard boxes.

"What have we got here?"

"Akai tape deck and speakers" the captain replied "Got a great deal on them. Once they're hooked up I'll be able to blast Charlie all the way back to Hanoi."

I climbed aboard and strapped myself in. For awhile I remained lost in thought until I noticed how low we were flying, barely scraping above the fields. We rose and fell with the undulations of the land, sending the grazing caribou running and bucking. We almost hit one.

"What the hell are you trying to do?" I yelled but they ignored me. Did they think I was a greenhorn who would scare easily? If so, they had plenty to learn. I had been in too many helicopters with too many pilots who had pulled the same stunt.

The co-pilot turned back towards me with a wicked smile "Everything alright back there ma'am?"

I yawned, exaggerated "Sure thing."

It wasn't the expected response, I suppose, for they changed direction and flew on until coming to a waterway. Dropping low over the muddy water they began tipping the chopper first left then right. 'Pretty bloody stupid' I thought. I'd been subjected to this stunt with other pilots but the props were now dipping frighteningly close to the water. I remained expressionless, even when a bridge loomed up ahead and I could guess what was coming. Sure enough, we flew under the bridge with little space to spare.

"Nice flying boys" I yelled into the headphones but they renewed their brainless jig above the canal. They gave another sharp tilt and the boxes slid sideways then shot out into space, before hitting the water with an enormous brown splash.

"Good thinking '99'," I yelled into the headset "Your new speakers are at the bottom of the canal." I had a good belly laugh before switching off.

It was my first trip to Dau Tiang, although I had spent much time at the divisions headquarters camp in Cu Chi. The 3rd Brigade camp was a great improvement after other camps I'd encountered. The Michelin Rubber plantation had been leased by Uncle Sam, undoubtedly at a higher price than any profits engendered from rubber tapping. The French owners had long since taken their windfall and high-tailed it back to France.

The handful of staff officers lived splendidly in the homestead, a rambling, white stucco building surrounded by wide, covered verandahs draped in Bougainvillea. Nearby, the officer's swimming pool shimmered within a bamboo enclosure. A second building was utilized as the Brigade Headquarters Office. Further back, white painted rocks bordered neat pathways, bisecting the small community of tents which were stacked waist high with sand bags.

There was no comparison between this and the larger Cu Chi camp. The plantation was extraordinarily neat, green and shaded; Bougainvillea adding splashes of color.

I followed the signs towards the headquarters building. Once inside, the office seemed deserted. I was wondering where everyone was when a tall, starched black man stepped through a doorway. I could see from his insignia that he was a lieutenant colonel. His name tag read Hunt. There were very few black officers in the army in those days. I hid my surprise beneath respect, aware of how difficult it was for black Americans to attain officer rank; partially because few of them had the education.

"Hullo Colonel Hunt. I'm June Collins. Is Colonel Daems around?"

The lieutenant colonel shook hands, smiling.

"He said you might drop by. You're too early ma am. He's out fighting the war but he should be back before sundown. I'm his exec. Can I get you some cold water?"

"Yeah thanks colonel. Maybe I'll just go out and sit near that pool I noticed. Don't see too many of those around Vietnam."

"We have a few perks but we pay the price. The plantation's rubber trees are a great hiding place for Charlie. He keeps us on our toes."

I took the water and headed towards the pool. A Poinciana tree offered shade. I pulled up a deck chair and must have dozed off. Voices woke me.

"Ah. Here she is, Sleeping Beauty." Larry grabbed my hand and pulled me from the deck chair "June, meet my old pal, Len Daems."

His dust covered friend was at least six inches shorter than Larry but he exuded charisma. His smile was cheeky, his stare impudent and he reminded me of the movie director, Mike Todd.

"What are you doing with this renegade?" Colonel Daems nodded towards Larry. "He'll sure as hell get you into trouble."

"I can find plenty of that for myself."

"Well the sun's over the yardarm. Let's go find a drink. The war's over for another day.....I hope."

The two friends had plenty of catching up to do. I tagged along, not part of their conversation.

Later, we relaxed upon bamboo chairs on the wide verandah of the spacious, homestead. Lieutenant Colonel Hunt, two majors and a captain joined us while an enlisted soldier served ice cold drinks. These brigade staff officers apparently observed the cocktail hour ritualistically. Two of the officers picked up some dice from a table and began playing liars dice.

"We unwind out here in the evening, whenever we can," Colonel Daems commented.

"You lucky son of a bitch! You've got it good." Larry jibed.

"You wouldn't say that if you saw our action sheets for last month." Daems turned serious "But I know you've got no picnic up north."

"Right on! But certainly none of these perks. How do you always land on your feet, you old bastard?"

Daems glanced at me and grinned lecherously "What are you bitching about?" He raised his glass "Let's drink a toast. To beautiful women everywhere! May they always brighten our miserable lives."

"Speaking of beautiful women Colonel Daems, Larry says you will speak to your club managers about putting my show in here."

"You bet your ass. How many of them are there?"

"Eight men and two women."

"Pity there's not a few more women." He swallowed a mouthful of Scotch then stared at me with such naked lust that I blushed "Are they as good looking as you?"

"Hey. Back off you bum. She's taken." Larry turned to me "You've gotta watch out for him and he's a married man."

"Well that's the kettle calling the pot black."

Their rivalry flattered me.

Colonel Daems called for music. The captain set up a tape deck on the bamboo table. Lieutenant Colonel Hunt glanced at his watch "Showtime, folks! The fun starts any minute now. Look in that direction." He pointed towards the camp perimeter and right on cue I saw a flash.

"Mortars!" I stated.

"Right! Charlie reminds us he's here every evening. These early rounds seldom reach far inside our perimeter. They get courageous after dark and sneak in closer. Right now they're far enough away that the sight reaches us ahead of the sound. Watch the next one then listen for the delay."

I sat back, soaking up the atmosphere. The slightest touch of pink was fading from the sky. Hundreds of fireflies flitted around us, their glinting wings creating silver, pink and blue pin pricks of light in the semi-gloom. A welcome breeze dispersed the day's heat, stirring the tangle of crimson bougainvillea. Frank Sinatra's voice soothed the soul and an ice cold gin and tonic tasted great. Beside me, two tough old warriors vied for my attention. How good does it get?

But the incongruity of it had not escaped me. I knew that a mortar could land in our midst any moment, bringing death.

"Do you mind if I borrow your woman, Mowery?" Daems asked "It has been a long time since I've held a woman and danced."

"It's up to her. Just don't hold her too close."

Colonel Daems bowed theatrically before me "Shall we?"

I was blushing again. He placed his arm firmly around my waist and waltzed me away.

"Your hair smells delicious." He murmured as I followed his lead. Moments later, his cheek rested warmly against mine. Before long, Larry was tapping him on the shoulder

"Don't hog her for yourself. I'm sure the rest of us would like a turn."

"Thank you Colonel Daems." He numbed my brain and I could think of nothing clever to say.

"Forget this colonel business. Now we're dance partners you've gotta call me Len."

By the time dinner was served I had danced with every man in our small group.

"After dinner let's cool off in the pool." Len Daems said.

Larry frowned. "We don't have swim trunks with us."

"Oh come on. What's wrong with underpants?"

"A lady present demands a certain amount of decorum." Larry spoke firmly.

"I'll forgo the swim." I agreed.

"Yeah!" Larry added "Let's have a one armed push-up contest. We'll see who is the better man."

I wondered what it was with Larry and his one-armed push up contests.

"I'm up to the challenge." Daems shot back "And we'll have the goddamn thing over at my officers club. May as well let my men watch me kick your ass."

"Get humiliated you mean. Put your money on the table. I'll wipe the floor with you."

"Are you a betting woman, June?" Lieutenant Colonel Hunt asked.

"Not on these two, they're like a pair of kids." The staff officers laughed.

CHAPTER 35

VIETNAM

Most of Larry's brigade was out on a big sweep. My Filipino's and I returned once more to the 25th Infantry Division Headquarters camp at Cu Chi. The custodian had not asked for a kickback so I assumed the corruption had not yet reached the 25th Division.

After so much contact with Americans, I had grown to love them, relating to their outgoing nature and generosity. Therefore, I was nonplussed by the numerous dishonest club sergeants. Were Americans as a whole abnormally dishonest? Or had I just stumbled onto a bad bunch that was somehow connected? I wished I knew.

Due to the frequency of our visits, the 25th Division had become special to me and my troupe. Regardless of whichever battalion we worked, we still slept nightly in the NCO clubhouse of the 1/27 Wolfhound Battalion; an attempt at stability I suppose.

A few weeks after meeting Larry's friend, Colonel Daems, my band performed our first show in Dau Tieng. Colonel Daems had arranged for two helicopters from his aviation battalion to pick us up then return us to Cu Chi before dark. Only afternoon shows were possible at Dau Tieng because of frequent, nightly mortar attacks. Even the Red Cross girls had to return to Cu Chi before dark if they visited the division's outlying brigade.

I had not seen Colonel Daems since the meeting with Larry and he was not present at our afternoon show. I assumed he was out chasing the enemy in his C&C (command and control) chopper. As the sun started to set, I supervised the loading of my band and equipment into the waiting helicopters. We were about to lift off when a major rushed over.

"The colonel has just landed. He sent me to bring you back to his chopper. He's taking you to Cu Chi."

I sighed heavily, told the pilot I was transferring and followed the major across the helipad.

Colonel Daems sat grinning aboard his C&C.

"I'm heading your way," he said. "I've got a meeting with Blaster 6, the Division Artillery Commander. Gotta exchange coordinates for tomorrow's operation."

I gave him a quizzical glance and climbed aboard, wondering if he could have used his radio phone.

"Sorry I couldn't get back in time to catch your show," he continued "It is the first entertainment my men have had. We'll have to get you back again when other battalions come in." He smiled, placing his hand lightly on my knee.

"Shall I tell Larry you send greetings?" I removed his hand.

"You're still in touch with that old coot, are you?"

"Certainly! We recently returned from Sydney where I accompanied him on R & R..."

That piece of information elicited a cocked eyebrow and a moment's silence.

"You do know he's getting short, don't you?" Daems recovered." On the other hand I've got a long time to go." There was no mistaking his meaning and I was surprised by a slight ripple of excitement.

"Do not be too presumptuous." I replied coolly, but apparently not cool enough. His leg pressed closer against mine.

Most days there wasn't much to do in the camps before evening. Some days I flew to other locations, setting up future bookings. Other days I tried to find a quiet spot and catch up on my reading.

It was becoming harder to discipline my emotions. Tears had been stifled for three years. Nights were still frequently filled with alcohol and laughter. Early morning reflections could be depressing.

I had never been interested in religion but too many body bags had me questioning what the point of life was. It seemed futile when so many good ones died young while worthless others took up space on earth.

Passing the 25th division chapel one day, I found myself drawn inside. I sat on the front pew, alone. Haltingly I began to whisper a prayer and then I started crying. My weakness was deplorable!

The Division Chaplain, Colonel Parker Thompson entered unnoticed. I felt his hand on my shoulder and jumped.

'These are confusing times for all of us." He said kindly "Perhaps you might find an answer in the bible."

I had briefly tried reading the bible after my pregnancy dramas but it never made much sense. I didn't believe God sat around listening to prayers and doling out favors.

"I have noticed your concern for the men" Colonel Thompson continued "I can see you have great love for your fellow man. Jesus would approve. He tells us in 1 Peter 4:7, 8 'Above all things love one another, because love covers a multitude of sins' It was for love of us that Jesus sacrificed his life."

I nodded dumbly, thinking that I had a few sins that could use a cover.

"Why don't you start bible studies with me? It may help you cope?"

"I doubt it Chaplain."

"It won't hurt. And try attending Sunday services with the men. You must praise God and give thanks if you want his blessings."

During our first lesson the monsoonal rain pelted the corrugated iron roof so violently that it drowned out the Chaplain's voice. Battling to hear over the noise and exhausted by the steamy heat, I fell asleep.

"I have that effect on a lot of the congregation". Chaplain Thompson chuckled when I awoke thirty minutes later. His quick wit and self- deprecating sense of humor kept him popular with the men.

"Why don't we call it quits for the day? I'm about to go over to the General's mess for lunch. Would you like to join me?"

Normally I would not have access to The General's mess. It was available only to the handful of headquarters' commanders. I routinely ate in the officers' mess. Colonel Thompson was one of several Chaplains belonging to the division but, as head chaplain, he was a staff officer.

When we passed by the guard, the Provost Marshall was coming from his office. He looked surprised to see me.

“Having lunch with one of your sinners, are you Chaplain?” he smirked. Colonel Thompson pulled himself up to his full height of five foot two inches, and replied “No colonel, having lunch with my FAVORITE sinner.”

Only weeks later, the chapel took a direct mortar hit. The Sunday service was underway at the time yet, miraculously, no-one was injured.

“It was the only time I ever got them down on their knees.” the chaplain quipped.

CHAPTER 36

MELBOURNE

In the year 1959 people had very different values from what they have today. Today, Australians are proud of Nicole Kidman despite her bared breasts in "Eyes Wide Shut." After all, isn't it art? In the name of art, we accept nudity, semi- nudity and very realistic 'simulated' sex acts in our movies and on television. Housewives sunbathe topless and teen-age girls from good homes now belly up in wet T-shirt contests and amateur strip shows. In the United States students are working their way through college by stripping.

Tolerance pervades the world; with the exception of society's outlook on strippers. The word still seems to be synonymous with prostitution. In truth, this has sometimes been the case but in my experience, it only occurred among a minority of the untalented. Talented strippers whom I knew, earned good money and were not lured into such proclivities.

When I began working at The Ritz Hotel, it was definitely the temptation of money and the dream of travel which I succumbed to. My upbringing had been so suffused with the pursuit of respectability that I knew I would now be a family outcast if they ever knew. And there was my own mindset to overcome. After all, I had grown up as a modest person and remnants of it still clung.

During the first week I threw up after each show. In the dressing room I never wandered about naked as some of the girls did. I felt out of place and initially, Ray was having regrets about hiring me.

"Bloody Hell" he exploded, bursting into my dressing after the first night. "I said to give them a glimpse. The customers are complaining that if they blinked, you were gone. You must hold a pose long enough for them to get a look before you duck behind that bloody feather fan."

"I'll try to do better." I quavered.

"You had better." He stamped from the room.

I was still shocked that I had taken up Ray's offer but my desire to escape my past, my life, myself, was overpowering. That damned streak of Puritanism was just a hindrance.

As the weeks passed, I marveled at my own expanding tolerances, remembering my married life and how I used to turn the light off before undressing and getting into bed with Peter. I recalled how childishly jealous and shocked I had been after learning he had indulged in a sexual encounter before meeting me. Our inhibitions had kept us from exploring each other's bodies and we never discussed sexual issues.

Whatever people now thought of me, I knew I must not let it trouble me or change the course of my life. With this greater versatility I should never be out of work again. Everything has its price.

I found a simple apartment a short tram ride from the hotel. Melbourne, like Sydney, was colder than Brisbane and not as colorful or laid back. But it would all be irrelevant once I left Australia.

Soon I began to settle comfortably into the new role. My position as 'head girl' boosted my ego and helped my adjustment.

During my short stay in Sydney I had become friends with a then unknown Italian/ Australian singer named Maria Venuti. After three months at The Ritz, Ray Bolwell told me the vocalist from the show was leaving and I suggested he audition Maria. She was an exuberant, glamorous brunette with a big voice and a bust to match. She would fit into the Ritz perfectly.

Once Ray agreed, I excitedly phoned Maria with an invitation to come down for a few days.

The big night arrived and we entered the Ritz while the 'old' singer was performing.

"Not a bad voice," Maria observed "but she lacks fire. The audience is talking instead of listening."

We took our place at the long table set aside for entertainers. I delayed eating and ordered my usual gin tonic. Soon Ray beckoned Maria to go on.

"Break a leg." I encouraged.

Minutes later, she bounced on stage, grabbed the microphone and belted out a huge note. The audience fell silent as she launched into her act with electrifying vigor.

"Not bad. Not bad." Ray said.

He left the table just as the regular singer strolled up and sat beside me.

"Who brung her?" she said, glancing disparagingly at the stage. "She's too fat."

Admittedly Maria was not exactly thin but she was voluptuous with most of it in the right place.

"She's very glamorous." I defended my friend.

"She's fat and she can't sing."

"She's a great singer." I was now annoyed "You're jealous. Shut your mouth and give her a go."

"Fat cow. Fat cow. Moo, moo."

"One more word out of you and you'll be sorry."

"Fat cow. Fat cow." She was enjoying getting a rise out of me.

I leaped up and dumped my gin tonic over her head.

Her mouth fell open and I was shocked by my own re-action. A slice of lemon hung drunkenly in her bee-hive hair-do. The gin dripped down her face and spilt into her cleavage, leaving her bodice a soggy mess. She screamed and Ray came running.

"Look what she's done." She yelled "I can't go back on stage."

Ray took one look and with a face like a thundercloud, turned on me snarling. "You're through. Get your things and get out."

I hadn't expected him to fire me. I had even thought he fancied me. As if he would! He was a worldly person and I was unsophisticated, still trying to acquire some polish.

"And take your friend with you." He added coldly.

Maria and I returned to the apartment. I was apologetic but she was unperturbed. The following day she flew back to Sydney.

Around four p.m. I was surprised to find Ray on my doorstep.

"Hi." I said tongue-tied.

"Can I come in?"

"Ray I'm sorry I lost my temper." I blurted.

"Yeah! The girls told me you were provoked." He lit a cigarette. I waited nervously.

"It's hard to lose my number one girl." He paused again and took a puff, "I guess I can understand loyalty to a friend but you have to learn to control your temper. Do you think you could do that if I took you back tonight?"

I sighed with relief.

"Don't do that again, Junie Moon. Right?"

"Right!"

Still a brunette, at the Ritz Hotel in Melbourne.

CHAPTER 37

VIETNAM

I had been Colonel Mowery's woman for several months when one evening I asked him to remind me of a second lieutenant's name.

"You know Larry. He was that red haired young man who spoke to us in the officer's club last night."

"I don't know his name." Larry dismissed me brusquely.

"Surely you recall him. He spoke about back-packing through Turkey. We both found him interesting."

"Well I can't remember. He is only a Second Lieutenant."

The words and the vehemence in them stung me. Had I misjudged this man? I thought he cared for his men. He was the very last person I would expect of arrogance over rank. I had been touched by how kindly he treated his young driver Ron, a Spec. 4. He took a fatherly interest in him. I couldn't reconcile that with his attitude now, finding this ugly characteristic appalling. It must have registered on my face for he seemed to read my thoughts.

"I avoid my Second Lieutenants. It's easier if I don't get to know them" he explained bleakly "They die too soon."

I regretted pressing the issue and misjudging him.

"Only two weeks ago" he continued somberly "A Second Lieutenant under my command was killed. His father and I went through OCS together. When the son arrived here my friend contacted me, asking me to keep an eye on him. He sighed heavily "You will never know how it twisted my gut to tell him his only son was killed….and under my command."

Indeed, if one looked at the weekly KIA lists, they contained mostly names of the youngest and least experienced; primarily,

PFC's with a few Spec. 4's or lower ranked sergeants. Any officers were mostly Second Lieutenants.

My next trip to the 101st Airborne Divisions Headquarters camp was a sad one. Larry was preparing for his hand over ceremony. His replacement had arrived.

My band was back in Saigon and I intended joining them a few hours later for a show in Binh Hoa that evening. My attendance wasn't necessary but I tried to check as many of their shows as possible.

Meantime, I felt I must be present at Larry's Change of Command ceremony. We had shared a warm and satisfying relationship which I was sad to end.

How often had I stood under the Vietnam sun watching these various ceremonies? I stood way in the background, as inconspicuous as possible. The Screaming Eagles stood in formation before the Headquarters building. The microphone pinged and echoed as the Commanding General fare-welled Colonel Mowery and introduced the new commander. He spoke glowingly of the Brigade's achievements under Colonel Mowery's leadership. The troops lamented the departure of their trusted leader, apprehensive about this replacement they knew nothing about. Their lives were now in his hands!

I planned to get out of there quickly and head back to Saigon after a hasty farewell. I hated good byes!

The ceremony ended, Larry strode back to his transit quarters to finish packing. I discreetly met up with him in the unfamiliar surroundings. It was awkward; neither of us knowing exactly what to say. He packed toothpaste and brush into a toiletry bag. The vibes between us were flat, his thoughts already back in 'the real' world, with his family and already I felt like an intruder. It was as if we were strangers. Had we really been so close? Yet only recently, he had chosen to spend his R&R with me, not his wife.

He hugged me roughly. We did not kiss goodbye. I escaped before he evaporated from my world completely.

I waited despondently at the helipad for the ride I had arranged back to Saigon. Swirling dust continually engulfed me as helicopters landed and took off. I needed a shower. When I bumped into a GI, a cloud of dust rose chokingly from my shirt.

Larry's cool farewell hurt. Had he never cared for me or was this how he had learned to steel himself against all forms of loss? After years of a military career, he had undoubtedly lost many close friends. We are molded by the life we choose. And hadn't I chosen to lead a single life?

Lost in thought, I was barely aware of the latest chopper to land near me.

I roused myself. The chopper had dropped in so close I was barely out of prop range. Two officers leaped out and ran in my direction, yelling and waving.

"Who the hell are these? I wondered. It was not the chopper or pilots I was expecting. Why were they waving at me? The lead major looked familiar but I couldn't place him.

"Come on quick." He called, drawing nearer. The chopper had not shut down.

"Quick,what? I'm not going with you. I've got a ride."

They reached me and grabbed my arms, tugging and dragging me towards the chopper.

"What the hell is going on?" I yelled, confused "I'm not going with you." I tried to pull away. They hoisted me off the ground and ran towards the waiting chopper, holding me tight. I kicked wildly, scared I was being kidnapped. The two pilots beckoned them to hurry; huge grins splitting their faces.

"Put me doooooown!" I was really upset now. The officers ignored me and threw me roughly into the chopper. I struggled as one held me down while the other tried to strap me in. The pilots lifted off even before we were settled. They couldn't have left any quicker if they were in a hot LZ (landing zone)

Panting, fuming, confused, I screamed above the combined noise of the engine, rotors and wind "Where the hell are you taking me?"

"To Colonel Daems."

I was stunned "What? Like hell you are."

"You betcha. He'd have our heads if we turned up without you. Not to mention our commissions." They too were grinning now and at last I recognized the major as one of Colonel Daems's staff officers.

"You can't just kidnap me. This is outrageous." My adrenalin was running amok.

"Sort it out with the colonel, Miss Collins. We were given orders to fly to Colonel Mowery's Change of Command and bring you back"

"What? I'm not going willingly." I choked.

"He said you might object. But we have our orders. We don't dare return without you. You may as well settle down and enjoy the ride. We've come a long way to get you."

"Who does that man think he is? And how did he know where to find me? He will get a piece of my mind when I see him."

"Well that won't be for quite awhile. According to the TOC, right now he's out in one shit-load of trouble."

"Then there'll be an even bigger shit-load when he gets back." I snapped.

"Don't worry ma-am. He told us to take good care of you; we'll bring dinner or whatever you need……" he paused, "but you can't leave Dau Tieng."

"Shit. What is this? The Wild, Wild West?"

Back at Dau Tieng I refused to eat dinner. I was still seething when the culprit himself bustled in.

"Ahhh. There you are, you wonderful, lusty wench. Thanks for waiting." He hurried towards me, throwing his cap onto a chair and grinning.

"I didn't wait and don't you lusty, wench me, you,… you…, you …you KIDNAPPER" I yelled. "I'm going to tell General Williamson about this. Just wait and see." My outrage had no effect.

"I thought you of all people would appreciate my unique approach to a highly desirable woman." He still smiled.

"Approach? Appreciate?" I spluttered "You must be crazy."

"So I've heard. Does that turn you off?" Unruffled, he poured two drinks.

'What the hell is wrong with this man?' I wondered. 'He is a strutting, smirking, short, unbearable maniac who needs to be put in his place, fast.'

He handed me a drink. I jerked my arm back to throw it over him but he guessed my intention. Before I could finish my move he grabbed me, bent me backwards and kissed me hard. I protested but he wasn't listening. He pressed my lips so hard they parted. Our breath mingled. It felt as if I was inhaling his wild spirit. The drink fell to the floor.

He smelled of cordite. I smelled of dust. It was wild. No showers. No aftershave. No build up. No leisurely drink. No music. No romance. What the hell was happening? My mind raced. This was new. I had always been in control. God help me!

Larry was probably still on the ground in Saigon, not yet out of the country, and his best pal was already seducing me. His audacity was shocking - the colonel wasn't even concerned that some of his men knew what he had done. Hell; not only knew but were conspirators. Larry had warned me, with some admiration, I suspected, that Daems was a renegade. What an understatement.

CHAPTER 38

It took a year but finally I received that overseas contract. The destination was Kings Theatre, in Manila, the Philippines. I was hired as a stripper, but I was told I could probably move onto Hong Kong after that contract finished. Hong Kong, part of the British Empire, excluded strippers and their night-clubs hired only dancers. Hoping to get back to jazz dancing, I signed on the dotted line. The agent, a Filipino named Pacita O'Jilla had signed me up, sight unseen, on the strength of my ten by eight glossies and a recommendation from Ray.

Leaving Melbourne, I flew into Sydney to start my Qantas overseas flight. My brother Russell and Nan and Pop came to Mascot airport to farewell me. Nan, looking embarrassed, pulled me aside. She whispered a disjointed warning about not getting cornered by some yellow heathen. (Australians spoke like that in those days- always worrying about 'the yellow peril', the heathens on our doorstep.)

These were the days when most Aussies were too impoverished to leave our sunny shores so my trip was a big deal. Pop made a few caustic comments about the pitfalls of dancing for a living. Fortunately, he was unaware I was carrying it one step further. He reminded me that good jobs were still going wanting in the post office. But realizing he had already lost the battle, he sounded half-hearted.

As anxious as I was to shake the dust of Australia from my feet, I felt a small tug at my heart as I saw their concern and love.

"Your mother sends her love. She cannot take time away from the farm" Nan said.

"She never can" I replied "Tell her I love her." Indeed, after all that had happened to me, I had stopped judging Mum and saw her with compassion. Now she no longer controlled me I was free to love her very much.

The flight between Sydney and Manila was a long one but I was too excited to sleep. For awhile I sat trying to envision what King's Theatre would be like. When we were children, Mum used to take us downtown to watch children's plays in the Tivoli or ballet in some of Sydney's grand, old theatres. Their interiors were marvelous, ornate spaces, hung with heavy, red and purple velvet curtains with thick, gold tassels. The gilded wall moldings and sparkling, antique lamps in those heritage buildings were pure fairyland to a child. I sure hoped Kings Theatre would be similar and I visualized luxurious curtains rising to reveal me in all my glory.

Slipping my shoes off, I settled further back into my seat. Fortunately the Qantas flight was not full and I had three seats to myself. I pulled the headphones on and switched to the jazz channel. The first music I heard was Thelonious Monk with his bluesy, piano rendition of Blue Monk. I often used that number for the opener of my strip act; swanning about the stage while slowly removing my skin tight evening gown for Thelonious. After he faded, my next segment was a Jazz routine, set to the upbeat rhythm of Peter Gunn. Finally, I slunk into the sounds of Harlem Nocturne with a sensual routine I particularly liked (except for the no-bra part). I wondered how my act would be received in the Philippines.

The cabin air dried my throat and I reached into my hand bag for a lozenge. Spotting my new, navy blue passport, I took the precious document out for another look. My eye wandered down the inside page to my name. Legally I was still Mrs. Skewes for I had never divorced Peter. Not planning to marry again, I thought a divorce was unnecessary.

Thought association led to my would-have-been babies and I quickly tuned them out by turning the headset louder. Lo and behold the next tune through the headset was 'The Stripper'. I hated that bump and grind song and never used it – another hang-up I suppose.

"Fasten your seat belts, ladies and gentlemen. We are preparing to land in Manila …………" My excitement stepped up a notch. Despite the sleepless night, my anticipation energized me as I prepared to disembark. Would they like me? Would I like them?

This was a far cry from driving a tractor, dragging logs onto the back of a truck in the outback of Australia.

Inside the drab, single story airport the economic differences between Australia and the Philippines were instantly apparent. There was no air conditioning to ease the heat but nothing could kill my excitement.

At that time in Australia we had the 'White Australia Policy' so other than a few Aboriginals; I had seldom seen non-white people. For the first time ever, I was surrounded by them and whilst they looked smaller and poorer than we Aussies, they appeared friendly and happy. I was thrilled to be among them.

Wiping perspiration from my face, I looked anxiously around for Pacita O'Jilla, the female booking agent. In my anxiety to go overseas I had rashly signed the contract with little background checking. Now I wondered what sort of a person she was.

Simply dressed Filipino men bustled around me. The better dressed ones wore embroidered shirts which I later learned were made of pineapple fiber and called barong tugalogs. These were attractive and practical in the heat for they hung loose and were not tucked into pants. Some of the wealthier looking ladies wore beautifully embroidered dresses with large, gathered sleeves and I was pleased to see that my height of five feet three and a half inches was not short in the Philippines.

The crowd began to thin. Was there no-one to meet me? In the distance, three people waved as they bustled forward. Leading them was a very short, plump, poorly dressed woman with straight, cropped, black hair. When she raised her arm, waving, I noticed a dark patch of sweat under the arm of her gray blouse. I squelched a quick sense of let down. Her two male companions looked like cheerful, slender teenagers.

"Juanita" she used my new stage name. I had selected it because my hair was black at that time.

"Juanita welcome to the Philippine Islands." Upon reaching me she leaned forward, extending a leis of sweet smelling, white flowers which she attempted to hang around my neck. I lowered my head.

"These are Sampagita, the flower of the Philippines."

The perfume was heady and intoxicating, befitting the moment. Even though this woman deflated my expectations, my spirit remained buoyant as she introduced me to her youthful employees.

Outside, the sunshine, exotic foliage, tropical perfume and waving palms were all that I hoped for. Pacita placed two fingers in her mouth and whistled shrilly for a cab.

"You must be tired "she said "We will take you to your hotel and you can rest until 3 p.m. We'll pick you up for a rehearsal at the Kings Theatre then. Tomorrow you start doing a daily matinee plus two evening shows."

I withheld my questions for later, not wishing to sound ignorant.

The taxi drove us along Roxas Boulevard around the Manila Bay. Pacita pointed out a big hotel on our left. "That's the grand old Manila Hotel where General Douglas Mac Arthur lived until the Japanese came."

Everywhere I looked, the colorful scene enthralled me. The boulevard was lined with lush, flowering trees and vendors dotted the pathways pushing small barrows of various wares. Wherever I looked I saw smiles and even an occasional wave. Poverty hasn't dampened their spirits, I noted.

The heavy traffic was full of great contrasts. I was surprised by the number of large chauffeur driven, American cars. Brightly painted jeeps were predominant and Pacita said these mini-busses were called Jeepneys. Passengers overflowed, clinging from the back step by a toe. A sea of St. Christopher medals and crucifixes swung alongside Sampaguita leis, from rear vision mirrors.

Crowded old buses displaying colorful, unfamiliar names spewed smoke over the many horses pulling flower decorated buggies.

When a traffic jam slowed us down, we were immediately beset by a handful of vendors. One grinning little fellow shoved his skinny arm through the open window, beseeching me to take what looked like a boiled egg. "What is it?" I asked Pacita.

"Baloot." She replied "A boiled chicken embryo. Don't buy it. You could choke on a bone and it gives you bad breath."

"A foul breath you mean" I said, attempting humor and shrinking from the proffered egg as my joke fell flat.

A small, ragged girl jostled the rotten egg vendor aside, shoving a pack of cigarettes through the window.

"I don't smoke." I declined.

"Go away." Pacita shooed her off.

"American cigarettes! We call them 'Blue Seal'. They are smuggled into the country, avoiding taxes. The smugglers get rich and buy fast boats to outrun the customs police." She waved her arm indicating the expanse of water to our left. "Sometimes we hear their shoot-outs at night."

I couldn't visualize anyone in Australia engaging in shoot-outs. Even the police carried no fire-arms in those days.

The traffic began to move and we pulled forward, heading away from the bay towards the down town central district. The excitement of it all overwhelmed me.

The Mabuhay Hotel was far from five stars. Pacita said the word meant 'welcome.' It was clean and acceptable and located in a very busy part of downtown Manila. It smelled of new timber and antiseptic cleaners. A male receptionist wearing a yellow Barong Tugalog shirt greeted us. I saw no other foreigners and assumed this hotel was not high on the tourists' list. They received me like a minor celebrity.

A miniscule elevator took us up three floors. My room was sterile and the veneered furniture looked new. A basic bathroom completed the picture.

The white jacketed room boy showed me an electric wall button to be used for calling room service. I peered about, flushed the toilet and checked that everything was satisfactory then Pacita and her minions took their leave. Pacita was not exactly what I had expected but I reserved my judgment, pleased that she and her boys spoke understandable English.

Alone again, I looked out the window at the narrow, bustling street behind the hotel. A man in dirty, tattered clothes stood in the middle of the busy road, unmercifully whipping his skeletal horse. The poor creature staggered up from the road and strained to pull an unbelievably overloaded cart. Huge, fleshy sores covered its back. My euphoria vanished and I stifled an urge to run down and grab the whip from the man and whip him. He spoiled my arrival.

If the hotel was acceptable, King's Theatre definitely was not. My expectations of a rather grand old theatre were shattered that afternoon. The place would make Abe Saffron's sleazy strip dives in the back alleys of Kings Cross look plush. I had once shuddered and vowed I would never work in a place like that. King's Theatre was worse.

It sat in a narrow, pot-holed alley in what was obviously a bad part of town. No chauffeur driven cars sped by here. There were plenty of old horse drawn carts and rats, as big as a cats, in the gutter. An overpowering odor of stale urine made my stomach heave as I followed Pacita and the boys across the pavement to the theatre. The glass in the front window was cracked and dirty. Gingerly I entered the dark interior. It smelled musty and I imagined I heard scurrying cockroaches.

The theatre, in between shows, was empty except for the musicians. They were waiting to rehearse. There were at least a dozen of them. A few spoke English. They looked at my music, began rehearsing and amazed me. They were great!

After rehearsing, we checked out the dressing room. It stunk of cigarettes, face powder and methylated spirits. Empty tin cans, overflowing with un-emptied cigarette butts were everywhere. I made an instant vow never to leave my costumes overnight.

I was packing my sheet music away when an attractive, blonde girl of Amazonian proportions strode towards me, her hand extended. I had seen her black and white photo in the foyer. She smiled warmly and I liked her immediately.

"You must be our new girl." She said with a strong accent. "Hi. I'm Julie, a kiwi."

"I'm Juanita but call me June." I answered, happy to find a touch of home.

She waved her hand around, "What do you think of this shit-hole?...Pretty bad, huh?"

Pacita grabbed my arm. "We've gotta get going."

"Just a minute Pacita." I turned to Julie "It is quite a let down. Are all the places in Asia like this?"

"Hell no! There are some good clubs along Roxas Boulevard and if you get to Japan you will find some really fab joints. Better than in Australia."

"I'm only booked here." I said, wondering how one got to Japan.

"If you're any good, the agents will find you."

"Then why does anyone work in this sleaze joint?"

"Money! They pay big money here for white strippers. There are not too many countries in Asia where we can work. Pretty much it is here and Japan. Strippers are banned in Hong Kong where the English are impossible. The police audition every show and even carry a tape measure to check the costumes are modest enough."

"Well that wouldn't bother me" I replied "I prefer working as a straight dancer – even if the money is a bit less."

"Well lucky you." She grinned.

"Come on." Pacita was frowning now and insistent.

"I'll catch you tomorrow." I said, following Pacita outside.

That evening Pacita took us to a bayside restaurant for dinner. The waiter hung yet one more Sampaguita leis around my neck. We sat outside beneath a beautiful, spreading Banyan tree strung with twinkling lights. A light breeze blew in from the bay. This is more like it, I thought.

Pacita ordered the house specialty, honeyed chicken. The popular place was crowded. The food was delicious. Pacita obviously thought so too, for she tore strips of chicken from the bone with great relish, ignoring her knife and fork. I pleaded a genuine fatigue as soon as I ate and returned to my hotel room.

CHAPTER 39

VIETNAM

Once again I was the colonel's woman only this time it was a different colonel. And although they had much in common, there were many differences. Colonel Mowery had not worried about the little luxuries of life but they were very important to Len Daems. He was pedantic about his dinner menu, personally selecting the food to be prepared for him and his staff officers; within the limitations of available ingredients. He had chosen the brigade's best mess sergeant as his personal chef and only the finest wine was served at his table.

The mess hall cooks hated to see him coming for he tasted everything while repeating, 'an army travels on its stomach' make sure you feed my troops well.'

After I recovered from my 'kidnapping' he brought in a tray of food.

"From now on, when you are not on the road with your band, you are staying here," he ordered.

"This camp is close to the 25th's Head quarters" I replied "Surely you can't keep me here in the villa without General Williams hearing about it."

"No I can't. I share the villa with my staff officers," he replied "But don't worry. I'll take care of it."

Before I left for Saigon the next day to get my clothes, he asked me to accompany him on a walk. He pointed to where a Chinook helicopter was descending with a heavy sling load. It hovered over an open patch of ground in the centre of the camp. As it descended lower, I could make out a forty foot trailer dangling in the net. It was identical to those used for living quarters for Cu Chi's headquarters staff officers.

Shielding my eyes from the dust, I watched a group of GI's maneuver the trailer into position.

"Why did you bring me to see this?" I asked, realizing I would now have to shampoo my hair again.

"Welcome to your new home." Len grinned smugly.

"Good God. How did you manage this? You must have told a few beauties."

"What if a senator or some other VIP dropped in? We had nowhere to put them up" he said with heavy sarcasm. "Give me two days. Return from Saigon with your things then. It will be air conditioned and safe for you to move in."

"Two days?"

"See the TOC over there?" he pointed.

"Sure." The TOC was barely visible, sandbags entirely covering this highly important nerve center.

"What of it?"

"I've ordered my men to protect your trailer like that. Charlie's mortars are becoming more accurate. I've gotta keep you safe. Tomorrow we'll build the timber framework. By the time you return, it will be covered with sandbags."

I was speechless.

"I'm sure you'll find the furnishings comfortable and tomorrow the air conditioner will be working. Any complaints?"

"Hell no!"

As I've said, the Michelin rubber plantation was a pretty unique campsite in Vietnam. If there were any others like it, I never found them.

While flying all over the country booking shows in the heat during daytime, I was always anxious to get back to Dau Tieng and that swimming pool.

Most nights the routine was the same; sitting around the villa's verandah playing liars dice while watching the sunset and bursting mortars. I was the only woman on base, unlike larger bases where there were nurses and Donut Dollies.

Some weeks after settling in I was having a nightcap with Len.

"One good turn deserves another." I said. "You gave me safe quarters; I'm about to arrange some shows for your men when they're back from the field next week."

"Well, woman, that's a nice thought but it will have to wait."

"Why? You said they could use a break."

"Too right! However, our choppers have taken too many hits lately and too many are in maintenance for repairs. We couldn't get your entertainers out here."

"I can handle the transport."

"How? This is not Cu Chi," he scoffed. "There's very little coming our way and road travel is out of the question."

"What would you say if I told you I could bring them in on a C123?"

"I'd say you're crazy woman. The big Hercs have never landed here. Our runway isn't long enough to handle them. I repeat, this is not Cu Chi."

"Well if there's any way to lengthen your runway, I can assure you my band will be here and they will play all day so every man here can see a show. The commanding General of Tan Son Nhut air base has promised me the plane."

Len's expression changed instantly, his eyes narrowing.

"The Commanding General? How did you manage that?" It sounded like an accusation.

"Surely you're not jealous?" I needled.

"Of course not. I'm just curious."

"You remember my band played at the Airmen's club in Saigon last week?"

"Yeah. I missed you."

"The General invited me to have dinner in his trailer."

"Ahha. You can't trust those fly boys."

"Don't worry." I stirred. "We had a lovely dinner. The Air Force sure treats their people well. An excellent chef does nothing but prepare the general's meals. And he even has a personal butler to take care of his trailer and uniforms. You should have seen it. Soft lights, - vases of flowers."

"Yeah. Yeah. Everyone knows those air jockeys are spoiled." He frowned "I met him once. Tall and good looking, quite the ladies man! How long did you stay?"

"Now, now! But all that candlelight and soft music was romantic. I couldn't very well eat and run….Besides, he's a smooth dancer." I let my words hang.

"Hrrmph!" Len made an angry sound, "I suppose I have no right to ask. I'm sorry for questioning you, he was trying to keep his cool and I enjoyed letting him stew for awhile.

"That was it." I finally laughed "I've got as much as I can handle with you. He was more of a gentleman than you. You crazy old fox."

I detected a relieved sigh.

"I returned to my apartment with my chastity intact and the promise of an empty C123. I have to call and tell him where and when I want it." I gave a sly look, "Of course, I left him hanging with the illusion of better luck next time."

Len shook his head and smirked broadly.

"Goddamn! You're a bad woman. And now if you will excuse me, I've got to make a phone call."

"Who are you calling?"

"My engineers, of course! They need to start lengthening the runway first thing tomorrow morning." He left the room chuckling.

The arrival of my show on a C123 was quite an event. The engineers had worked long hours on the runway, excited to be getting rewarded with a show. When the plane was due, troops lined the runway on either side. The first Hercules to ever land at Dau Tieng was a big event. Even lengthened, the runway was barely the required minimum length and would have been insufficient if the plane was loaded.

At first sight of the plane, the troops cheered. It descended over the far end of the runway, hit the ground and bounced along, breaking hard. The troops held their collective breath until, with only inches to spare; those skilled pilots brought it to a halt. A roar of appreciation went up amid, applauding and whistling. I'm sure, in the annals of the Vietnam War, it was the only time that an empty Hercules was commandeered to carry just one small group of entertainers.

Returning to camp after a booking trip to Cam Ranh Bay, I took a shower and picked up my Hemingway book. Len was often late getting back from the war.

It was totally dark when I heard choppers landing. I put the book down and headed for the villa and a late dinner.

Mortar attacks were becoming more frequent and I was grateful for the sandbags around my trailer. The previous night they had closed in around the villa whilst we were having our evening cocktail. I watched the troops running for the bunkers before asking "Shouldn't we go to the bunkers?" I hated the prospect. They were dark, dank, mosquito filled places and I was claustrophobic.

"No!" Len replied "The French built this place as solid as a fortress. Maybe we should just go inside."

I had noted during an earlier mortar attack that while the men were running helter-skelter, Len walked calmly to the TOC as if he was out for an evening stroll. I surmised he was a fatalist and he seemed indestructible.

My hair was freshly shampooed and, unbraided. I wore a pretty pink chiffon dress and sandals.

I was half way to the villa when mortar rounds began dropping behind me. "Damn" I thought, nervously, here I am out in the open. Mentally, I measured the distance to the nearest bunker, the villa or my trailer. They were about the same.

I decided to try to make it to the safety of the villa with its rock like walls. The next blast shook the ground. I quelled my fear and hastened my step, forcing myself not to run. I was the colonel's woman; I would not show fear.

Suddenly the mortars were all around me, polluting the air with flying missiles and filling my nostrils with acrid smoke. It was too late to run. I remembered someone telling me that shrapnel from mortars usually cut through you at waist height. I threw myself to the ground and covered my head with my arms. My nostrils burned, my throat stung and hot pebbles fell upon my back. My feet had a mind of their own, scratching the earth, like a rabbit digging in. Every muscle in my body tensed as I waited to feel hot shrapnel tear into my back.

Why hadn't I run sooner? What foolish pride! I gasped for clean air and my eyes watered as the pungent fumes seeped into my throat. My heart beat like a frightened bird and I was coughing into the dirt. At last it stopped but still I lay there as if paralyzed. Belatedly the siren started up and above it I heard Len's voice. I climbed shakily to my feet, dirt and small pieces of debris falling from me. Len was running. He grabbed my arm and spun me around, searching. "Are you alright, darling?" His voice was husky. He had never called me darling before. That was too much admission.

"Yeah. I'm fine." I said, trying hard to sound normal "I must look a sight."

"What a Goddamn dumb thing to worry about." He sounded almost angry. "Come on. You can clean up over at the villa. You need a brandy." I didn't disagree with that.

Later that night, back in my own bed (Len never stayed at my trailer and rarely came there) I thought about our relationship. I was sure he cared deeply about me but we never voiced such things. He was the first serious threat to my vow never to live with any man again. I wondered what his wife was like and I couldn't imagine him in civilian life. I knew him only as a larger than life warrior and I didn't want it to end. Every day held an undercurrent of excitement as I anticipated his return and I thrived on every second we spent together. At last I had met my match. I loved it! I hated it! Love hurts!

Everything today is so different from the time I'm covering. Today we have women going through infantry combat training and fighter pilot training. We have women CEO's of major companies. England has had a female Head of State and the USA almost did.

No longer are little girls given only dolls to play with and influenced to become a mother, wife and homemaker. No longer is a woman's success measured by the whiteness of her sheets or the dust free environment of her home.

Television shows like Sex and The City would certainly not have been tolerated in the 60's. Women now boast openly of sexual conquests which previously were a shameful secret capable of destroying them.

Because of the times I lived in and the lifestyle I chose, I rejected 'normal society.' I did not need its approval, finding it boring and hypocritical. Maybe that is why I stayed so long at the war.

Years later when I saw the movie, 'Patton' I had goose-bumps. George C. Scott was brilliant and I felt sure I knew Patton. He certainly reminded me of Len, even in his stature and mannerisms. In one scene he controversially slaps a cowardly soldier across the face with his gloves, I could relate. Courageous men find it difficult to tolerate or understand a coward.

I dislike 'judgment' and tried to make allowances for weakness but I too, found cowardice distasteful. I'd known of one who shot himself through the foot for an early 'out'. Many times the weak cause the death of the stronger ones.

After watching Patton I left the theatre on a high. Nostalgia brought that old excitement rushing back for a moment. It also brought a wave of sadness.

Lifting the morale of some of the men of the 725th Maintenance Battalion, 25th Division.

Outside the TOC at Dau Tieng

My trailer at Dau Tieng, ready to be sand-bagged.

CHAPTER 40

MANILA

My nerves were on edge as I accompanied Pacita to the Kings Theatre. We arrived early but gradually the other performers straggled in and introductions were made. The banter between them was so crude that I felt like a nun in a whorehouse.

Monique, a beautifully svelte, dazzlingly blonde New Yorker, had the filthiest mouth I had ever heard. She seemed delighted whenever I looked shocked so I tried to remain expressionless no matter what.

Another American, Karen, was tall, loose-fleshed, and grubby. Bruises sprinkled her arms and legs and her bleached hair resembled straw. Purple hickeys dotted her neck and a half empty bottle of bourbon sat on the dressing table in front of her. She was the roughest looking female I had ever seen and I could not believe anyone would pay to see her perform anywhere. She appeared drugged and ignored us as she went about putting on her blue, fringe- beaded costume which was missing several strings of beads. A cigarette dangled from her mouth and the ash accumulated at the end before finally falling onto her chest. I recoiled from the fumes of methylated spirits and cheap whisky when she shoved past. Julie whispered that Karen did a baton twirling act which explained the metho smell.

Both Julie and Monique looked tall and glamorous after donning their expensive gowns. Julie, whom everyone called Big Julie, adopted a protective attitude towards me; maybe because I was small and looked lost. Or maybe she was just helping a green horn from Down Under.

Mike Walker, another American, was a good looking, smooth talking singer wearing a nicely tailored Hong Kong suit.

The last ones to arrive were two other Aussie's. Art, a wrinkled, grey haired, rough, tough character, billed himself as Ned Kelly and did a wild-west act with whip, rifle, and knives. I've forgotten the name of his female assistant. Art was abruptly outspoken and would have been at home swatting flies under a gum tree out in the bush. Indeed, he referred to himself as The Bastard from the Bush. He must have been at least sixty years old. His partner looked eighteen and rarely spoke, probably as much out of her depth as I.

A couple of short Filipino men did a slapstick comedy routine in Tugalog, the local language. They spoke English and were friendly.

The co-ed dressing room was screened off at one end for anyone inhibited by modesty. Few were. I disappeared there to change into my costume, a bright red, tight fitting, strapless, fringed number. Next to Julie's and Monique's gowns it looked cheap.

Approaching show time, I peeped through the curtains and saw the room silently filling with poorly dressed, solemn men. I shuddered, imagining busy hands in the dark and quickly thrust the unpleasant picture from my mind.

Mike doubled as emcee. He announced 'Showtime" and I stood in the wings, watching my competition perform. Julie was the opening act and just the look of her tall, statuesque figure as she twirled onto the stage brought thunderous applause. She was the Ice Queen; moving gracefully, her pale blue gown glistening under the lights. An accomplished stripper with class!

I had not mastered the art of stripping but I could out-dance most strippers and my ample breasts usually compensated for any lack of bump and grind.

Mike returned and gave a good rendition of 'Beyond the Sea' a Bobby Darrin number. He was a polished performer but his best efforts barely raised a hand. The Filipinos followed and although I didn't know what they were saying, the audience responded with salacious laughter. I was grateful they had warmed up the audience for I was on next.

There was anticipation when the regulars awaited a fresh act.

Mike introduced me with great fan fare and suddenly I was out there, pinpointed in that dark space by red spotlights. I could not see the audience for which I was thankful. Once my dress was off, I danced with freedom, feeling the music and forgetting the dingy surroundings. The other performers, I knew, would be crowded into the wings, watching to see how the new girl did. I think I went over Ok. There was certainly loud applause when I removed my bra. I heard Monique offstage yelling "Good for you, Tits Aplenty!"

Ned Kelly followed. His partner was dressed in a blue and white, fringed cowboy outfit and white, straw, Stetson-style hat. He whipped cigarettes from her mouth, barely missing her lips. I wondered how she could remain so still while he threw knives at the board behind her, tracing her silhouette like police chalk lines around a dead body. Art spoke to the audience throughout his show but aware they spoke no English, he said anything at all. In one trick he shot the chalks from between his assistant's fingers with the commentary "And now Gentlemen, I shall attempt to shoot the young ladies fingers from between the chalks."

Next, Karen the baton twirler stumbled out half drunk. Her tattered costume did not look so bad under the lights but her body should have stayed under wraps. Streaks of charcoal, presumably not washed off from her previous day's performance were visible.

The audience remained stony silent. Somehow she managed not to drop the batons. Then it was time for the grand finale with flaming batons. She bent, and dropped a match in the tin of Metho. The tin must have been overfilled. It shot into the air with a fiery explosion. I watched wide eyed, as sparks shot out in all directions. Flaming droplets of metho hit the floorboards creating a myriad of small fires. It was a finale hard to beat! .Someone screamed "Fire, Fire!" and the two comedians, musicians and half a dozen stage hands jumped into action with extinguishers. They frantically sprayed foam everywhere and thankfully, the heavy curtains did not catch alight.

As smoke filled the theatre, panicked customers clambered over chairs, trampling each other as they rushed for the exits. The manager ran on stage, calling the fleeing audience back in an attempt to salvage the show. The fire was extinguished, and order was restored in the smoke filled theatre but the noisy chorus of coughing was disconcerting.

After the unscheduled intermission Mike yelled to the orchestra that he was switching his next number to that old favorite, "Smoke Gets In Your Eyes." Backstage, our eyes streaming, we doubled over in laughter and I realized that even if it was a sleazy joint, at least I would not be bored.

Monique was the last act of the day and the star. She was raunch sublime and the customers loved her. The glint in her eye and the smirk on her face indicated she was enjoying herself. Gyrating to the strains of "Night Train," I feared the enthusiasm of her bump and grind could cause injury. Just before exiting the stage she mooned the crowd and yelled "Kiss My Arse". I was pleased I did not have to follow her act.

CHAPTER 41

VIETNAM

We hear these glorified tales of long ago when brave commanders led their foot soldiers or cavalry into battle at the forefront of the charge. A poor idea! If the leader is killed, who directs the men? In Vietnam the commanders directed the battle from above—looking down and giving orders from their C and C (command and Control) helicopters. Of course the enemy knew who was in those bucking helicopters and they did their utmost to bring them down. A commander killed would bring great glory.

I had fallen asleep beside Len and not yet returned to my own trailer as I customarily did before dawn. Two phones sat beside his bed; a black one and a red one. If the red one rang 'LOOK OUT' that meant trouble. It must have been about three in the morning when the red phone rang. In an instant he was up, alert. In a flash he finished the call then contacted his pilots to have the chopper on the pad warming up. I was wide awake, the tension infectious "What's happening?" I asked, sitting up as he jumped into his uniform.

"One of my fire bases is being over run. I've got to get out there ASAP."

"Can I come?" my heart pounded. It was a stupid request but I wanted to share his life in every way. He laced up the last boot.

"Only if you can walk out this door in sixty seconds!"

I was running at his heels, hair uncombed, shirt open, as we leaped into his command chopper. Lieutenant Colonel Hunt was already there. His eyebrows flew inordinately high when I jumped in but he recovered quickly, turned to Len and handed him a map. Len jerked earphones on and before we were even strapped in, the pilots headed, nose down, off into the night.

The door gunners peered keenly into the darkness while the sense of urgency in the dark cabin was tangible. Colonel Daems barked into the radio while Hunt studied the map by the light of a flashlight. The only other light came from the small yellow bulbs inside the choppers control panel. I was merely a forgotten bystander yet my adrenalin raced at super-car speed. The atmosphere felt electrified but not fearful. There seemed to be a razor sharpness to all thought and speech.

We could see the battle ground before reaching it. The sky was lit up bright as day from flares. Another C and C was already twirling in the sky ahead of us.

"Looks like Blaster 6 beat us here." Colonel Daems said to his XO. I knew that Blaster 6 was the radio call sign for Colonel Sumner the Division Artillery Commander. We whirled into the melee and immediately our brilliant pilots started the chopper twisting like a mechanical bull. The other C and C was doing the same crazy gyrations. It was necessary to fly low enough for the commanders to see the battle through their binoculars yet somehow avoid the enemy fire. The pilots' skills left me speechless.

I too wore a headset, privy to the many yelled commands and profanities flying back and forth. We jerked through the air sideways and every which ways except up, giving us a view of the battle in snatches. I watched in brilliant light as the little black figures ran scrambling in all directions. To my inexperienced eye, it was difficult, at first, to distinguish just who were our men and who were the enemy.

Streams of red tracers flew by on all sides as the enemy tried hard to hit our bouncing target. Small, phosphorous, white, parachute flares filled the sky in such numbers that some almost drifted into our chopper as we tilted sharply to one side. Momentarily, we were bouncing close, and almost parallel with Blaster 6's chopper. As the artillery commander looked up and saw me in the bright light, his head jerked in a double take, shock clearly written all over his face.

Only then did I realize the full enormity of what my renegade lover had done. It could certainly destroy his whole career if there were any loose lips among his men or if Blaster 6 chose to add my presence to his report. I knew Blaster 6 well and he was a very 'by the book' kind of fellow, just the opposite of Len. I prayed he would say nothing.

Belatedly I considered the possibility of getting shot down. The enemy was trying desperately to do just that. What a scandal it would cause! Not only Colonel Daems career would be ruined but his marriage as well…….. if we survived.

I don't know how long we were out there that night. We saw the enemy withdraw, dragging off their dead and we headed home, passing our Dust Off's on their way out to pick up our wounded. It felt like we'd been gone an eternity but we were back by daylight.

When it was over I felt euphoric. Now I understood the enlisted men I had watched come in after a battle. They were bodily exhausted but overdosed on adrenalin. I had seen them stamp about their tents like caged lions, talking loud and excited. I'd heard them turn the music on but switch back and forth, settling on nothing. They dragged out the beer---or in some cases, the drugs. Once more, they had survived! Eventually booze (or drugs) settled them down.

It was different when they lost their mates. Dark and somber, they hid grief behind silence or, in some cases, cussing and raging anger. Enlisted men have always been the sacrificial lambs. The officers and NCO's, career, long term soldiers had learned the stiff upper lip. Unfettered emotions only hampered clear thought. Responsibility for the lambs is a daunting role.

A week after my night battle, I was paying off sergeant Higdon in the Long Binh office. He was wearing his ostentatious jewelry, a Cuban cigar smoldered in the ash tray. The strains of Merle Haggard blasted from the Teac tape deck as a hooch maid squatted on her haunches, polishing his boots.

Suddenly I shuddered, a vivid picture of other army boots springing to mind. Those other boots were covered in mud. They poked out from beneath the army blanket covering a gurney. Two young, orderlies at the 3rd Field Hospital in Saigon were laughing and joking as they pushed the gurney through a wide hallway, on their way to the morgue. Angrily, I stopped them.

"Can't you show some respect?" I snarled "This young man has lost his life and you are making jokes. How heartless are you?"

They looked startled and a bit guilty then one spoke up "I'm sorry ma'am. We don't mean to be disrespectful but we do this every day. We can't let it get to us or we couldn't do our job."

"Oh!" was all I could say. But those muddy boots told the story. His last hours had been spent slogging through the jungle mud, undoubtedly filled with fear and a desperate desire to live. I hoped his mother would never see those boots.

Remembering that incident, I felt like spitting on the sergeant's shiny boots but I controlled myself and handed over the greenbacks.

In recent months I had worked occasionally with the crooked club sergeants but my anger still simmered on the back burner.

"You must do something." I reminded myself, "How much longer will this shit go on?" I had spoken to so many officers about the kickbacks; even to Major General Williams, commander of the 25th, but like the rest, he was too pre-occupied with the 'more important' aspects of the war. Rear echelon capers took a back seat. What could a mere civilian like me do?

Off to work by helicopter.

Headquarters of the 3rd Brigade, 25th Infantry Division, Dau Tieng.

Relaxing at the Officer's Swimming Pool in Dau Tieng

CHAPTER 42

MANILA

The grand title of Ching Imperial belonged to the number one booking agent in the Philippines. Ching was large, a half Chinese Filipino with a commanding presence and an American college education. He was sitting in his office on Roxas Boulevard talking baseball with Mike Walker when the phone rang.

"Just a moment while I answer this," He said, lifting the receiver. Mike continued perusing the sports page of the San Francisco Chronicle, checking out the Anaheim Angel's stats.

Ching cursed and slammed the phone down.

"Bad news?" Mike asked his old friend.

"Business" Ching growled "I had a French adagio act booked into the Bayside club next week and they just cancelled. Visa problems! God knows how I can replace them at this short notice."

Mike folded the newspaper and placed it back on Ching's desk. After a short silence he said "So you need a replacement in a hurry?"

"Yeah. I wonder if there's anyone available in Hong Kong. I'd better call my buddy, Benny Tung and see if he has any foreign acts in between engagements." Hong Kong was the favorite gathering ground for the foreigners working the Asian Entertainment Circuit. It was perfect for renewing wardrobe while taking a breather.

"Maybe I can help" Mike replied "There's this Australian dancer working at Kings Theatre. I think her contract is up for renewal."

"King's Theatre?" Ching scoffed. "They ought to burn that goddamned joint down. Old A.P would have a fit if I offered him an act from that rat's nest." He stopped himself and coughed "Sorry Mike. I forgot for a moment that you're doing a gig there….. I can't understand why."

"Their money's as good as anyone's and it's been good for a few laughs before heading home." He paused and lit a cigarette.

Ching smirked, eyeing Mike's Zippo lighter with the picture of the nude girl.

"Giving them free advertising, are you?" He said, pushing an ashtray towards Mike.

"There's nothing wrong with the female form my friend. But seriously Ching, you ought to consider this dancer. She doesn't belong in Kings. She has talent and I know she's unhappy there."

Ching thought for a moment before replying. "Well I suppose there's no harm in taking a look at her. Can you bring her around tomorrow? What's her name?"

"She goes by Juanita but her name's June Collins."

"Well if she's any good we'll have to drop the Juanita and she will need different costumes. Maybe a change of hair color. Can't have it known she worked at King's. Anyway, how did she get there?"

"She was signed up by some old lesbian named Pacita O'Jilla."

"Oh, she's small fry. If this girl's any good I'll buy her contract out. It might just get me out of a bind. As you know, the Bayside is Manila's best club and old A.P. is pretty particular about who he puts in there. Fortunately the clientele is from a different planet than King's so they're not likely to recognize her. Just don't tell A.P."

"I've never met the man. Well, do you think you can close up shop for a bit and join me over at the Manila Hotel." He looked at his watch. "It's about time for lunch?"

One week later, after dying my hair blonde and getting fabulous new costumes made, I started at The Bayside. The club was located on the boulevard across from the Manila Bay. Exotic gardens of bird nest ferns and Plumeria led to the ornate, double door entrance. Passing beneath the canvas awning, I stopped short after reading the prominent sign. In bold letters it said;

PLEASE DEPOSIT ALL FIRE ARMS AT THE DESK BEFORE ENTERING THE CLUB.

I wondered was the place a hang out for those smugglers Pacita had warned me about. But by now I knew that Filipino's carried guns as routinely as Aussie's carried bottle openers.

The interior of the club smelled sweet, devoid of stale booze or tobacco stench. The expansive room was air conditioned and in the dim light, I could see tables covered with clean, starched cloths. Each held a soft lamp and a small vase of Hibiscus blossoms.

The Philippines had countless talented musicians but the Bayside was reputed to have the best band of all. There were at least thirty members, the most that ever backed me. They looked well groomed in attractive green blazers and white trousers. From Kings Theatre to this was sheer happiness. No longer was I Juanita, the brunette stripper. I was June Collins, a blonde, Jazz dancer.

The clubs in Asia employed dance hostesses. The Philippines was no exception. These pretty, showily dressed young girls kept their distance from me, probably considering me a rival.

The club was always so popular that the dance floor could barely contain the energetic bodies. People of all ages were loose hipped and full of rhythm, unlike my countrymen in Australia who would rather drink beer than dance. The Latino rhythm was funky and hot.

My two gay seamstresses were geniuses. They made fantastic, Vegas style, beaded costumes which would have cost a fortune back in Australia. Most of my Kings Theatre money went on new gowns for on and off stage.

I had new music written for my routines, covering all bases from arrangements for small quartets right through to the large group at the Bayside. This totaled hundreds of sheets. Trumpet players had ruined my earlier music when their saliva blew out onto the sheets, bleeding the ink. This time I laminated the new arrangements, eliminating one problem but creating another of weight.

At last I had flexibility, world class costumes and arrangements for all occasions; even if it was all so heavy it could barely be moved.

Life was wonderful. I loved the climate and the friendly people. I was earning good money, working short hours and dancing from sundown to dawn with no shortage of dance partners.

At last I could write a letter home with photographs of me performing and not resort to lies or subterfuge.

During my third night the club manager asked me to come in the following afternoon and meet A.P. Reyes, the owner.

"Why can't he see me at night, in the club?" I asked.

"He is not a young man and he seldom goes out at night. Anyway, he comes in here for an hour or two each afternoon to dance. He loves to cha-cha."

"Alone in an empty club?"

"Not at all. He pays the band and a handful of the hostesses to come in at three o'clock each day for his enjoyment. You will join them won't you?"

"Certainly! I'd like to meet my boss."

"Yes he is a good boss." The rumor was that A.P. was wealthy enough to buy the Taj Mahal. The Bayside was only one of his many toys. He was a family man with many children and grandchildren. Besides dancing, his pleasures were horse racing and he owned a stable full of fine horses. I was curious to meet him.

The following day I arrived at The Bayside, casually dressed in white linen slacks and a blue button down blouse. Entering the dim, empty club I spotted half a dozen dance hostesses sitting around, glittering in their evening attire. The band, at half strength, was playing a rhumba and A.P was on the dance floor, swinging it with one of the Filipinas. He was a portly man of medium height in a lightweight cream suit. I marveled at the flexibility of his overly fleshed hips. His smile was perpetual and I guessed his age at late sixties. He reminded me of a happy Buddha with hair.

The band took a break and he wandered back to the table. He mopped his brow with a large white handkerchief then noticed me standing there, unsure of myself.

"Come, come" he called "You must be my new floorshow. Take a seat."

A hostess reluctantly relinquished her chair.

"What's your name again?" he asked.

"June. June Collins" I found my tongue "And it's my pleasure to meet the man I've heard so much about."

We quickly established an easy rapport.

"Are you going to dance for me then?"

"Of course! I'll change and be ready in five minutes."

"That's the girl! And after you finish, please join me back here."

I remembered Ching telling me that A.P. owned a second Bayside Club on Nathan Road in Kowloon. I hoped to move on to Hong Kong after Manila. My private performance for A.P. would be as good as if there was a packed house. The band struck up the first strains of Peter Gunn and I shot out onto the floor, glittering from head to toe in a black, sequined body stocking, only my white face and heavily made-up eyes visible.

After changing, I returned to the table where a tall glass of coke was already waiting for me.

"Thank you for the drink Mr. Reyes."

"None of this Mr. Reyes, please! If you are going to be a member of my family you must call me A.P."

One of the hostesses left her seat and stood behind him, gently massaging his shoulders. He bestowed his Buddha smile on her before turning back to me.

"My manager tells me you are from Australia, June. I know your country well. I keep a string of race horses down there and I often go down to watch them race."

He lifted his coke and my eyes widened. The ring on his finger held a marble sized diamond.

We chatted for awhile and I watched him dance with another pretty Filipina hostess. Then it was my turn "Would you like to dance this cha-cha with me?"

"I was hoping you would ask" I flirted a little.

The band played a perky arrangement of "Its Cherry Pink and Apple Blossom Time". We finished our dance and I sensed he was preparing to leave. Thanking him, I turned to go.

"I like you" he said "We will be friends. Where are you staying?"

"Downtown at a small hotel called the Mabuhay."

"And how are you traveling about?"

"By taxi."

"Well, not anymore. From now on you will have the use of one of my cars. What make is your favorite?"

I didn't have a favorite and I didn't drive. "I don't know." I replied.

"Well never mind. I will send you a different one for each day of the week. Tomorrow I will send a Rolls Royce Silver Cloud. Your driver is named Alfredo. He will be waiting for you in front of the hotel from 11 a.m. each day."

This was most unexpected. He smiled, pleased by my stunned expression. A fleet of luxury cars at my disposal was something I had never imagined. It may be common place for celebrities but I was no celebrity.

Rudy Aguilar was my duo dance partner in the Philippines for many months.

CHAPTER 43

VIETNAM

Colonel Daem's Change of Command Ceremony was a black day in my life and I did not attend. No tears were shed but that night, for the first time, I thought about leaving Vietnam.

Len had gone back to that other world, making him a stranger to me as surely as if he had died. The future loomed flat and empty. I couldn't bear to think that I now meant nothing to him; just a brief memory overshadowed by those of battle. Yet I was certain that our relationship must have been as unique to him as it was to me. His memories of me would fade, starved out by secrecy. I, on the other hand, thought of him constantly.

For days I could not focus, unprepared for this emotional onslaught.

I tried telling myself that although we seemed so perfect for each other, it would never have been the same in civilian life. I could not even visualize him as a civilian. Outside, we would both be different, I thought, strangled and brought back to earth by the very mundaneness of normalcy.

The night before he left he was in a pensive mood and said "You will have a difficult time finding any man who satisfies you back in civilian life June. Here you have known some real men, the likes of which are extremely rare. You will no longer be satisfied with less. The sad thing is…no man knows if he will measure up until he is put to the test……………You have seen great men at their best! It's a privilege most wives seldom have. Civilian life will be extremely hard for you." Unfortunately I was to learn that his words were too true.

Of course, I had to move back to my Saigon apartment

on Plantation Road. I carried on booking my bands. The recently acquired Vietnamese band didn't have the talent or professionalism of my Filipinos. I plodded on through the motions but life had lost its zing.

Although my disgust at the corruption had not abated, my happiness and pre-occupation with Colonel Daems had weakened it. Repeated disinterest in my revelations had made me feel helpless in the matter and I shrugged it off.

It was strange how I had never considered life after Vietnam. Had I expected the war to last forever? Had I expected to die there? Whatever it was, I now had no plans and nothing tempted me. I tried drawing on my dreams of adopting a child from the streets. That too, no longer aroused a spark. For years I had used the excuse that I could not bring a child to Vietnam, promising myself I would take action the moment I left the country. That time was maybe now but the motivation, like the rest of me, was dead.

I would never dance or strip again. I couldn't go backwards and outside of Vietnam I had no future as a talent agent. Was it time to return to Australia?....... And do what?

Life seemed pointless. Previously I thought I was doing some good in Vietnam, but my bands were no longer necessary. During the last year dozens of new entertainment groups had arrived.

Increasing my despair, the corruption had finally entered my stronghold at Cu Chi and my business had dried to a trickle. I debated my options; play ball with the crooks, quit Vietnam, or fight. It was difficult for me to hide my contempt for the powerful custodians. I spoke tentatively to my Filipinos about going home. Some of them seemed ready; others did not.

My band members were paid a weekly salary, regardless of the number of shows they worked. Compared to what they made in the Philippines, they were rich. With insufficient bookings we gradually gave more and more free shows at the hospitals. This didn't affect my entertainers but of course, it hurt my bank balance.

I was spending more time hanging around Saigon at the I House on Tu Do or at the Officer's Club in a small Special Forces compound called CLD (Command Liaison Detachment) on Rue Pasteur. CLD was off limits to all but Special Forces officers and comprised a couple of red brick villas of various sizes. Major Chuck Darnell and a handful of Green Beret sergeants ran the place. These men had seen their fair share of fighting and were given this cushy assignment as a respite. One of the buildings was used as in-transit accommodation for high ranking officers or visiting VIP's.

The 3rd Field Hospital off duty nurses often hung out in the small lounge where nobody bothered them. Occasionally, Major Chuck Darnell hired my band to provide evening entertainment. Hamburgers and hot dogs could be bought from the bar.

After buying a drink I moved to a table in the half empty lounge. A little later Chuck Darnell stopped by.

"You look as if you've lost your best friend" he said.

"Haven't we all?" I gulped half my drink.

"Hey, hey, cheer up."

Major Darnell was some sort of hero who had been written up in Time magazine. He was a crazy guy. I'd seen him break up a fight in the lounge one night by leaping across three tables and banging the brawler's heads together then single-handedly throwing them out.

"I think I am ready to leave Nam" I said "I've got too few bookings and too much time on my hands. Nobody here gives a shit about the corruption in the army clubs. I'm just spinning my wheels."

I had spoken to Darnell before about the corruption and he had loaned a sympathetic ear but offered no solutions. The Special Forces were distinctly separate from regular army so the crooked army custodians had no foothold in their clubs.

"I never thought of you as a quitter." The major replied. "I don't think you've given it your best shot."

His words riled me "I'm not a fool. Would you volunteer to fight against overwhelming numbers without back-up? What chance have I got?"

"You keep complaining to the army officers, you say, but have you gone to the CID?"

Before I could answer, Darnell was called to the phone and after he left, I thought about his words. Why hadn't I gone to the CID? Was it because I thought they might not believe me?

The major returned with two beers "Here, have one on the house." He said handing over a can of Coors. I poured mine into my empty glass and thanked him.

"Well, have you?"

"No. How can I, without evidence? The army pricks won't take a check."

"Then get other evidence. Cozy up to one of them and see what you can learn. You will gain more with honey than vinegar. Have you never heard of tape recorders?"

"Pretty bloody dangerous! They don't trust me."

"Well give it some thought. No battle is won without good planning. You need to change your tactics."

"Cheers" I said, lifting my glass "I'll think about it. I've got plenty of time on my hands."

"Then why aren't you out there visiting more of our men. I hear you used to visit some of the A teams. They really appreciate it when you drop in on them for a few hours. You and Martha Raye are the only ones who ever have."

"It's damned hard to reach them. They're scattered too far out and there's no transport."

"The pay chopper does the rounds once a month. I'll give you the names of a couple of our pilots." He paused "Anyway, I've got to get back to work. Can I get you anything else?"

"Thanks. Your encouragement is enough. Maybe I will buy that cassette recorder."

CHAPTER 44

Long before we ever heard of The A Team television show, the Special Forces A teams were around. In fact, the show of that name was based on a fictional group of retired A Team soldiers.

These small A Team encampments of only twelve men were isolated, out in the boonies. Usually they could be reached only by helicopter.

In my experiences, the entire team was never in camp. Several men were always reconnoitering the jungle, searching for enemy activity. Hence, the regular army boys somewhat derisively nicknamed them Sneaky Pete's, motivated no doubt by jealousy of their well earned reputation.

I loved these guys – true warriors—real survivors. They were a breed apart and some of the older ones were pretty damned eccentric. It took a different type of person to join the Green Berets. These specialist soldiers did not count the days, hours and minutes to board that 'Freedom Bird' the way the regular army boys did.

Back in President Kennedy's day when the Special Forces were formed, the group was even smaller and more elite than what they are today. Their training still is far more stringent than most. They do jump training, are encouraged to learn foreign languages and are trained to kill silently, such as with a garrote. They know how to live off the land.

My first involvement with Special Forces occurred when I was running the Waltzing Matilda in Nha Trang. The A Team members sometimes passed through their 5th Special Forces Group Headquarters on their way to and from assignments. The 5th was commanded by Colonel Fred Ladd at that time and located not far from my club.

I was always welcome on Colonel Ladd's base and made many friends. Occasionally I ran into Martha Raye, the old movie star, who was a champion of the Green Berets and visited them often. She had been known on one occasion to utilize her nurses training by helping out with the wounded. The men adored her and I never could match drinks with her. Her capacity for alcohol was legendary however she sometimes ended up under the table.

The Special Forces clubs (there weren't many) were not part of the organized corruption that ran rampant in the Army Clubs. Unfortunately, including the Air Force and Marines, there were insufficient clubs to keep my bands working continually without the army.

I took Major Darnell's advice. The next pay day found me on a chopper heading for a small A Team. Two of my guitarists were adventurous enough to come with me. We carried several loaves of French bread fresh from the Saigon bakery as well as huge slabs of cheese.

After a long ride over the jungle, the pilot set the chopper down on his first leg of the 'pay run'. A Captain Michaels was the only other passenger. He leaped out ahead of us.

A deeply tanned soldier in shorts and boots emerged from a small above ground building. Spotting me and my two band members, Joe and Ding, he looked surprised

"Goddamn! Money and visitors in one day," he exclaimed. "Welcome to our humble home."

"Let's get this money taken care of." Captain Michaels said, unbuckling his brief case and placing a large book on a tree stump. Seconds later, four more soldiers, materialized. They greeted us laconically and ambled over to sign for their pay packets. It was impossible to tell what rank any of them were.

"That's all of us here today," one said "The rest of our team is out on recon." He turned his attention to me.

"Who are you little lady? And what brings you to our God forsaken neck of the jungle?"

Introductions were made. I had not previously met any of them but a couple knew who I was; part of that active 'in country' grapevine.

The Captain snapped his book shut, had a few words and headed for the chopper. He turned and shouted "We'll be back to get you later."

"Don't forget" I answered, looking at the dismal surroundings. My two Filipinos looked as if they wanted to climb back onto the chopper right then.

"I brought lunch" I said, handing over the bread and cheese.

"That bread smells great," said the oldest one. He was missing a front tooth. There were no dentists out here.

"I don't remember when I last tasted fresh bread." A younger one added. " It's good to know we're not totally forgotten."

"Yeah! You're the only woman ever been out here." Said the tall one "Let's show you around and maybe we should crack open that bottle of Bourbon I've been saving."

"Save your liquor" I said "It's a long way to the nearest PX. Meet Ding and Joe. They're part of my Filipino band and they volunteered to play for you, if you'd like."

"God almighty, of course we'd like? Pritchards over there considers himself a bit of a guitar picker." He nodded towards the youngest of the group.

"First, come see the camp."

We followed him past the only building, down into dank, underground bunkers. These were not the cement bunkers I was accustomed to. They were merely dirt caves. The men's boots lay covered in thick, green mould.

"Not the greatest quarters," one said "But survival means more than comfort."

"Look" said another, lifting a mouldy boot from the ground. "We can't put our foot into these without checkin' for fuckin' Tarantulas first."

I was relieved to climb back into the sunshine.

The timber building was surrounded by a sea of tree stumps all encircled within a perimeter of coiled barbed wire. My attention was caught by white objects hanging on the wire. I walked over for a closer inspection and discovered they were sun bleached human skulls.

"Don't let them scare you June. They visited us many moons ago. Now they're a warning to trespassers."

"Yeah," added one. "They arrived with hot lead, not hot bread."

"It's macabre decor." I replied, thinking I wouldn't want to spend a night there.

"What brings you here June? Occasionally one of the army brass might drop in briefly to get intel before sending their leg battalions through the area. Other than the pay chopper, we seldom see others"

I laughed "I admire what you guys do and thought you might like company."

"You and Martha Raye"

"Well the chopper will be back soon enough so how about we listen to Ding and Joe for awhile?"

We sat on stumps in the only shaded spot we could find. Those trees had been cleared for safety purposes. The boys gave a nod, struck a chord and sang California Dreamin' from The Mommas and The Poppas. The small audience quieted down. Pritchard hummed along, joining in here and there.

I was grateful that my young Filipinos had accompanied me.

"You guys deserve a drink." Our tall friend said. "Bring the bottle out James."

James ducked inside and reappeared with ice filled plastic glasses and a bottle of Bourbon. My boys frowned.

"You don't have any water, do you?" Joe asked "We don't drink alcohol."

"Shit buddy, you must be sick. And let me tell you, if you drink any water around here you sure as hell will be sick. Come and look." He beckoned us to follow him out past the barbed wire until we saw a slow moving creek. Unlike the dirty brown waterways of Vietnam, this was plugged with sluggish green slime.

"That's our water supply. Our ice cubes are made from that crap so ya hafta drink up fast before the stinkin' stuff melts. If you don't wanta get hepatitis you betta have a real drink."

We gingerly took the drinks.

"To all the gooks I've killed and those still waitin' for me." One toasted boastfully. I knew they liked to shock. Then I noticed the ice cubes inside the plastic tumbler actually were green and as they melted, they did stink. I downed my drink before any more ice could melt and I spotted Ding tipping his drink out when he thought no-one was watching.

"June, are you any good with a weapon?"

"Not very."

"Well shit woman, there's no time like the present. Everyone needs ta know how ta handle firearms out here."

"Yeah!" another agreed "Let's hit the firing range."

I followed them to a couple of rusty 44 gallon drums.

"Here! Have a go with my M16."

I took the weapon as directed and aimed. I was shocked at how fast it fired and the bullets sprayed wildly without control. Eventually I managed a little better so I couldn't understand why the men began yelling.

"Holy Cow."

"She almost got it."

"Look at that mother-fucker move."

Joe, his eyes popping, pointed to the biggest python I'd ever seen. Its fat twenty foot body slithered fast along the ground in front of the drums. My stomach lurched.

Still, I agreed to have a go with an M79 grenade launcher. They warned me it had a kick. I held it tight and aimed at the drum; the recoil almost knocked me backwards. My shoulder really hurt but I bit my tongue.

"This is more my size." I said, pulling my small Browning 25 from my fatigue pants pocket. The men went hysterical.

"Christ almighty. They'd havta be right on top of you before ya could do any damage with that." One ridiculed.

We walked back just as the pay chopper landed.

Special Forces Camp Bien Hoa.

A Special Forces A Team in Thuong Thoi

Sam, a Special Forces A Team member at My Da.

Special Forces A Team Pleime. With pilot and a Special Forces sergeant.

Meeting a fellow Aussie at Co Chao.

CHAPTER 45

MANILA

AP. was as good as his word and every day of the week I found Alfredo waiting in a different luxury car.

Another long night of working and partying at the Bayside came to an end and I sank comfortably into the leather seat of the Daimler and closed my eyes.

"Straight home, Miss June?" Alfredo asked

"Of course, Alfredo. I'm sorry for keeping you so long."

"No problem Miss. I sleep in the car same as in my bed."

I had never lived such a pampered lifestyle. Each day my hair was styled at a nearby salon. After every show, the masseur for the Philippines National Basket Ball team came to my dressing room to give me a massage. It cost a pittance and hurt like hell but felt great later.

I glanced down at my gown. It fit like a glove and shimmered spectacularly over my body. Every bead was hand-sewn. It would have cost a fortune back home.

As we sped through the empty streets I pondered the contrasts of my life and I realized that fate completely ruled my destiny despite my plans.

Earlier that day, AP. had approached me with a new proposition.

"My manager tells me you stay on and dance until closing each night. Is that correct?"

I worried momentarily that this did not please him. "Yes I do. I love to dance and there is nowhere else I can safely go alone except back to my hotel."

"Did you know that I own a gambling casino not far from here?"

"I had heard something."

"It is quite a grand establishment. Unfortunately, gambling casinos aren't legal here so I run it as a private club. Our members are the crème of Manila society." A touch of pride tinged his voice.

"As you must be aware, Filipino men greatly admire pretty white ladies and there are not many around here."

I nodded.

"And my customers are great gamblers. Your presence should keep them gambling longer"

Seeing my blank stare he flashed that Buddha's smile.

"Could you drop by the casino after your floor show some nights and act as my shill for a couple of hours. I think it would be good for business."

"Well A.P. I don't know what a schill is?"

He laughed heartily.

"My dear girl, it is merely a lure to keep the gamblers spending. My staff can teach you how to shoot craps and play Twenty One."

"I hate gambling" I said hesitantly "My father gambled our house away."

"Gambling is for suckers. Suckers always lose. You my dear will never lose. My cashier will give you a hundred US dollars worth of peso chips each night. If you win, you return the original hundred and the winnings are yours. If you lose, we write it off. You've got nothing to lose so you're not exactly gambling. Right?"

I hesitated briefly, "I will give it a try A.P. I've never been inside a casino before."

"That's the girl." He patted me on the shoulder. "Start tomorrow night, please"

A.P.'s wealth was acquired from gamblers, be they in the Casino or race track. To this day, the Manila suburb of Makati has an "A.P. Reyes Avenue" named after him and it was for many years, the location of the Philippine Turf Club.

The Daimler slid in before the Mabuhay hotel.

"You are home Miss June, have a good rest."

"And you too Alfredo. What will you be driving tomorrow?"

"AAhh, that's my secret, Miss."

The night doorman was missing from his post, apparently sleeping. I stepped from the car then leaped back, repulsed as a huge rat scurried by my feet. Shuddering, I lifted my shimmering skirt, and for the first time noticed three ragged figures sprawled across the cement sidewalk.

I gasped as I recognized the tiny beggar girls. Every morning they waited for me, angering the doorman who chased them away with a broom. They made it a game, laughing and taunting the harried man.

They were vibrant and cheerful then. Not now! I looked at their tiny, soiled bodies, crumpled in sleep like discarded rag dolls. They lay uncovered, on sheets of newspaper, helpless prey for predators, human or animal.

We joked each morning as I gave them my loose pesos while the doorman attempted to discourage me.

"They're little scammers" he once said "Don't you know that baby the oldest one carries on her hip is rented out daily so she can get sympathy?"

I admired her more for being so enterprising at such a young age.

Thoughtlessly, I had assumed they retreated at night to their parents shack, adding the day's takings to the family's coffers.

I stepped around their pitiful bodies and hurried inside; my high spirits doused.

Unable to sleep, I compared their lives with my own and felt sad. The cost of one of my gowns could feed those waifs for a year. I hadn't done much to help them.

I wondered if there was a God and, if so, why were some children born into hell while others were born to be coddled and over-indulged. I recalled hearing Mike Walker say "I'm proud to be an American." Why should anyone feel proud of their birthplace? They should feel privileged, not proud. As far as I knew, none of us could choose where, or to whom, we were born, or into what circumstances.

I thought of my own lost babies and for the first time in ages, I cried. I cried for children who were sick or hungry, who were alone and unloved. I cried for children of unfit parents. Shouldn't all children be fed and loved and protected?

My vow never to marry again hadn't changed and I would never attempt to carry another child in futile pregnancy. Adoptions were as rare as snowstorms in the tropics and single parents even rarer. But a voice inside me screamed "Can't you do something?"

I tossed and turned all night. My 'Grand Adventure' was just starting and I wasn't prepared to make sacrifices. Yet as daylight crept in, I compromised. Somewhere in the future, I would take a little orphan off the street.

CHAPTER 46

VIETNAM

It was mid afternoon when I slipped into the back office of the Wolfhound's NCO club in Cu Chi. Sergeant Delaney, the custodian, sat alone at his gray, metal desk, making entries in a thick book. A pedestal fan in one corner rustled the papers on the desk as it blew hot air about.

"Am I interrupting?" I asked "I can come back later."

He closed the book and looked up "I can always make time for you, honey."

"That's the best news I've heard today."

"But I've got a bone to pick with you." He grinned.

"What's that?"

"Both my knees are skinned from rug burn. I can't take any more nights on this office floor."

"Oh,you poor baby!" I derided. "Maybe I shouldn't come again."

"You are joking, and is that a double entendre? But anyway, I've taken care of it and bought a roll up futon. It's hidden it in the cabinet."

"Aaahhh. So I'm not a one night stand?"

"Are you kidding? But you have ruined my plans to return home a straight arrow."

"Do you feel guilty?"

"A bit, but I'm not complaining."

"The other Custodians don't seem to suffer guilt when they pick up any number of Vietnamese bar girls."

"Well I'm different." He hesitated "I've never picked up a bar girl. I love my wife and I'm not bringing her any goddamn disease."

"Don't make me feel like Jezebel. Maybe we shouldn't see each other again."

"Too late! Hung for a sheep, hung for a lamb." He eyed me hungrily before walking around his desk and encircling me in his arms "I can't get enough of you."

A shiver tingled my spine but quickly faded at his next words.

"My wife has been very sick and that is why I am not extending my tour."

I broke out of his arms, feeling guilty.

"Until you came along, I was a monk."

"Let's have a coffee." I changed the subject "Anyway, I just dropped in to check what time you want my group to start at the Aviation Battalion tonight."

Later that day, I rested on a narrow, iron bed in the Red Cross Girls quarters. This privilege of occasionally sharing the Cu Chi Donut Dollies quarters was arranged by Chaplain Thompson.

Delaney's compassion for his wife had given me a jolt. I had to remind myself that although he was not as bad as the other custodians; he was still ripping off the system. I must not weaken but my procrastination was already a bad sign.

Prior to Colonel Daems departure, no-one from the 25th Division's club system had ever asked me for a kickback. I hadn't known if this meant that the Division was not involved in the corruption, or if I was exempt from kickbacks because I had a commander's ear. Immediately after Len's departure, Delaney had demanded the usual kickback. I sighed heavily and rose to take a shower and dress for the evening.

The Donut Dolly's communal shower was thankfully empty. I, who had danced semi naked before men felt uncomfortable when showering among a roomful of naked women. Go figure!

The weeks passed. My small cassette recorder worked reasonably well and I kept making excuses about why I hadn't turned my information over to the authorities. Delaney and I continued our lustful, late night meetings, two or three times a week.

Gradually, his suspicion of me faded as his penis conquered his brain. We went to great lengths to keep our trysts secret. Most of the 25th's troops would eventually get back to their home base in Hawaii and he certainly did not want gossip reaching his wife. His hooch mate, must have wondered about his frequent late nights at the club.

Little by little I was gathering information; reading invoices left on his desk, listening in to phone conversations. I still did not understand what linked the custodians together. Clearly they were an organization. But someone else could unravel the ins and outs of it once an investigation was started. My goal was merely to light the fuse.

The one name that kept popping up in conversations I had taped between Delaney and the salesmen was Maredem Ltd. My instincts told me that this was an important piece of the puzzle, if only I could fathom it out.

My Vietnamese band entertaining the troops.

Sitting with the M.P's keeping an eye on my Vietnamese band.

After traveling a long hot, dusty ride by convoy. Photographed with a guitar player from my Vietnamese band.

CHAPTER 47

MANILA

Visiting the casino, I felt as if I was in a spy movie. As A.P. had said, the casino wasn't exactly legal and to access it I had to climb down a narrow stairway into the underground. Accompanied by Alfredo, we reached a solid metal door and stopped beneath a dim yellow bulb. Alfredo tapped out a signal and a center spy hole slid open, revealing dark eyes.

"I'll leave you now." Alfredo said "Let the manager know when you need me." He disappeared into the night and I stood nervously alone as the door, which looked remarkably like a bank vault, clunked open. Two barrel-chested, surly faced men stood with rifles slung over their shoulders.

They beckoned me inside. Within minutes a man in a white Tuxedo hurried from the brightly lit room and introduced himself as the manager.

"A.P. told us you were coming Miss June. Before we get started, would you like something to eat or drink? Our chef's are excellent."

I thanked him but declined as I looked around the gigantic room. After the dinghy, frightening stairwell, the opulence was surprising. Male customers wore white or beige suits and the ladies sparkled in gorgeous gowns and flamboyant, real jewelry. The air held the scent of French perfumes. Champagne glasses clinked beneath an arbor of crystal chandeliers. I teetered across the thickly carpeted floor, following the manager between the gaming tables.

It didn't take me long to get the hang of Craps and Twenty One. Soon I was looking forward to my nights at the casino. It made me feel like Rita Hayworth in her 1940's role of Gilda. Playing with house money I seldom lost, and if I did lose I quit immediately. Gambling was fun but I remembered what it did to my family. Occasionally when I lost and was about to leave, a punter would push a stack of chips over, saying "Don't leave. You bring me luck."

Weeks after I started at the casino I received a visit at the Mabuhay Hotel from Monique and Ned Kelly.

"What brings you two here?" I asked, surprised.

"Have you heard about Big Julie?" Monique asked.

"No! What?"

"She's in the fucking Manilla lock-up."

"Good God. What did she do?"

"Some bloody little bastard put the hard word on her and she told him to piss off, that's all." Ned used his colorful Aussie vernacular.

"We're going to the joint now. We thought you might join us." Monique added.

"Of course! But why would they jail her just for rejecting some bloke's advances? And what can we do?"

"I had a yarn with her. She's not eaten - says they feed them like pigs with slop out of a bucket." Art spoke harshly. "I'd like to take my rifle to the bloody pig that did this."

"We're taking her fruit" Monique added "but we hafta raise bail and it's pretty fuckin steep."

"Of course you can count me in but I still don't get it."

"She overstayed her friggin' work visa by a month" Art explained "It's no big deal. Ordinarily you just pay under the table and they turn a blind eye but the mongrel in the immigration office wanted a bit of nookie. She told the shit-head where to go."

"You know Big Julie" Monique added "She comes on like gang busters. After blasting the shit out of him, she socked him in the jaw for good measure."

"Has anyone called the New Zealand Consul?" I asked

"They don't have one here."

"Then how about the Aussies?"

"We're on it!" Art replied.

I had never seen the inside of a third world jailhouse and it was beyond my worst nightmare. We three followed a prison guard along a passageway between the men's cells, before reaching the female section. The stench of urine made me gag and the inmates in the small, overcrowded cells yelled and jeered at us. The excitement of our arrival surged through the halls like a Mexican Wave. Inmates scrambled up the cell cages, clinging to the wire like a sea of dirty, long haired, monkeys. Almost naked, they stretched their dark arms through the bars, clutching desperately at us and I don't intend this as disparagement of Filipinos for whom I have a great affection. Severe living conditions alter us in every respect. In Vietnam I once visited lepers banished to an island colony. I cannot even describe how unearthly those poor neglected wretches looked.

I recoiled from the sea of grasping hands and hastened my steps, looking straight ahead, filled with a mix of pity and horror.

Our escort stopped in front of the cell housing Julie. She sat slumped on an old rug in a corner. Her blonde hair was tousled and she had dark circles under her eyes. Seeing us, she quickly stood, towering above the dozen pitiful Filipinas with whom she shared the cell. She strode forward like a grimy, white giant.

"Thank God you're here" she gasped "Are they gonna let me out?"

"Not yet" Ned replied "The Aussie Embassy was closed when we left here last night but I saw them first thing this morning. I've hired a lawyer and don't you worry about the damned bail."

Monique produced the fruit from her bag and the guard grabbed at it, tearing the paper bag. Apples and bananas rolled all over the filthy floor.

"You fucking shithead." Julie yelled.

"Don't waste your breath," I bent to pick them up and handed a banana through the bars. Repressing a shudder, I didn't tell her that a huge cockroach was climbing up her hair.

"You've gotta get me out of here, quick." She begged "Or I will go bloody stark, staring mad. Look," she waved her hand around "we have nowhere to sit, nowhere to sleep, only the floor. That hole in the middle of the cell is our toilet. There's no privacy and we can't escape the revolting stink."

Indeed, one wretched soul was squatting, peeing as she spoke.

"Some of these poor creatures have been in here for years" she said "I'd kill myself first. Look." Even as she spoke, she pointed to where a hairy, fat, red-eyed rat was scurrying along a high window sill.

"We've gotta go" Art said "I'll prod those Embassy blokes again. They shoulda been here by now."

"Here" Monique said "I've brought you a hair brush, some soap and a toothbrush." She showed them to the guard who inspected them, piece by piece. When he didn't pass them on, Monique grabbed a few pesos from her bag and angrily waved them at him. Stony faced, he stuffed the money in his pocket then passed on the items.

We said our goodbye's and as we hurried away we could hear Julie cussing out the guard. The hellhole stench filled my nostrils and I tried not to inhale deeply. It was hard not to bolt for the exit and fresh air.

After the Aussie Consulate's Office had Julie released she was deported the same day. I never saw her again.

Realizing how different the law in the Philippines was from in Australia, I decided to find myself a protector.

My three months work visa was running out. There was no way I would rely on an under the table payment. I spoke to Ching about the possibility of extending for another three months.

"Even if I can get you a further three months," he said "You would need to change your act and do something fresh."

"Like what?"

"Can you sing?"

"God no!"

"What about working with a Filipino as a duo dance act?"

"If I knew someone suitable, I would like that."

"I know a young man called Rudy Aguilar. He has just returned from six months in Vegas where he danced in Steve Parker's Philippine Revue at The Sands Casino." He scratched his head "I'll talk to him."

"That would be great. Thanks Ching."

"If he's agreeable, I will send the two of you away for a couple of weeks to Bacolod City. They've just opened a waterfront Casino and they are looking for acts. It will give you a chance to break in the new act."

I left his office in good spirits.

Ching was as good as his word. Rudy was a great dancer with a fine body which looked good on stage. He was a virtuous catholic boy who didn't smoke or drink. He frowned upon my drinking and refused to work with me unless I agreed not to drink before a show. Married with five children, out of money and still in his twenties, he was pleased to work again.

Our duo was an improvement over my solo act and A.P agreed to engage us for his Hong Kong club when my six months finished.

Soon after returning from Bacolod City, I found my protector. He was a powerful man, second only to President Macapagal. In fact, many people called him 'the little president.' His name was Feny Henchenova and he was The Minister for Finance. Married of course!

Our affair was very discreet and few people other than A.P and Feny's bodyguards knew about it. Feny was cunning, quick witted and sexy. In a country where most men wore light, colorful clothes he wore dark, conservative suits and traveled in a black, conservative sedan. Of course, he had a second car and an army of body guards.

I enjoyed the intrigue of our afternoon trysts. We met regularly right up until I left the country. Occasionally this caused me to miss my rehearsal with Rudy, infuriating him, but I could never reveal where I had been.

Feny and I had no emotional entanglement. In Hong Kong sometime later, I read in The Hong Kong Standard newspaper that he had been murdered and I felt sad. His wife found him with a woman in 'our' secret hideaway and shot him. I was pleased I wasn't there. I have always believed that if a man is going to play – a man is going to play; if not with me, with someone else. Feny's wife must have felt that if a man is going to stray, a man is going to pay.

It was my last night in The Philippines. Ching had promised me a return engagement the next year.

"You left early tonight Miss June" Alfredo said as we approached the hotel. "Are you tired?"

"No Alfredo. But I have to finish packing." I leaned forward and dropped an envelope onto the front seat "There's a little something in there for you. Thank you for the wonderful job you have done."

He thanked me self consciously and slid the Aston Martin deftly into the curb in front of the hotel.

Inside the hotel bedroom I closed my suitcase and climbed into bed in my underwear. I was sad to leave but other travels, other adventures beckoned. My travels had started badly at Kings Theatre but that was behind me now. The last few months had been an education and I had friends and contacts in Asia now. From here on there would be no more dives. I planned on traveling for the next few years. When I had my fill of fun and a pocket full of money I would return and take one of those little girls back to Australia and settle down. That was the plan!

CHAPTER 48

VIETNAM.

It was never my intent to write about the war – only my role in it. However, one could not stay as long as I did, traveling around as much as I did, observing and listening at all levels and not form opinions. For more qualified opinions than mine, there are plenty of military commanders, historians and others, who have written about the war and its politics. Some tremendous documentaries were produced, revealing the truth in later years.

Over time I had grown to empathize with and love the American troops. Although the war was eventually lost – they did not lose it. Personally I blame it on the commander in chief, President Lyndon Johnson. He at least contributed. The American troops were consistently victorious in battle, including Tet when they speedily pushed the enemy back.

The Vietnam War was fought differently from previous ones. Whereas past wars measured progress by territory taken and held, that was not the goal in South Vietnam. Whilst the NVA and VC ran amok all over South Vietnam, our troops were not allowed to cross the border and chase them back into North Vietnam. We never attempted to take their territory. Our missions were always 'Search and destroy". Millions of NVA's and VC were destroyed but immediately, the North was able to effortlessly replace them – unlimited fodder! Allied victories were judged by body count. Our commanders were given goals of a ten to one kill ratio. They continually surpassed this, which indicates the high performance of our troops. The plan didn't work yet was left unchanged! A constant complaint amongst the troops was that they were expected to fight with one arm tied behind their back. These orders of restricted pursuit came directly from President Johnson's office. What we didn't know then was that he was too scared to push on into North Vietnam for fear of stirring Russia and China. His fears of starting WW111 are understandable but you can't win a war with half measures. Either get in or get out.

I recall the words of some of our young troops. One war weary PFC spoke to me after returning from battle "I killed a gook" he said "and when I took his weapon, I saw he was only a kid."

"Did that make you feel bad?" I asked.

"Hell no. His bullet kills just as dead as mine."

Another time, late at night, I was flying over a hamlet in a chopper when we came under fire. The door gunners, anxious to return fire, swung their mounted guns in preparation - but they were ordered to hold off until receiving radio permission. When an answer finally crackled over the radio it was 'NO'. They were not to risk hitting innocent women or children. The enemy operated under no such concerns.

"Shit" the young gunner spat" It's too Goddamn late now anyway. Charlie's had plenty of time to dee dee mau.. What sort of a fuckin war is this?"

So much for morale! Our troops can hold their head high. As for the pilots, whether fixed wing or rotor, their skills and courage were second to none. The military never lost the war - Washington did! And that's the opinion I'm entitled to.

A Korean band was just finishing up as I entered Delaney's NCO club. Seating myself on a barstool I ordered a coke. Delaney emerged from the office.

"How did your group go over at the Aviation Battalion?" He asked.

"Good. They're just packing up now. They'll bunk over there."

"Yeah. I'll send these Kim Chee eaters over to join them."

Gradually the club emptied and the workers cleared the tables, carrying back the empty glasses. Delaney opened the till and started counting the night's takings.

"I won't be long. Do you want something stronger?" he indicated my coke.

"No. I'll wait for you."

Fifteen minutes later, the workers left and Delaney turned off the overhead lights and locked the doors.

"Would you be okay if I left you for a few moments?" he asked.

"If you must."

"I smell of beer and sweat. You might like me better if I took a shower."

"I'll wait in the office and get the futon ready." My mind raced at the opportunity presented.

"I won't be gone long." He said, closing the back door behind him. Immediately I raced into the office, opened the cabinet, dragged the futon out onto the floor then sat at his desk. He would be gone for at least fifteen minutes. The troops' community bath house was several hundred yards from the clubhouse.

I was lying on the futon in my underwear when he returned, bare-chested with a khaki towel slung around his neck.

"You smell nice." I said.

He shot me a lascivious stare, threw the towel onto a chair and unbuckled his belt.

Thirty minutes later we were in the throes of passion when the familiar whoomp, whoomp sounds warned of incoming. The club house had little to no protection. The rounds were dropping really close, the sirens were blaring and my heart pounded as I waited for Delaney to climb off me so we could dash for cover. Instead, he excitedly renewed his efforts with a fervor that was catching and ignited my own excitement. 'We are crazy' I thought as my heart seemed to thump in rhythm with the wailing sirens and bursting shells. As I considered the possibility of shrapnel raining down on us, the thought flashed through my mind that I was in the safer position on the bottom. Adrenalin had me shaking and vaginal muscles spasmed; again and again. He made one violent thrust as the 'All Clear' wailed and he shrieked loud enough to drown it out.

"Wow," I gasped "a mortar attack makes one helluva aphrodisiac. That was worthy of champagne."

"You'll… have… ta. ..settle… for.. beer." He croaked before rising and tottering off.

I was dressing to leave when he returned, "I had a visit from O'Halloran today. What did you ever do to him? The man hates your guts."

"Old history. He offered me a job and didn't put all his cards on the table. It's just sour grapes."

"Unfortunately some of my friends' feel the same way about you."

"I know all that. I've never fraternized like the other agents do, so they call me a snob and officer material. Anyway, I was here before any of you. In those days I never had to pay kickbacks and I don't like the change. Can you blame me for complaining?"

"Well it doesn't help you win any popularity contests." He scratched his head "Just makes me wonder why you're with me?"

"Do you want the truth?"

A frown crossed his face and he nodded hesitantly. I wondered was I being rash in risking a half truth.

"I wasn't getting many bookings for all the above reasons. I've always thought you are an attractive man and I wanted to keep my people working out here. Truthfully, I never expected this combustion between us. You are a terrific lover."

He finished his beer and threw the can across the office, missing the waste basket before replying

"So you're using me! I thought it might have been something like that."

I ruffled his hair. "Don't be mad. Aren't you using me?"

"I should be pissed off .....but the benefits are too good."

"I need to get back to the Donut Dolly's quarters; I've got an early start tomorrow."

"Before I forget, can you meet up with me in Saigon next Thursday night?"

This was a surprise. We made a point of never being seen together.

"What's the occasion?"

"A big deal! Sergeant Major Woolridge is having a birthday blow out. It will be a blow-out to end all blow-outs and he has invited all the club managers."

"I've never met him. He might not welcome me."

"If you're with me, of course you'll be welcome. He and I go all the way back to Augsburg Germany. I guarantee you won't want to miss this. He has a sharp Villa in Saigon, and he goes first class all the way."

"Then how can I say no?" I smiled, thinking of my un-trusty little tape recorder.

"Bye the way," I added "I haven't paid you for this month's shows but I'm all out of green. I can either give you a check now on my American bank account or get some green before Thursday. Take your pick."

"You know I don't take checks." He answered quickly.

"Oh what the hell! Aren't we friends and lovers? Write me a check."

I reached for my handbag on the back of the chair, carefully removed the American checkbook and filled in a leaf while hiding my shaking hands. He stared at it for a moment before saying "I'm no longer comfortable taking your money."

Half hoping he would tear it up, I heard him say "After tonight, I don't want you to pay me."

His words made me feel like shit. Why did it have to be him? He was the best of the bunch. But if I caught one, I caught the lot.

CHAPTER 49

SAIGON

Unfortunately, there are patches of vagueness in the following events. My recall has been good in most instances so it is disappointing that it fails me at this crucial stage. Certain incidents that occurred on this night however, are indelibly engraved into my mind while others are hazy. I have filled in the hazy parts with what I THINK happened. My only explanation is that someone must have drugged one of my drinks, for there is no way that I would have been careless while in the Lion's Den.

So as I recall it;

Delaney sat at the wheel of the jeep as we bounced along the road between Cu Chi and Saigon. During daylight hours the road was usually safe. He glanced across at me then broke into a deep, peal of laughter.

"What's so funny?" I asked.

"Do you carry a mirror in that friggin oversized handbag of yours? If you do, take a look."

I pulled my compact out, careful to keep the fabric covered cassette player out of sight. Snapping the compact open, I looked in the mirror then laughed. The clouds of red powdery dust churned up by our vehicle had coated my face. In the mid day heat, sweat had pooled inside the lower frame of my oversized sunglasses, quickly turning to mud. Two muddy semi-circles beneath my eyes overflowed at the centre, dripping down my cheeks in two vertical lines.

"You look like a cross between a clown and a raccoon" he laughed.

"Well thank God we are stopping at my apartment to get cleaned up." I giggled.

"Yeah!" Delaney agreed "We should sleep there tonight. This party will go late."

"You know Del, you are so different from the other custodians. I sometimes wonder why you are all friends."

"Of course we are. We've worked together here, the States, Germany, you name it."

"But there must be over a million men in the American army."

"There's not so many club managers," he said testily "Anyway, what's it to you?"

I quickly backed off "Nothing really. Just idle talk."

"Well, where we are going, I'd forget the idle talk. I've tried to set them straight about you but don't give them grist for their mill."

I finished the trip in silence, my mind racing. If only it was Higdon or one of the other hateful ones I had entrapped but I doubted I could have bedded any of them.

I hated the sexual magnetism between Delaney and me. It was like a drug which had to end. I hoped this party, with alcohol flowing, might loosen tongues and finally tie up a few loose ends.

At four p.m. Delaney parked the jeep in the driveway which ran alongside Woolridge's two-story, colonial villa. Several jeeps were lined up ahead of us.

"We will be hemmed in if we want to leave early." I observed.

"We won't be leaving early."

I was wearing a white leather, mini skirt and matching boots. Sliding carefully out of the jeep I jerked to a sudden halt as a deafening roar rent the air.

"What the hell......" laughter erupted from the back of the house.

"It must be feeding time" Delaney grinned, "Let's go take a look."

We squeezed between the wall of the house and the row of jeeps until, rounding the corner, I saw four Americans dressed in civvies. They crowded around a mesh cage, banging on the heavy wire, teasing the magnificent tiger inside. It padded back and forth, its muscles rippling beneath the shiny coat as it roared impatiently for dinner.

Moronically, they were holding out slabs of fresh meat then quickly withdrawing them. I gaped at a tray stacked high with T Bone steaks,- the best I had seen in years.

"That damned tiger eats better than we do!" I murmured.

"I told you, Bill goes first class. He gets whatever he wants."

"Why would he want a tiger?"

"People give him gifts. The tiger is good image I suppose."

For a few moments we watched as the steaks were finally relinquished and the beast devoured them.

"Let's go and meet Bill" Delaney muttered, leading me away.

We entered the crowded room unnoticed. About forty or fifty people, mostly men, were milling about. White jacketed Vietnamese waiters weaved among the guests, carrying trays of canned beer and bottled champagne. Waitresses in black mini skirts offered the guests steaming dim sum and Vietnamese spring rolls from bamboo trolleys.

Long haired, heavily made-up Vietnamese girls clung to many of the guests. I recognized a tall, middle aged American woman on the far side of the room. It was Levinia, the only other female booking agent in Vietnam. She and her husband were talking to O'Halloran.

Spotting me, they put their heads together and I guessed I had become their focal point of interest. She and I were the only 'round eyed' women present.

"Let's grab a drink then go find Bill to wish him a happy birthday." Delaney pulled me further into the room.

"Yeah. I brought him a boomerang as a small gift. Of course, it won't compare to a tiger."

"No. But a nice thought. I never know what you are going to pull out of that goddamned bag."

The bag he referred to was large, square shaped and conspicuously gold. The top did not close. I had chosen it hoping an open topped bag might prevent any muffling as the cassette recorded. If anyone decided to look inside, a fastener wasn't going to keep them out.

Delaney scooped a can of beer from a passing waiter then said "I'll go to the bar and get you a gin tonic."

I squeezed his hand appreciatively and looked around the room. It was large and comfortably furnished. The walls were adorned with military awards and photos. One wall held some fine looking paintings. There was nothing as undignified as a Playboy centerfold here. I stepped closer to one painting to get a better look.

"Do they meet your approval?" a deep voice caused me to turn. The man was tall, stately, with strong features and intelligent eyes.

"They do." I replied "although I'm no expert."

"Neither am I" he said "But I buy what pleases me."

I nodded in agreement. "Am I to guess that you are Sergeant Major Woolridge?"

"Correct. And am I speaking to the infamous Miss Collins?" he smirked.

"Yes. Isn't it amazing we've never met before?"

"I'm a very busy man. And I've heard that you're an old timer here."

"I guess."

"Well there are more guests arriving. I had better go and greet them."

I reached into my hand bag.

"Before you go.... here's a small birthday trinket. Happy Birthday!" I handed him the tissue wrapped boomerang.

"Ah. I think I can guess what this might be. Thank you for the thought. Have Delaney show you around. There are more paintings on the upper level."

Delaney returned with my drink. "I see you've met Bill."

"Yes. I'm duly impressed. He said you can take me upstairs to look at some more of his paintings."

"Then follow me."

There were fewer people upstairs. I greeted some of the club managers who had booked my bands. Delaney sat waiting on a brown leather sofa while I wandered around the room, looking at the paintings. When I rejoined him, he was arguing the merits of the various American football teams with a group of men. Bored, I looked around the room and noticed one guest sitting on the edge of a billiard table. He looked already drunk and his legs were spread eagled. I was thinking what a slob he was when a head popped up from his crotch area. Involuntarily, I gasped as I realized she was on her knees giving him oral sex.

"God it's started already." I blurted bitterly "I'm going back downstairs Del."

Del looked up frowning and saw the uninhibited couple

"Jesus Christ!" He jerked up off the sofa "This ain't no whorehouse." Striding towards them he yelled "Give Sergeant Major Woolridge some respect can't you?

There are bedrooms down the hallway. Get into one of them before I call him."

The man pulled the girl to her feet "Thanks for spoiling my blow job you asshole."

"You're the asshole." Del said, shoving his face menacingly forward. I ran over and grabbed his arm.

"Come on Del. Let's go downstairs. They're not worth it."

"I should tell Bill" he said angrily "I'm sorry you witnessed that. It makes us all look bad."

"Unfortunately, doing business with some of your cohorts, I've seen it all before."

"I hope you don't think I'm like that."

I was about to answer when there was a stir in the room. Looking towards the entrance, I saw the Dragon Lady enter on the arm of General Hare. Four pretty, young, long-haired Vietnamese girls trailed her. The sergeant major strode forward to greet them.

"That's the Dragon Lady" I said to Del "I've met her before at Bill Crumm's place."

"Who's he?"

"The wealthiest carpetbagger of the lot! He owns all the Sego slot machines."

"She's a looker."

Indeed she was! All eyes were glued to the couple as she stood posing in a crimson, figure hugging ao-dai. Her two inch long painted fingernails drew almost as much attention as the sea of glinting diamond rings on her hand which rested possessively on the General's arm. With coiffed hair and flawless make up, she totally eclipsed the four younger girls accompanying her.

"Would you believe she is fifty nine years old?" I said.

"No I don't."

"Well underneath an inch of make-up and several face lifts, she is." I said cattily. "And if I was ever going to write a book, I could write a whole book about her exploits over here. I think she even outdoes Bill Crumm as the biggest carpet bagger."

"Isn't she the owner of the massage parlor on Long Binh Post?" The penny dropped.

"You've got it! That great white monstrosity with its nude statues out front and 200 sexy 'ladies' inside! Are there any other American army posts like that? She has the General to thank for that. But let's forget her."

"You sound damned bitchy. Lower your voice."

"Don't worry. Her proclivities are no great secret. I suppose if you have enough power you don't have to worry who knows what."

"How about introducing me?"

"You're not wearing stars on your collar. I'm surprised to see her here. Probably just delivering the birthday present" I nodded at the four long haired girls.

An hour passed. I ate spring rolls greedily and drank slowly; aware I had to remain alert in the Lion's Den, especially while looking for taping opportunities. Delaney circulated but kept returning to my side. His time was short and he said this was a good time to tie up a few loose ends with other managers.

I was becoming frustrated that I had not yet encountered any loose lips. My frustration I remember clearly but this is where it starts to get hazy. Time passed and the steady stream of couples going up and down the stairs increased. With all the giggling and butt slapping, it was easy to guess why they were disappearing.

It just didn't make much sense. The sergeant major seemed to be a cut above the behavior in his home. He didn't flirt with any of the willing women and he certainly didn't disappear up the stairs. As predicted, the Dragon Lady and the general had not stayed long and she left the four 'masseuses' behind.

It dawned on me-there was not a black face in the crowd. That seemed strange, considering the army had quite a few black sergeants. And then I realized, this was the 'Good Ole Boys Club'. They were southerners and there was not a black club manager among them.

A gruff voice interrupted my reverie "What's a girl like you doing in a nice place like this."

I looked up into the florid face of O'Halloran. He blew a cloud of cigar smoke at me.

"It's nice to see you too" I coughed "And how is your wife doing back in the States."

"She's as happy as a pig in mud. All that shopping! All that money! That could have been you if you'd been smart."

"Lay off O'Halloran. That's water under the bridge."

"Yeah! Well I've told Bill, you shouldn't be here. You've obviously suckered Delaney in."

"Nobody suckered anyone. Get over it and leave me alone. I'm going to find Del." I slipped off the stool and went in search of my escort.

Finding Del I placed my arm around his waist "Don't leave me again. I'm feeling a little dizzy. Do you suppose they serve coffee here?"

"I have to talk to Bill. He leaves for Washington with the General tomorrow. You just sit here while I go find him and I'll try to bring back a cuppa coffee for you."

Ten minutes later he returned with a mug of the steaming brew.

"I'm going upstairs to wait for Bill in his office." He said "You can come up with me and drink your coffee but you will have to leave when he arrives. This is business talk."

We climbed the stairs, and I had to ask him to carry my cup. I needed to hold the banister for support. Entering the office at the end of the hallway, I took a corner seat then began rifling through my large bag.

"Want a mint?" I said, producing a roll from my gold bag. He shook his head. I put the mints back in the bag and as I did so I slipped my hand inside the thin fabric cover and switched the cassette player on. After leaning down, the room swam and my heart began thumping. I felt as if I was moving in slow motion and I knew I was no longer alert enough to do this. But it might be my only opportunity. Grabbing the coffee cup, I took a huge swallow. The door opened and Sergeant Major Woolridge entered. He looked at me and frowned.

"You will need to leave young lady. We have business to discuss."

"No problem." I smiled and rose unsteadily to my feet. Closing the door behind me, I resisted the urge to glance back at my purse which sat on the floor between my chair and the wall. Walking unsteadily towards the bathroom, I entered as a Vietnamese girl departed. A gray haze had taken hold of me, pierced by a few vivid vignettes. The first vignette was of urine on the toilet seat. Taking hold of the toilet paper, I unintentionally unraveled half the roll before putting it on the seat, lowering the lid and sitting. 'If they see my bag and look inside, I'm dead, I thought.'

"Are you still in there?" Del's voice roused me. I must have passed out.

"What's wrong with you?" he asked when I opened the door.

"I don't know. I feel sick."

"How much did you drink?" he demanded.

"I don't know. But I want to go home."

"We can't leave before the dinner and Bill's presentation." He said. "They're sitting down now."

"I'm really sick Del."

"Drunk is probably more like it" he said irritably. "If you want to leave you will have to take a taxi. I can't leave now. Try and make an effort for one more hour."

"I'll try" I said reluctantly "But first I have to go back into the toilet and to Bill's office."

"Why?"

"I think I'm going to throw up and I've lost my purse. It must be in the toilet or the office."

He shook his head exasperated and the following space is blank until I recall sitting before a table set with food. I'm not sure why that food detail penetrated my fog so vividly. Narrow tables stretched the length of the room. Roasted turkeys sat on platters every few feet. There was cranberry jelly, stuffing and pale gravy. Bright orange yams danced before my eyes with dollops of white marshmallows floating on them. In Australia, at that time, people did not eat turkey. Maybe that is why I clearly remember it.

The sea of faces around the table struck me forcefully. Gaping mouths seemed to cover entire faces as they masticated food, talked and guffawed. So many large, open cavities held me mesmerized. A man was pawing the breast of a giggling girl. His image waved in and out hazily. Only the hand and the breast were clear. Another girl was hand feeding her escort a turkey drumstick while her straight hair dangled, unnoticed in the gravy on her plate.

My vision was impaired but my emotions ran riot, broiling beneath the surface. 'I don't belong here' I remember thinking. 'What am I doing? I've got to get away.' I felt sick and despised everyone, including myself. Suddenly, with no forethought, no self control, an explosion like a brain aneurism shuddered through me. I leaped to my feet, knocking over my chair.

"Look at you" I screamed "You blood sucking, bastards. How can you live with yourselves? You're nothing but filthy animals and I'm going to get the lot of you." (I remember this outburst vividly)

There were a few moments of astounded silence and blank expressions before my sanity returned and I sprinted for the door. Somehow I knew I was running for my life as my heart throbbed in my ears and I heard shouting behind me. Fear propelled me down the driveway and into the heavy traffic of the busy thoroughfare.

Blank spots drifted in and out but I recollect the sense of being chased. Maybe that is just an assumption but I believe I was chased by three men in a jeep. Vividly, I recall the incredible fear and urgent need to escape. Somehow I knew not to go to the apartment. That thought is clear. Less clear is being saved by a traffic jam. When all larger vehicles were forced to a standstill I think I switched from a Renault taxi to a Cyclo. My one clear thought was escape. I believe I turned off the main drag and headed down a dark side street, away from the traffic. I don't remember anything else. Just the fear and panic!

CHAPTER 50

I dreamed I was playing the drums in the Tamworth High School marching band. Boom. Boom. Boom. The drumming penetrated the heavy fog and brought me back to life. Opening my eyes, I discovered I was lying on my tummy between crisp white sheets. The sound of my steady heartbeat continued.

I sat up slowly and bile surged up through my esophagus. I choked it back and stared at the unfamiliar surroundings.

"Where the hell am I?"

The room was elegantly masculine with high ceilings, tall timber doors and heavy, drawn drapes. The furniture was oak.

My head throbbed and I could no longer ignore the nausea. I ran towards one door, hoping it was the bathroom. It was! Falling to my knees, I threw up in the oversize commode as sweat beaded my forehead and my body shook. For several minutes I crouched there, resting my head on the cool rim and occasionally spitting up.

Eventually I stood. My knees were stiff and I noticed they were scraped raw. I tottered to the old fashioned, pedestal basin. Cupping the tap water in my hands, I gargled and rinsed my mouth. My reflection in the mirror showed tangled hair and smudged mascara. Grabbing the soap, I washed my face vigorously and reached for a fluffy towel.

Again, I wondered where I was. The bathroom was enormous and brilliantly white. Everything was large, from the bathtub to the bidet. I realized I was wearing only bra and pants. Grabbing one of the thick towels, I wrapped it around myself like a sari.

Back in the bedroom I saw my mini skirt lying on the floor,

covered in dirt. Vague recollection gave me a jolt. Almost immediately I saw my gold bag on a chair and I raced to it. With a sigh of relief, I pulled the cassette player out and pushed the rewind button. Damn, Damn, Damn. The batteries were flat.

Someone banged on the second door and I recognized Chuck Darnell's voice.

"Open up if you're alive. I come bearing coffee." He called cheerfully.

"Thank God it's you "I said, relieved. "Where am I?'

"Sshh! You're in the VIP villa and the shit would hit the fan if the brass knew I let you stay here. Luckily the senator who was here last, flew back Stateside yesterday so it was empty."

"You're a real friend" I said "Are you sure no-one will turn you in?"

"I've got loyal non-coms" he replied "and no-one except them and the guards know you're here"

"How did I get here?"

"Apparently by taxi. You collapsed in the driveway and the Nung guards called me out. I shook you to life and you started hyper ventilating. Now, drink your coffee and tell me what happened."

"Turn the light on" I said "It's gloomy in here. Look, the answer might be in that little machine" I pointed towards the cassette player on the bed. "But the battery is flat and I left the electrical cord at home. I'll bring you up to date on what I can remember."

Fifteen minutes later Major Darnell said "Sounds like you're in a shit-load of trouble. You can't go home. They're probably watching the place."

"Yeah. And I need my clothes and other things from there."

"I'll go and get them. Don't worry. But you are going to have to find somewhere else to stay. Another big wig is coming in tomorrow. Is there anyone you can stay with?"

"No. I'll talk to the CID then go and stay with friends in Hong Kong. Once the CID investigates these crooks and they are replaced by honest club sergeants, I'll return. Meantime, my Filipinos will have to go home to their families."

"You take a shower and rest a while longer. I'll take two of my men with me to collect your clothes."

I looked in my bag for the keys and handed them over.

"And bring me a couple of aspirin before you go." I said," At the apartment you'll find a suitcase on top of the wardrobe in my bedroom. Pack as much as it will hold. And you will find the cord to the tape player in the kitchen drawer." I hesitated, "One more thing. There is a silver kettle on the gas stove beside a teapot. Be sure and bring the kettle."

"Why in hell's name do you need a kettle?"

"That's where I keep my passport, cash, important stuff."

He shook his head and left the room.

It was 1 pm when Major Darnell returned.

"Your landlord tried to stop us going in until I showed him your key. He told us a jeep load of assholes showed up last night and tried to break in. He called the white mice and they ran them off."

"They wouldn't have liked that." I replied "Now. Do you want to listen to this tape with me?"

"You betcha. Let's hear what shit this bunch have been up too."

The tape was scratchy and skipped here and there but it was audible. Del had sat closer to my handbag and his words were clearer than the Sergeant Major's. As the conversation unfolded my mouth dropped open and Darnell kept shaking his head. When at last it clicked off Darnell said "Those flea bags are a disgrace to the uniform."

I sat silently a few moments more, mentally replaying what I had heard.

"And to think I felt guilty about turning Delaney in" I finally spoke. "The bastard is no better than the rest of them. As well as turning this over to the CID I think I should call Colonel Sumner and let him know what's afoot at the 25th. Not that it's done any good in the past."

"This fucking Maredem Ltd. takes the prize," Darnell said. "Can you believe Woolridge and his senior sergeants formed a sales corporation to sell to themselves, purchasing with profits from the money paid by the poor friggin troops?"

"It boggles the mind." I agreed "They are buying from and selling to themselves. And what about Sergeant Delaney? Can you believe his scheme?"

"I didn't quite grasp that bit."

"He's going home but he didn't want to miss out on future kickbacks from the next twelve months. Apparently Woolridge, not expecting him to leave already, has none of their group ready to replace him at Cu Chi. The Corporation's partners are placed in strategic divisions and when Delaney goes, they are a man short and may lose the sales from the 25th. Can you believe the sales on bar snacks alone are worth half a million dollars per year per division?"

"Wasn't it Marie Antoinette who said "Let them eat cake? This seems to be a case of 'Let them eat peanuts."

"God my head hurts….. Look….. that slimy Delaney told Woolridge he is going to order a year's supply in advance. The bar snack orders are to be shipped over in monthly increments and Delaney's cut will continue to be deposited into his Swiss bank account each month. I can't believe I thought he was a cut above them."

"I would think the new custodian, not being one of them, would smell a rat. At least he would find the pre-ordering an insult to his ability."

"They don't seem to care. Someone must be protecting them."

"Well, it will be out of your hands in another hour. "I've called on Agent Winthrop from the CID. He and his partner are coming here. You can meet in my office. Once you give your deposition and sign it, your part is over."

"I can hardly believe it's over. Meantime, if you will excuse me, I'm going to throw up."

Later that evening, when I signed that deposition, I felt as if a huge weight had been lifted from my shoulders. The two agents had tried not to look shocked as my revelations unfolded but I knew they were excited about stumbling onto something so big.

"As soon as your department removes these men, I will be able to start my business again." I said optimistically before they left.

CHAPTER 51

"I've booked a flight into Kai Tak." I informed Major Darnell the following morning when he came to hurry me out of the VIP quarters. "I should head for the airport in a couple of hours."

"I'm afraid you will have to alter your plans" he said frowning "There's a new development."

"What now?"

"There's been a leak somewhere. Word is out that there's a $5000 price on your head. That's a lotta lettuce in a country where you can have anyone fragged for $50 but I suppose the stakes are high."

"That is just great!" I absorbed this shocking news.

"It has all been for nothing. I've tossed away three and a half years of my life. The sooner I go now the better." I spoke bitterly. "I really trusted agent Winthrop. Had no reason not too."

"It couldn't have been him. He's the one warned me. Tan Son Nhut airport is being watched. You've stirred up a hornet's nest."

"Got any more good news? And how on earth did the bloody leak get out?"

"I don't know. Agent Winthrop is outside now. He wants to apologize. Come join him for a coffee or a wake-up shot."

"Maybe both." I said grimly. "I should have known it was too good to be true. I've had opposition or disinterest the whole way."

Warrant Officer Winthrop was nursing a mug of coffee in Major Darnell's office when I entered.

"How can this have happened?" I asked, omitting the courtesy of greeting.

"Miss Collins, believe me, I wish I knew. I would stake my life on my fellow CID agents."

"Then you might not live long."

"The only other people to see your deposition were the Provost Marshall's people. Our investigations pass through their office."

"I thought you were the investigator." I accused.

"Well I am…..I mean I was."

"What do you mean 'was', can't you carry on with the investigation?"

"I'm afraid not. General Carl Turner, the Provost Marshall himself told me I had to sanitize your file."

"What sort of bullshit is this?" I burst out "Isn't there any bastard in the whole damned world who cares about what's going on over here? I can't believe this." I jumped up angrily and left the room, slamming the door.

Pacing back and forth in the courtyard I felt bewildered. A few minutes later Chuck Darnell came looking for me.

"He's gone" he said. "Try not to blame him."

"Then who the hell do I blame? And where do I go from here? I'm damn well ruined….and trapped."

Darnell didn't answer.

"I've got to leave here today. I guess I'll just take my friggin useless Browning 25 and go back to the apartment and take my chances."

"Now don't be stupid. I'll talk to our colonel about the situation and see if I can get permission for you to stay here, even if one of us has to give up his room temporarily. The army boys will never get at you in here."

"Well, maybe I should just risk getting onto a plane but I'll hang around a bit longer. Please help my kids get out of here this week, will you? They're all paid up."

"I'm already on it. Try to calm down. You can't make good decisions with your knickers twisted in a knot."

There was no more I could do. Nobody, not even the CID, had helped me. I had tried to buck something much bigger than all of us.

My business was over and I had no future. Maybe I should just risk the airport and let a bullet finish me off. The thought was fleeting but never the less…………..

I would have taken hope had I known that in another world far away, there was someone who did care. In Washington D.C. a senator named Abraham Ribicoff (D. Connecticut) was as troubled about the corruption breeding in the Vietnam War as I was.

A group of Texan businessmen and oilmen had years ago formed a group which they called 'The 8F Group.' The name was taken from room '8F' where they met regularly in a Texas hotel. President Johnson was one of the leading members of this powerful group. When the Vietnam War started up they formed a new company called RMK-BRJ, a company which included Halliburton. These are familiar names to anyone who spent time in Vietnam during the war. RMK, as we referred to it over there, was awarded the contracts to build jet runways, hospitals, prisons and communications facilities; also the contracts to dredge channels for ships, and build the American army bases from Danang to Saigon. RMK garnered 97% of all construction work in Vietnam. Three percent went to local Vietnamese contractors. The money made by RMK was astronomical and they employed tens of thousands of multi national civilian workers.

When it was clear much of the money the government was paying for these jobs was going missing, Senator Ribicoff, a senator who had a history of fighting corruption and who opposed the war, attempted to expose the scandal. He claimed that millions was being paid in kickbacks and called for an investigation by the United States General Accounting Office. They discovered that by 1967 RMK-BRJ had 'lost' $120,000,000 but the G.A.O. could not identify who the people obtaining the kickbacks were. Put that into perspective with the value of the dollar then and now. Beginning in 1964, RMK-BRJ was spending $15,000,000 a month. This had jumped to $67,000,000 a month only two years later. When looking at the total figures from this gigantic company, the money is staggering and the opportunities for graft, mind boggling.

The Senator was left frustrated by any lack of convictions from those investigations. Then more recent reports had seeped back to Washington about corruption in the U.S. Army's Clubs and Messes System. This was not about stealing money from the government but from the pockets of the troops who were doing their duty. Once again, the righteous senator wanted to know more.

Knowing none of this, I was unaware that the fate, which had continually altered my life, was about to put me and the good senator on converging courses.

While I tried to decide what to do, my good friend, Major Darnell arranged for me to lie low with a Special Forces B Team in Moc Hoa.

Each 'B' Team held eleven men. The Moc Hoa team leader was Lieutenant Colonel Wes Heerlein. He, Sergeant Hernandez and I took an air boat out onto the canal running alongside the camp. These two men clearly had a high regard for each other. They had served together for years and they joked back and forth. Sergeant Hernandez was at the controls of the noisy, aluminum boat. We were on the return part of the journey, approaching a bend on the waterway when a sniper opened fire from the bank.

"Jesus. My leg has been hit" Sergeant Hernandez" said, rather calmly I thought.

Herrlein jumped forward and grabbed the controls, gunning the engine. We shot around the bend, out of firing range.

"Take a look at his leg and see if the bone was hit." Herrlein yelled above the noise. Hernandez was sitting by then. I loosened the laces to his boot and carefully rolled up the leg of his fatigues. Heerlein multi tasked, driving one handed while calling in a medvac on the box-like radio.

"Is it hurting much?" I asked

"Not yet." The sergeant replied. I was surprised how calm we all were, especially me who hated the sight of blood. I saw that the outer calf of his leg was missing a large chunk of flesh, four inches in diameter. The raw, fleshy wound wasn't bleeding and I could see the white of bone amid the red pulp.

"I can see the bone" I screamed to Herrlein. "It doesn't seem to be shattered."

"The fuckin' things enough to get me a flight stateside though." Hernandez complained "Fuck it!"

I shook my head. Only a S.F. troop would cuss at being sent home.

"The medvac team said they'll meet us at the landing in fifteen minutes."

"How about a cigarette?" the sergeant asked "It's starting to hurt now."

The lieutenant colonel reached into his pocket and handed me a pack of cigarettes and a zippo. I took out a cigarette, lit it and put it in Hernandez mouth. He smiled gratefully and I was amazed at how he downplayed the moment.

"You don't think those bullets were meant for me, do you?" I asked Wes Herrlein.

"Naw. No-one knows you're here. It was just a lucky sniper. There's plenty about."

The camp came into sight and we could see the chopper with the Red Cross sign had beaten us. Two medics were already running to the waters edge with a stretcher as we pulled up onto the muddy bank. By now Hernandez was hurting, but with help, he got onto the stretcher and lay back, still smoking his cigarette. As they carried the stretcher up the grassy incline, Herrlein and I ran alongside.

"Throw that damned cigarette away and groan a bit" Herrlein ordered. "If you don't sound hurt real bad, they won't come so fast next time I call."

Hernandez did not throw his cigarette away but he did give a feeble groan and then smiled.

"Groan louder, damn it. Louder! And for God's sake stop smiling."

I couldn't believe these crazy bastards. I knew Hernandez was now in pain but they played the game until he was lifted aboard.

A short while later we got the message. His leg was permanently damaged. His war was over.

I was drinking gin an hour later and watching Heerlein feed rats to his twenty foot caged python. It wasn't my favorite pastime but Heerlein had asked me to accompany him and hold his glass while he fed the brute. I averted my eyes and listened as the lieutenant colonel talked about what a good bloke Hernandez was. A team member joined us.

"Of by the way" he said "June is needed back in Saigon urgent. Group has given permission for her to stay at the CLD. The call came in while you were away but in all the excitement I forgot to mention it."

"What the hell now?" I said "I should have gone in with the medvac."

"Well it's too late now. I'll call the C camp in Can Tho and see if they can get you back."

CHAPTER 52

Chuck Darnell and his first sergeant were waiting at the helipad for me.

"Let's get out of here quick." Darnell said, grabbing my duffle bag off the chopper.

I hitched my fatigues and ran after him, jumping into the jeep. We took off so fast I almost dislocated my neck.

"What's the hurry?" I asked after jerking forward again.

"There are a couple of men waiting back at the CLD to talk to you."

"Who would know to find me there?"

"Agent Winthrop brought them over. You're not gonna believe this."

"Then don't keep me waiting. What's the big secret?"

"They are two investigators from Washington."

"Wow! How did they hear about me?"

"They didn't. But a Senator Ribicoff has called for an investigation into the running of The Clubs and Messes System. His senate committee has higher power than the army. It seems he has sent these investigators out to see what they can find. They went straight from USARV to the CID. Agent Winthrop called them aside and told them about your 'sanitized' statement."

"Thank God for Winthrop," I said "I shouldn't have been so hard on him.

"He brought them to CLD. The three of them are there now, waiting for you in my office. We expected you back last night."

"The best plans of.................." I trailed off.

The Nung guards waved us into the compound. Chuck hustled me through a side door into a meeting room. Agent Winthrop was seated at the table with two strangers. They looked imposing and hot in their dark, serge suits.

I hurried over to Winthrop and gave him a peck of gratitude. He was not expecting the familiar greeting and looked uncomfortable.

"Miss Collins, these are two investigators from the United States Senate. I believe they will be able to help you much more than I have been able too. Please meet Fred and Duffy."

I was surprised at the informal introduction to two such formal looking men.

"It's nice to meet you!" I said "What brings you to our exciting war zone?"

"Partly this" Duffy said, indicating the papers spread before him. I recognized the transcript I had signed in what seemed a lifetime ago.

"I can't believe you are interested in my story? I've been beating my head against a brick wall for so long." I tried to keep the emotion from my voice.

"We certainly are interested Miss Collins. Depending on what we uncover whilst here, we may arrange Senate Hearings into what we believe is widespread corruption in the NCO and EM army clubs systems here."

I was stunned and without warning my eyes filled with tears. Was something really happening at last?

"Thank God! You have no idea what I have been up against."

"And that is what we want to hear, Miss Collins." Fred spoke up "We need to verify all the claims you have made here. Are the tapes mentioned still in your possession?"

"Yes."

Re-asserting his position as number one, Duffy cut in "Right now would you be kind enough to retell your experiences to us, starting at the beginning?"

"I'd be happy to."

"I should leave you now" Major Darnell stood.

"Before you leave Major Darnell, I just want you to know how grateful I am. If it had not been for Agent Winthrop's warning and your protection............who knows? I owe you both a lot."

Darnell brushed it off and left. Winthrop looked uncomfortable; maybe worrying he was being disloyal to his office by assisting us.

"I hope you gentlemen can do some good and I hope my department is not too tarnished. We have some very fine, dedicated people."

"I don't doubt that." Duffy replied.

For the next two hours I answered all the investigators questions, far more fully than in the affidavit submitted to the CID. It poured out of me- all that pent up anger- all that sense of injustice - all the myriad of things I had witnessed and stored away. I was amazed by the little things I thought I had forgotten

When it was over, Duffy stood to shake my hand.

"Thank you Miss Collins. You have been most helpful."

"Yes, most helpful, June..." Fred re-iterated.

"We need to meet with you one more time before we leave Saigon." Duffy spoke again "Once we get back to Washington, the senator will set a hearing date."

I took a deep breath. It was finally happening.

"Yes" Fred cut in enthusiastically "We will need you as our star witness."

Duffy glared at him. "We most likely will need you to testify." He agreed.

My pulse rate went up a notch or two. Was I about to get out of here and this God awful mess I had made of things? Then one last doubt surfaced.

"I may not get through the airport alive." I reminded him.

"Major Darnell assured me they can handle it."

"How long must I wait?"

"Not long."

"Who's paying for all this?" I asked.

"The committee will pay for your airfare and hotel while you are in Washington to testify" Duffy spoke coldly, as if financial considerations were beneath him.

"First class would be nice." I prompted.

"Don't press your luck. We have a budget."

CHAPTER 53

WASHINGTON DC

Thursday October 9th, 1969

The day of the hearings arrived. After barely sleeping the previous night, I took a long shower then ordered coffee, juice and scrambled eggs from room service. After carefully dressing, I sat on the edge of the bed, waiting for my breakfast. I plucked a carnation from the vase and tucked it into my headband for luck.

I could hardly believe I was in Washington, about to tell my story to the world. So much had happened. I wondered was it all a dream.

The fact that I planned to digress from the rehearsed script Duffy and Fred had prepared for me was making me nervous. I knew Duffy would be angry but I was sure I could tell this story much more effectively from my heart.

The waiter entered with my breakfast. I poured some coffee and uncovered the scrambled eggs but could only pick at the food.

Fred had warned me there would be a "full house" and plenty of newsmen and TV cameramen. I took a last look in the mirror then stood and braced myself.

Fred was waiting in front of the Senate Building with a security guard when the taxi stopped. We shook hands and hurried up the wide steps.

The hallways were crowded with onlookers unable to get into the already packed hearing rooms. Pushing ahead, the security guard made way for us. This had to be the performance of my life! With television coverage I would have an audience of millions. I hoped my sincerity and outrage would come through.

We had almost reached the big double doors into the hearing room when a woman broke free from the crowd and rushed towards me screaming, "You lying, scheming whore. You're destroying decent men. They shoulda killed you." Before I could move she spat in my face. This distressed me for we had just reached the time of Aids paranoia. Quickly, the security guard jumped forward and grabbed her by both arms. I wiped her saliva from my cheek with a linen handkerchief as he dragged the woman from the building. She twisted her head, trying to see me and continued screaming. I guessed she was the wife of one of the sergeants.

Entering the hearing room, a bit shook up, I saw the distinguished senators sitting up high, behind a polished timber partition. My legs began to shake. Duffy was standing behind the partition, whispering into the ear of an elegant, grey haired man.

"That's Senator Rubicoff" Fred informed me. "He is the Acting Chairman of The Committee and he is one of our country's most powerful men."

Every seat in the room was taken. Cameramen stood against the walls. I felt as if I was dreaming.

"I've got to leave you now." Fred said. "You'll be fine. Just be yourself and tell the truth. Don't let them trip you up. You've had plenty of rehearsal with the statement."

The enormity of what I was about to do hit me and I felt another wave of panic ...What am I doing here? I am just a simple Aussie girl. Not that long ago I was married to a sheep farmer, living in the bush. I took a deep breath. Get a grip you idiot! I mentally chided. After all you've been through, don't blow it now. You'll never get another chance. The panic evaporated and I was confident, even eager, to have the floor and tell my story.

When my name was called, I took the oath then looked slowly along the row of senators before speaking.

"Gentlemen, my name is June Collins and I have before me a transcript which I may refer to from time to time, but as I have lived this nightmare for such a long time, I know it well and prefer to speak from my heart and memory if that is allowed."

The senators looked mildly surprised but nodded agreement. Duffy looked apoplectic.

With barely contained emotion I launched into my story, telling how the club sergeants' greed and uncaring attitude towards their wounded and dying disgusted me. I spoke of the kickbacks I and all others doing business with them had to pay – Every salesman selling beer and whisky or bar snacks, bar stools, tables and chairs--- we were all required to pay the kickbacks. Every booking agent providing entertainment to the clubs must pay. It eventually ran into hundreds of millions.

You could hear a pin drop. I spoke of the half a million troops in country, all of them drinking beer and catching a floor show when not in the field.

Time seemed to stand still until finally I ran out of steam and reached for a glass of water.

"This has certainly been a moving testimony Miss Collins." Senator Ribicoff spoke. "You have shown great courage in doing your best to expose these things. Can you tell us Miss Collins, was there anything in particular that made you go to the C.I.D. and report this dreadful story? After all, you obviously were giving up your livelihood."

I thought for a moment before continuing.

"There were several incidents that finally put me over the edge sir.

One such incident was the death of a major who was a mate of mine. He was a professional soldier who believed we had a good reason to be in Vietnam. I always disagreed but our opposing views never impaired our friendship. He was not the first of my friends to be killed but he was the only one I actually witnessed lying dead. And it occurred soon after I came from paying a kickback.

This man belonged to the 101st Airborne division. I was in camp when someone ran out of the Tactical Operations Centre and said we had just taken several casualties in battle. I rushed to the helipad as the first Dust Off's landed. Standing in the whirling dust I heard someone mention the major's name. The wounded were being placed on stretchers and carried away. I recognized the major. I ran towards his stretcher, hoping to comfort him but someone pulled me away. It was too late. He lay unmoving with a gaping raw, ghastly hole at his mid section." I stopped speaking, momentarily choked up "The contrast between him and the custodian I had recently paid was so great that I was filled with a boiling rage. My friend's hollowed body was like a stuck movie reel going round and round in my mind. I remembered what a colonel once told me. He said "The body is only the empty house where he used to live." There were too many empty houses and too many military criminals building mansions on those empty houses. I had to act."

While recounting that story, a tear slid down my cheek. A short silence followed.

Breaking the tension I spoke up again "Before I finish Senators, may I add a footnote to my testimony about Sergeant Delaney and his transaction for a year's worth of bar supplies. I have a tape of him planning this unorthodox order and I wasn't actually in Cu Chi when the order arrived so this next part is hear say only, although it can be verified by most of the 25th Infantry Division's troops."

"I don't think there are any objections" Replied Senator Ribicoff after glancing around at his colleagues for confirmation.

"You may recall that a year's worth of supplies were to be sent in monthly increments? Well even though I had warned the division staff officers of what was afoot, they ignored my warning.

There's an old saying about many a slip….but this was more like a landslide. When that bar snack order was received back here in the States, someone at the warehouse made a monumental blunder. Instead of sending the shipment in monthly increments, they sent the lot at once. A year's supply! I have the following on good authority. --- General Williamson looked out his window one morning and saw his camp in total chaos. The largest convoy ever to reach Cu Chi was circling the camp. Monstrous clouds of red dust enveloped the camp as the semi- truck drivers searched, reversed, carried on looking for the non existent warehouses. Jeeps, tanks, army trucks all came to a standstill in the ensuing traffic jams. Vehicles stalled, military personnel, unable to pass were yelling and shaking their fists. The civilian drivers of the big trucks kept stopping and starting, climbing in and out of their cabs, scratching their heads, as they looked about lost. Nobody knew what was happening.

I'm told General Williamson turned to his aide and bellowed "Find out what the hell's going on will you."

The aide soon returned looking perplexed "It seems Sir, it's a… a whole bunch of peanuts sir."

The general spluttered. "Peanuts? Peanuts? Are they fuckin crazy. There's Goddamn truckloads there. What are we? A goddamn army of monkeys?"

But it WAS a convoy of bar snacks, mostly peanuts and there was no where to store them. The division was stuck with all these perishable bar supplies. The honest custodian replacement knew nothing about them, had no money to pay for them and nowhere to keep them. The Keystone Cops had arrived in Vietnam. General Williamson was forced to pull a major from his regular duties to become a salesman. They had to be dispersed to camps from one end of Vietnam to the other before the humidity could destroy them. Shelf life is short in the tropics. I pity that poor major when his children later ask him, "What did you do in the war daddy?"

"Oh. I sold peanuts." I laughed as I finished speaking and the spectators laughed with me. Even the senators were smiling. Suddenly I was aware of flash bulbs popping and flashing.

"Our investigators checked this story" Senator Ribicoff interjected "And they verified it was all true." His words can be found in one of the newspaper copies at the end of this book.

He then harrumphed loudly. "Well you have painted a very funny picture Miss Collins but of course, this is no laughing matter. Now, before you go, would you mind answering any questions that the panel may have?"

"No sir. I'll do my best."

The senators had plenty of questions. I believe I answered them fully and well. At last Senator Ribicoff thanked me on behalf of the committee. Then he added "Although you are not an American; you have done our country a great service at much personal risk, Miss Collins. I'm sure everybody here joins me in thanking you."

It was over. I finally did it.

In a daze I left the senate building. It was over.

FOOTNOTE TO THE HEARINGS;

Sergeant Major William O. Woolridge, and three other senior sergeant custodians took the 5th Amendment. They were dishonorably discharged from the army with loss of all pensions and medals. The investigations showed that Maredem had been formed years earlier in Augsburg Germany. I had not known these details. In Germany, the sergeants had been selling to themselves to a tune of $380,000 a year. An earlier investigation into Maredem, while the group was still in Germany, had been quashed by the very same Major General Carl Turner, the Provost Marshall (Top Cop) from Vietnam. Thus 'The Khaki Mafia' was allowed to grow until reaching Vietnam. At the time of his arrest, Major General Turner had retired from the army and was holding the prestigious position of Head of the United States Marshall's Office. The investigation showed that he had pilfered hundreds of guns from the military and had been selling them for personal gain. That information was turned over to the U.S. Tax department.

The group was all convicted but none served prison time. They were placed on probation and ordered to do hundreds of hours of charity work. The Federal judge said "I want the defendants penniless. I just want to make sure they don't have anything." Another quote went "When you are responsible for lives and well-being of soldiers, you should not take advantage, especially for your own gain and greed."

For awhile after the hearings, all slot machines were removed from army bases. Of a more lasting nature, changes were made to the way investigations were handled between the C.I.D. and the Provost Marshall's office so that no such cover-up could happen in future, even by the man at the top.

I sometimes wonder would I have become a whistle-blower had I known they were not individual bad guys but a powerful and organized group. However, towards the end, I don't believe anything could have stopped me. I was too obsessed to fear even death.

This brings me to another thought. In Melbourne when I accepted Ray Bolwell's offer to become a stripper, I thought 'We all have our price and I've just accepted mine.'

But I do now believe that for most of us, there is a line beyond which our conscience will not allow us to go. People doing business in Vietnam quelled their conscience so they could get rich. I was one of them but my conscience could not allow me to continue and I lost the money I had made. So maybe, after all, we don't all have our price.

NIGHT OWL

DAILY NEWS

NEW YORK'S PICTURE NEWSPAPER ®

8¢

10¢ OUTSIDE L.I. AND SUBURBS

Vol. 51. No. 92 — New York, N.Y. 10017, Friday, October 10, 1969* — WEATHER: Mostly sunny and mild.

SENATE UNIT OKs HAYNSWORTH

Mary Jo Autopsy Ruling Today

Stories on Page 2

UPI Telephoto

No Time for Sergeants. Australian June Collins laughs during Washington Senate hearing on alleged mismanagement of Vietnam enlisted men's clubs. She told senators some sergeants managing clubs demanded "sexual favors," and that she was driven out of business as booking agent when she complained. —*Story on page 4*

The Washington Post
Times Herald

FRIDAY, OCTOBER 10, 1969

Phone 223-6000 Circulation 223-6100 Classified 223-6200

Index
Amusements B
City Life C
Classified C
Comics E
Crossword B
Editorials A

's
ne
gs

Roberts

Henry Cabot at the stalled shington "for

a few hours had opened to be the ad- ffort to blunt xt week's Viet- n. Secretary of P. Rogers will on Sunday on 'ress" program, ppearance. hilip C. Habib, to Lodge, will hite House on iday, Press Sec- L. Ziegler an- moratorium to gainst the war r next Wednes-

the President port from Gen. er, chairman of fs of Staff, who from Vietnam. will be Laird embers of the

esterday again e peace-in-Viet- when he said, g Medals of Vietnam veter- dedicate our- o bringing the all want." of the word in referring to it home came er South Viet- ent Thieu said ady to discuss a the Commu- not a unilateral the allied side isisted that it sary to "discuss for effecting a h the Commu-

United States cease-fire offer of a package to he Communists licate any inter- p.

NT, A9, Col. 1

ths
Low

was merely re- preparing for a ttacks. he casualty sta- l today by the ith Vietnamese

that ended last Americans were ed to 95 the also a very low umber of U.S. 00.

M, A21, Col. 1

Czechs Curtail Travel

Most Trips To the West Are Banned

From News Dispatches

PRAGUE, Oct. 9 (AP) — Czechoslovakia has barred its citizens from most private travel to the West. The cutoff went into effect at midnight Wednesday and caught hundreds of travelers at airports and frontier crossings.

Relatively free travel to the West was allowed even before the ouster of the Stalinist Antonin Novotny as president in 1968 and had been one of the last freedoms remaining after the Soviet-led invasion in August of last year.

Officials say about 50,000 persons, many of them intellectuals and skilled workers, have settled in the West since the invasion. A major reason behind the restrictions was said to be "the danger to the stabilization of the economy."

The new restrictions, which are subject to alteration, allow private visits to immediate members of families who are legally in the West. They bar visits to the estimated 28,000 Czechoslovak refugees who stayed abroad without government approval after the invasion.

Private visits to friends abroad, which in the past accounted for the bulk of travel to the West, now would be prohibited.

Foreign travel is expected to be limited largely to official trips by Czechoslovaks doing state business, attending scientific meetings and cultural events or making foreign lecture tours. Approval will not be given for Western trips for professional reasons, for study or for work.

Airline and travel officials were informed early today that all exit permits in private passports had been declared invalid, effective immediately.

A sign at police headquarters proclaimed that the passport and exit permit office was closed for the day. Small knots of travelers, some with their suitcases, gathered outside.

At Prague's airport, Czechoslovak passengers were removed from all flights to the West, except for those holding passports for official business.

A number of passengers had already been aboard their plane, Sabena Flight 786 for Brussels. It had loaded up yesterday on schedule, then was postponed until today, because of fog. Private Czechoslovak travelers were left behind when it took off.

See CZECH, A21, Col. 1

By Bob Burchette—The Washington Post

Impresario June I. Skewes testifies before Senate investigations subcommittee.

GI Club Kickbacks Charged by Blonde

By Morton Mintz
Washington Post Staff Writer

An Australian woman impressario charged yesterday that a kickback racket in Army servicemen's clubs in Vietnam rewarded their noncom custodians with "Swiss bank accounts and expensive liquor and spacious villas and beautiful women."

She told Senate investigators that the racket became "a personal tragedy" because it killed her business of booking commercial entertainers—but that "a far greater tragedy" was the multi-million-dollar annual exploitation of GIs who risk and give their lives."

The witness, known professionally as June Collins, was June I. Skewes, who for two years in Saigon booked bands and shows for noncom and enlisted men's clubs. Miss Collins, voluptuous, 34-year-old blonde in a brown knit minidress, appeared at a hearing of the Senate Permanent Investigations Subcommittee.

She gave a clean bill of health to Green Berets and Marine Corps clubs during the 2-hour matinee hearing.

See CLUBS, A14, Col. 1

Hill Unit Bars Tax on Bonds

The Senate Finance Committee yesterday voted to eliminate from the comprehensive tax reform bill a provision that would indirectly tax state and municipal bonds.

Details on Page A2

Nixon Urges Hill Action on D.C. Crime

By Peter Braestrup
Washington Post Staff Writer

President Nixon yesterday urged a bipartisan Congressional push for his anticrime proposals for Washington amid a record wave of armed robberies.

Over coffee in the White House Cabinet room, Nixon told a gathering of Congressional leaders, including Senate Majority Leader Mike Mansfield (D-Mont.) that District of Columbia crime was not a "partian" matter.

"It has run through all administrations and today it has reached crisis proportions," he said.

Neither the Senate nor the Senate District Committee, headed by Sen. Joseph Tydings (D-Md.) has approved a House has voted on the administration's crime package. The court reorganization plan, but decided to deal separately with other Administration proposals strengthening the pow-

Court to
Plea Aga
School D

By Peter Milins
Washington Post Staff Writ

The Supreme Court rejected N arguments yesterday and agreed to ate attention to an appeal against segregating Southern schools.

The court's action made plain th as urgent, and was an indication it n the pace of desegregation in the South.

The appeal was brought by the NAACP Legal Defense and Educational Fund after the administration sought and got a delay in desegregation of 30 Mississippi school districts late in August.

In a move that provoked strong criticism from civil rights organizations, the administration said the delay was necessary to avoid "chaos, confusion and a catastrophic educational setback" for the pupils involved.

The fund replied in its appeal that the 30 Mississippi school districts "have had 15 years to eliminate barriers to desegregation, and that is enough."

The fund's lawyers asked the court for a ruling that, in effect, would apply all across the South, and they asked for an immediate ruling.

The immediate questions were whether the court would hear the case at all, and when.

The administration asked the Supreme Court to wait at least until Dec. 1, when the 30 districts are under orders to submit new desegregation plans for next year.

The court turned down this suggestion yesterday, and scheduled a full hearing on the case Oct. 23.

The date is such that the administration's current and controversial nominee for associate justice, Judge Clement F. Haynsworth Jr., will probably not be able to take part in the case even if confirmed by the Senate. The vote to confirm him now seems about two weeks away.

The Supreme Court has set forth several timetables for desegregation over the years. The first and most famous, "all deliberate speed," came in its original desegregation decision, in 1954.

The latest came two years ago in Green v. New Kent County. A less patient court said then that "the burden on a school board today is to come forward with a plan that promises realistically to work, and promises realistically to work now." The italics were the court's own.

The fund has suggested even stronger language, of the sort used by Associate Justice Hugo Black last month.

See SCHOOLS, A16, Col. 6

Hi
A
No

By
Wash

The S mittee 7, to cl nominat Haynsw floor, w pected t But w said t "please vote "s nee was ing Sen Hollings hearted see the Repul Democr South ently loss of days, prompt timetab matter two wee Comp head co support camps. Chairm (D-Miss. confirm ble" m than 30 This wa timate ponents NAACP Mitchell care wi said the against likely a leanings The Charles was cas the tw sion. N vote al ment tl Associa meeting the mat Lawr man of on the that th in New See

SYDNEY BLONDE HITS AT RACKETEERS

"SEX BRIBES TO U.S. ARMY MANAGERS"

WASHINGTON, Fri.–A Sydney woman said today U.S. Army sergeants demanded sexual favors as well as bribes in a Vietnam club rcket.

[illegible]

"Kickbacks"

[illegible]

Peanuts

[illegible]

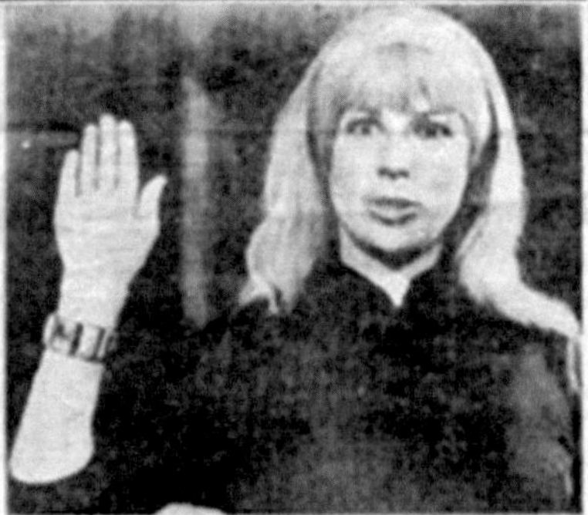

AUSTRALIAN JUNE Collins taking the oath before giving evidence at a Washington Congressional committee inquiry into alleged graft in U.S. Army clubs in Vietnam.

Booking Agent Describes Army Club 'Kickbacks'

By ROBERT M. SMITH
Special to The New York Times

WASHINGTON, Oct. 9—An Australian booking agent for entertainers told a Senate inquiry today that "corruption is widespread" throughout the United States Army service club system in Vietnam and that "the most common form of corruption is the kickback."

The agent, June Collins, a 34-year-old former dancer, told the Senate Permanent Subcommittee on Investigations that she had paid the custodians of various service clubs in Vietnam $8,000 to $10,000 over a two-year period.

She said she was forced out of business when the custodians would not hire her entertainers after she had reported some of the sergeants' activities to the military authorities.

Miss Collins testified that she had heard one sergeant tell a group of people that he was extending his tour because he could not afford not to.

"Being a club custodian," he allegedly said, "is worth $150,000."

"Nobody blinked an eye," at this remark, Miss Collins said. "Frankly, I think custodians make quite a bit more. Many of them have Swiss bank accounts, and they live very well."

The booking agent's testimony was supported by an

Continued on Page 27, Column 1

June Collins, an Australian booking agent, taking oath prior to testifying before Senate subcommittee yesterday.

EPILOGUE

After it was all over I returned to the hotel, physically and mentally drained. Celebration was the last thing I needed. I fell into an immediate, deep sleep.

The hotel phone woke me. I looked around to get my bearings. I had slept for twelve hours. Memories of the hearings flooded back as I reached for the phone.

"Hullo" I stifled a yawn.

"Miss Collins?"

"Speaking." I leaned over; smelling the perfume from the carnations the investigators had given me.

"This is James Mansfield calling from the Australian Consulate's office."

"What?" I wasn't quite awake.

"The consul asked me to call and congratulate you."

"What on earth for?"

"For your dignified conduct at the Senate Hearings yesterday."

"Were you there? How do you know?"

"From the news of course! You are on every television news program and your photo is front page of the newspapers."

"This is news to me." I was stunned. I had been aware of flash bulbs going off and I thought I might receive a mention, but I certainly never expected front page coverage..

"Yes. Now, is anything we can do to help you. I suppose you will be returning to Australia?"

"What?" I blurted "Oh, right. Well frankly, now I'm here I may as well stay awhile and take a look at the country."

"Indeed, yes. Well, take care. Good bye."

I jumped into my clothes and raced down to the small shop in the foyer to buy a paper. Photographs of me stared out from every newspaper. "Why the Dancer Sang" and "No Time For Sergeants" and "The Great Peanut Convoy" screamed some of the headlines. Speechless, I grabbed a bundle and carried them back to my room.

Then the phone started ringing off the hook. People I hadn't seen in years had somehow discovered my whereabouts. And during my many years in Asia I had made a lot of American friends.

"Hullo Bob? Yes I have arrived with a splash. Oh, you expected as much? Yes, I do miss Hong Kong but I will definitely come down to San Francisco to see you. Give me your number… I love you, Bye."

"Geraldine Raye? I haven't seen you since Hong Kong. You married a billionaire? One of your Johns? Oh congratulations. Sure! Once things settle down. Give me your number?"

"Oh hi. Yvonne Dunleavy. Are you still writing for the National Enquirer? Is Steve here with you? Working in New York for Rupert Murdoch? Is he as wild as ever? I can't wait to see you both."

And so it went on for hours. Fred came by in the late afternoon to take me out for a coffee.

"It's nasty outside." I said "Let's have it downstairs. Where's Duffy?"

"After yesterday, he hates you."

"Too bad. I couldn't have garnered more news coverage for your hearings, scripted or not. He ought to be happy."

"That's not a word in his vocabulary."

We had reached the elevator.

"What will you do now?" Fred asked.

"I need some quiet time to think things out."

We seated ourselves in the coffee shop and placed our orders.

"Unfortunately the committee can't pay for your hotel past the end of the week so you will need other arrangements."

"That's a bummer. Becoming a whistle blower has cost me plenty."

"It usually does. That is why most people go along with things and don't rock the boat."

When I returned upstairs the red light was flashing on my phone. I called the operator.

"Oh yes. There's a message for you. A Mr. Robin Moore left a number. He wants you to call him back. Shall I place the call now?"

"Please do." I mulled the name over. I didn't know anyone by that name yet it sounded familiar.

"He's on the line Ma'am."

"Hullo Junie Moon" he said

"Robin, I'm sorry" I said "I can't remember where we met. Please jog my memory."

"We haven't met. That's a pleasure still in store for me Junie Moon."

"Then why are you calling me Junie Moon. I haven't been called that in years."

"I saw you on television and the name just seemed to fit." The hairs stood up on the back of my neck.

"Your own name sounds familiar."

"Have you read the Green Berets or seen the movie with John Wayne? That's me."

"Oh. Of course. I've done both."

"Now the reason I am calling. You have quite a story. Have you thought of turning it into a book?"

I couldn't believe my ears. I had thought about recouping some of my losses that way but I didn't know if anyone would be interested or if I could write well enough.

"Not really." I replied.

"Well I think it has the makings of an excellent book. Maybe even a movie. Can we get together to discuss it?"

"I'm free tonight."

"Can you wait until tomorrow? I'm having dinner with Gene Hackman tonight. One of my books, The French Connection, is being made into a movie and he is playing the major role."

"Oh my God. Yes. Tomorrow will be fine. See you then Robin."

"Oh! And one last thing?"

"Yes?"

"If we come to an agreement on this book, would you be free to travel?"

"To where?"

"Port Antonio Jamaica! I do most of my writing at my property down there."

"As long as the climate's warmer than here, you won't have to twist my arm."

I hung up. I was almost broke yet once again fate was mapping my path.

Calling room service, I ordered a champagne split and a pair of scissors. I would cut out some of the headline stories and mail them to Mum. That would explain why she hadn't heard from me much during the last year.

Propping up the pillows on my bed, I lay back against them. This book with Robin Moore was sure to get me financially sound again. Funny about money, I thought. I kept making a lot of it and then losing it again; always up and down and seldom in between. I thought about the tens of thousands I had spent on jewelry. Lately I hadn't had the lifestyle to wear it. Soon I could buy a new piece. But somehow the anticipation didn't thrill me quite the way it used to.

That small voice of my conscience was bothering me again. Have you forgotten your promise to go back and get one of those children off the street in Manila? You can't buy more jewelry when they need you."

Slowly I smiled. Soon I would have money again and I could keep that promise. That would be more precious than any gemstone. I would need to make changes to prepare for motherhood. I needed to find a home--lead a more stable life, modify my vocabulary. It felt great to have a goal again. I closed my eyes. Thank you God! You've heard me after all!

And true to my nature, I was unable to stop with only one child but that is another story!

To be continued... Sequel; Junie Moon Rising, available on Amazon books

ARMY TIMES DECEMBER 22, 1971

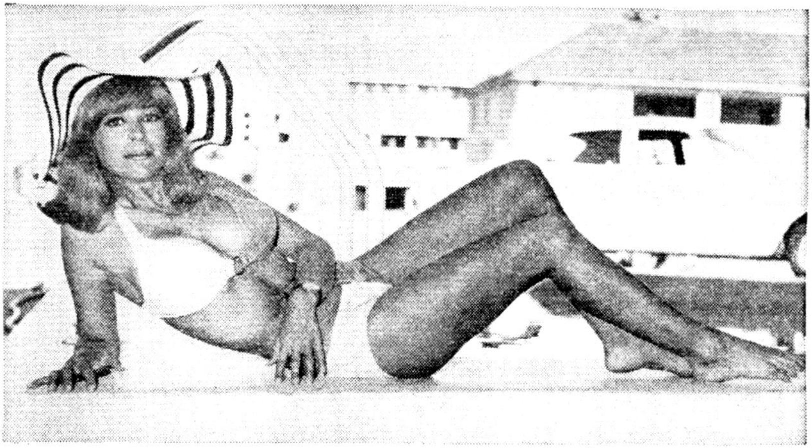

Literary Figure

THE LATEST AUTHOR to hit it big in the book world is June Collins, who made worldwide headlines last year when she testified that club managers in Vietnam were demanding kickbacks and favors before signing entertainment contracts. Miss Collins, an Australian who switched from exotic dancing to show business booker, now has moved to Spain to write a second book. Her first book, written with former Green Beret Robin Moore, is "Khaki Mafia," which was reviewed in Army Times last week. It's a fiction version of the Senate investigation into the military club and exchange scandals by the Senate Permanent Investigating Subcommittee.

BLOG: www.memoirofjuniemoon.wordpress.com

Author's contact: juniemooncollins@hotmail.com

GLOSSARY

NCO	Non commissioned Officer (sergeants)
Non Coms	As above
EM	Enlisted men
OCS	Officer Candidate School
MACV	Military Assistance Command Vietnam
USARV	United States Army Vietnam
CID	Criminal Investigation Department
'in country'	How the troops referred to being in Vietnam
The real world	The U.S.A.
R & R	Rest and recuperation sometimes spoken of by the EM's as I and I (intercourse and intoxication)
Deros...	Date of finishing their tour of duty and returning to the USA
Freedom Bird	Reference to any plane taking them out of Vietnam
Gook	Disparaging way some GI's referred to Vietnamese
Slopehead	As above.
Charlie	The enemy
VC	Viet Cong. Enemy; black pyjama wearing civilian guerrillas
NVA	North Vietnamese Army. There were 2 distinct enemies, the VC and the NVA
ARVN's	Army, Republic of Vietnam (South)

ROK	Republic of Korea troops
GI's	Government Issue
Nam	Vietnam
Round eye	Caucasian or black; any western females in Vietnam
Grunts	Infantry soldiers
TOC	Tactical Operations Center; Off limits, protected area in which battles were monitored.
HQ	Headquarters
MP	Military police
in the field or in battle	Out of camp. In the jungle on reconnaissance
White Mice	Vietnamese police (wore white uniforms)
Lt. Col.	Lieutenant Colonel. Rank just below full bird colonel but addressed as Colonel
W.O.	Warrant Officer. Often the rank of helicopter pilots
PFC	Private first class
Spec. 4	Specialist 4 rank
Leg	Scornful term used by airborne troops to describe non-airborne troops.
LZ	Landing zone
Hot LZ	Landing zone under enemy fire.
Boonies	Remote, undeveloped areas of Vietnam.

Spotter plane	Small single engine planes used in search for enemy activity.
Herc	C130 or C123 Hercules
Hooch	Tent or other structure which housed the troops. Usually two or four to a hooch.
Hooch maid.	Vietnamese women employed in the larger American bases to clean the hooches or do laundry. Australian troops did not allow Vietnamese onto their bases.

9 780646 582726